ASTRONOMY

McGRAW-HILL
SCIENCE
MACMILLAN/McGRAW-HILL EDITION

ASTRONOMY

RICHARD MOYER ■ LUCY DANIEL ■ JAY HACKETT
PRENTICE BAPTISTE ■ PAMELA STRYKER ■ JOANNE VASQUEZ

NATIONAL GEOGRAPHIC SOCIETY

McGraw-Hill School Division
New York   Farmington

PROGRAM AUTHORS

Dr. Lucy H. Daniel
Teacher, Consultant
Rutherford County Schools,
North Carolina

Dr. Jay Hackett
Emeritus Professor of Earth
Sciences
University of Northern
Colorado

Dr. Richard H. Moyer
Professor of Science
Education
University of Michigan-
Dearborn

Dr. H. Prentice Baptiste
Professor of Curriculum and
Instruction
New Mexico State
University

Pamela Stryker, M.Ed.
Elementary Educator and
Science Consultant
Eanes Independent School
District
Austin, Texas

JoAnne Vasquez, M.Ed.
Elementary Science
Education Specialist
Mesa Public Schools,
Arizona
NSTA President 1996–1997

NATIONAL GEOGRAPHIC SOCIETY
Washington, D.C.

CONTRIBUTING AUTHORS

Dr. Thomas Custer
Dr. James Flood
Dr. Diane Lapp
Doug Llewellyn
Dorothy Reid
Dr. Donald M. Silver

CONSULTANTS

Dr. Danny J. Ballard
Dr. Carol Baskin
Dr. Bonnie Buratti
Dr. Suellen Cabe
Dr. Shawn Carlson
Dr. Thomas A. Davies
Dr. Marie DiBerardino
Dr. R. E. Duhrkopf
Dr. Ed Geary
Dr. Susan C. Giarratano-Russell
Dr. Karen Kwitter
Dr. Donna Lloyd-Kolkin
Ericka Lochner, RN
Donna Harrell Lubcker
Dr. Dennis L. Nelson
Dr. Fred S. Sack
Dr. Martin VanDyke
Dr. E. Peter Volpe
Dr. Josephine Davis Wallace
Dr. Joe Yelderman

Invitation to Science, *World of Science*, and *FUNtastic Facts* features found in this textbook were designed and developed by the National Geographic Society's Education Division.

Copyright © 2000 National Geographic Society

The name "National Geographic Society" and the Yellow Border Rectangle are trademarks of the Society, and their use, without prior written permission, is strictly prohibited.

Cover photos: *bkgnd.* John Foster/Science Source/Photo Researchers, Inc; *inset* images copyright © 1999 PhotoDisc, Inc.

McGraw-Hill School Division
A Division of The McGraw-Hill Companies

Copyright © 2000 McGraw-Hill School Division,
a Division of the Educational and Professional
Publishing Group of The McGraw-Hill Companies, Inc.

All rights reserved. No part of this book may be reproduced or transmitted in any form or by any means, electronic or mechanical, including photocopying, recording, or by any information storage and retrieval system, without permission in writing from the publisher.

McGraw-Hill School Division
Two Penn Plaza
New York, New York 10121

Printed in the United States of America

ISBN 0-02-278234-6 / 6

2 3 4 5 6 7 8 9 027/046 05 04 03 02 01 00

CONTENTS

UNIT 4 ASTRONOMY
EARTH SCIENCE

CHAPTER 7 • OBSERVING THE SKY 289

TOPIC 1: THE TOOLS OF ASTRONOMERS 290
- **EXPLORE ACTIVITY** Investigate How We Learn About the Universe 291
- **QUICK LAB** Needs in Space 301
- **NATIONAL GEOGRAPHIC WORLD OF SCIENCE** Free Falling 304

TOPIC 2: EARTH AND THE SUN 306
- **EXPLORE ACTIVITY** Investigate What We Learn from Shadows 307
- **QUICK LAB** What Time Is It? 310
- **SCIENCE MAGAZINE** The Chain of Life 316

TOPIC 3: THE MOON IN MOTION 318
- **EXPLORE ACTIVITY** Investigate Why the Moon Changes Its Appearance 319
- **SKILL BUILDER** Making a Model: Model of the Tides 325
- **SCIENCE MAGAZINE** Straddling Worlds 328

CHAPTER 7 REVIEW/PROBLEMS AND PUZZLES 330

CHAPTER 8 • THE SOLAR SYSTEM AND BEYOND 331

TOPIC 4: THE INNER SOLAR SYSTEM 332
- **EXPLORE ACTIVITY** Investigate How to Tell Planets from Stars 333
- **SKILL BUILDER** Experimenting: Paths in Space 335
- **SCIENCE MAGAZINE** Be Your Own Weather Forecaster 342

TOPIC 5: THE OUTER SOLAR SYSTEM 344
- **EXPLORE ACTIVITY** Investigate How the Planets Are Arranged 345
- **QUICK LAB** A Planet Model 346
- **SCIENCE MAGAZINE** Looking Skyward 354

TOPIC 6: STARS 356
- **EXPLORE ACTIVITY** Investigate if Stars Are at Different Distances from Earth 357
- **QUICK LAB** How Parallax Works 358
- **SCIENCE MAGAZINE** The Stuff Stars Are Made Of 368

TOPIC 7: GALAXIES AND BEYOND 370
- **DESIGN YOUR OWN EXPERIMENT** How Can We Tell Where the Sun Is? 371
- **QUICK LAB** Expanding Dots 375
- **SCIENCE MAGAZINE** When Galaxies Collide 380

CHAPTER 8 REVIEW/PROBLEMS AND PUZZLES 381
UNIT 4 REVIEW/PROBLEMS AND PUZZLES 382–384

REFERENCE SECTION

HANDBOOK R1
    MEASUREMENTS R2–R3
    SAFETY R4–R5
    COLLECT DATA R6–R10
    MAKE MEASUREMENTS R11–R17
    MAKE OBSERVATIONS R18–R19
    USE TECHNOLOGY R20–R23
    REPRESENT DATA R24–R26

GLOSSARY R27

INDEX R40

UNIT 4
ASTRONOMY

CHAPTER 7
OBSERVING THE SKY

When you look up at the Moon, you may be used to seeing different shapes at different times of the month. On the right is a picture taken by a spacecraft from Earth. You can see the Moon and, beyond it, Earth. What shape does Earth seem to have? Why?

In this chapter find out how scientists explore space. Learn about Earth, the Moon, and the Sun.

In this chapter look for examples of cause and effect. One event—the cause—makes something else happen—the effect.

Topic 1 EARTH SCIENCE

The Tools of Astronomers

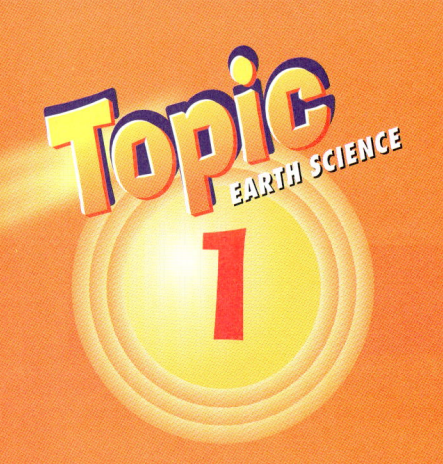

WHY IT MATTERS

People have been "looking up" for centuries, with just their eyes and then with tools.

How do you observe something that's very far away? If you attend a soccer game, how do you see what's going on? Maybe you use binoculars. How do they help you?

What do these two pictures of Mars show? Which one gives you more information? How do you think each was taken? From what observation point was each taken? What tools were used? How can you tell?

SCIENCE WORDS

universe everything that exists

telescope a device that collects light and makes distant objects appear closer and larger

refraction the bending of waves as they go from one substance to another

reflection the bouncing of waves off a surface

wavelength the distance from one peak to the next on a wave

frequency the number of waves that pass through a point in a second

electromagnetic spectrum waves of light in order by wavelength

EXPLORE

HYPOTHESIZE If scientists wish to learn about an object in space, how do they do it? What methods are available? What are the advantages of each? Write a hypothesis in your *Science Journal*. Test your ideas.

EXPLORE ACTIVITY

Investigate How We Learn About the Universe

Find ways to explore a mystery planet.

PROCEDURES

1. **MAKE A MODEL** Use a newspaper-covered shoe box as a "mystery planet." Place it as far away as possible, such as at the end of a hall.

2. **OBSERVE** View the mystery planet through a sheet of thin, colored, transparent plastic. This simulates looking at it from Earth, through Earth's atmosphere, using an Earth-based telescope. Describe the planet, and draw its picture in your *Science Journal.*

3. **USE VARIABLES** View the mystery planet without the plastic. This simulates looking at it from space, with no atmosphere, using a telescope that is in space. Describe what you see, and draw a picture.

4. **USE VARIABLES** Someone in your group walks near the mystery planet to observe it and report back observations. This simulates a space vehicle making a "flyby" of the planet.

MATERIALS
- newspaper-covered shoe box
- sheet of thin, colored, transparent plastic
- *Science Journal*

CONCLUDE AND APPLY

1. **COMPARE AND CONTRAST** Describe the differences between viewing the planet from an Earth-based telescope and from a telescope that is in space. Explain what causes the differences.

2. **EVALUATE** What new information were you able to get from the flyby? Explain some of the limitations of a flyby.

GOING FURTHER: Problem Solving

3. **COMPARE AND CONTRAST** How is this Explore Activity similar to the way scientists have learned about Mars?

4. **USE VARIABLES** What additional kind of observation was made to learn about Mars?

What Is Astronomy?

Look up in the sky some clear night. What do you think is up there? What would you like to know about it?

The branch of science that deals with "what's up there" is astronomy. Astronomy is the study of the **universe**. The universe is everything that exists—Earth and all the things in space. The contents of space include the planets, stars, and galaxies.

An astronomer is someone who observes the universe and tries to explain what is observed. The universe is a huge place and has many different parts. This means that no one astronomer can study everything. Different astronomers study different parts of the universe.

- What are the planets made out of?
- How fast do planets move?
- Why do stars shine?
- How hot are stars?
- How many stars are there?
- Did the universe always look as it looks now?

We will learn which of these questions can be answered with some certainty and which cannot.

Astronomers

What does it take to be an astronomer? Can you be an astronomer? Some people are professional astronomers. That is, they have made astronomy their careers. Other people are amateur astronomers. They buy telescopes and observe the stars and planets just for their own enjoyment. Professional or not, they all make observations that might lead to some new understanding.

Much of what astronomers discover has no practical benefits. Why then do they study astronomy? The reason is curiosity. Human beings have a need to explore and understand the universe. Not only are the stars beautiful to look at, they also make people ask where they come from. Astronomers try to answer these kinds of questions. However, there are some practical benefits to studying astronomy. For example, navigators use knowledge of star position to tell direction.

An amateur astronomer observes the stars through a telescope.

Brain Power

Could you be an astronomer at your age? Is a university degree needed? Explain.

Johannes Kepler (1571–1630), discusses planetary motion with Emperor Rudolph II, sitting. Kepler's work helped change people's view of their place in the universe.

How Do We Learn About the Universe?

All sciences, including astronomy, are based on observation. There are several ways in which astronomers observe the universe. Which method is used depends on what astronomers wish to observe. The Explore Activity showed the benefits of several ways of making observations.

One method is to use the eyes. This is good for such things as observing day and night, the position of the Sun and Moon in the sky, and the location of some planets and stars. Of course, you cannot look at the Sun directly because the light can harm your eyes.

A second method is to use a **telescope.** A telescope is a device that collects light. It makes distant objects appear closer and larger. Most of our knowledge of the stars and planets comes through using telescopes.

Another way of observing objects such as the Moon is to send a robot or a human there. Both robots and humans have traveled to the Moon. Only robots have been sent to or close to the other planets.

Models, Hypotheses, Theories

Once observations have been made, we try to understand and explain what we have observed. Scientists use models, hypotheses, and theories to help them understand observations.

Models are a way of simplifying the world so that we can understand it better. For example, Earth is not exactly a sphere. However, we often use a sphere to represent Earth, because that simple model helps us understand many observations.

A theory is an idea that explains old observations and also predicts new ones that we have yet to make. For example, the theory of gravity explains the past motion of the planets. It also allows us to predict their future motion.

A hypothesis is a statement that can be tested by observation. As more and more evidence is gathered through observation, our certainty increases. However, we can never prove a theory with complete certainty. Science can only tell us what is likely, not what is certain. Sometimes, though, evidence may disagree with a theory's predictions. In that case the theory is disproved.

What Is Light?

How can people learn about the universe? Most of our knowledge comes from light. Light is also called electromagnetic radiation, or electromagnetic waves, because light is related to electricity and magnetism. Light not only means light that we can see. It also means radio waves, infrared waves, ultraviolet waves, X rays, and gamma rays.

When light travels through empty space, it always travels at the speed of 300,000 kilometers per second (186,000 miles per second). This is the universe's speed limit. No matter or energy can travel faster.

When you turn on the light switch in your classroom, it seems like it takes no time for the light to reach your eyes. However, the Sun is so far away that it takes about eight minutes for light to travel from the Sun to Earth. Other stars are so far away that it takes years for their light to reach Earth.

Light as a Wave

It will help you understand light if you think of light as a wave. A wave carries energy from one place to another. Some waves need a medium to carry the wave. For example, water waves travel through water. Sound waves can travel through solids, liquids, or gases. Light waves are different because they do not need a medium. They can travel through empty space, which contains no solid, liquid, or gas.

One property of waves is called **refraction** (ri frak′shən). *Refraction* means "the bending of waves as they go from one substance to another." For example, when light travels from air to glass, it changes direction in a predictable way. Refraction of light is the basis of eyeglasses and some telescopes.

Another property of light is **reflection** (ri flek′shən). *Reflection* means "the bouncing of waves off a surface." Mirrors and some telescopes use this property of light.

The wavelength of a vibrating string

NATIONAL GEOGRAPHIC

FUNtastic Facts

Proxima Centauri, the star nearest our solar system, lies 40 trillion kilometers (25 trillion miles) away. Light traveling from the star takes about 4 years and 3 months to reach Earth. If a spaceship traveled 10 kilometers per second, how long would it take to get there?

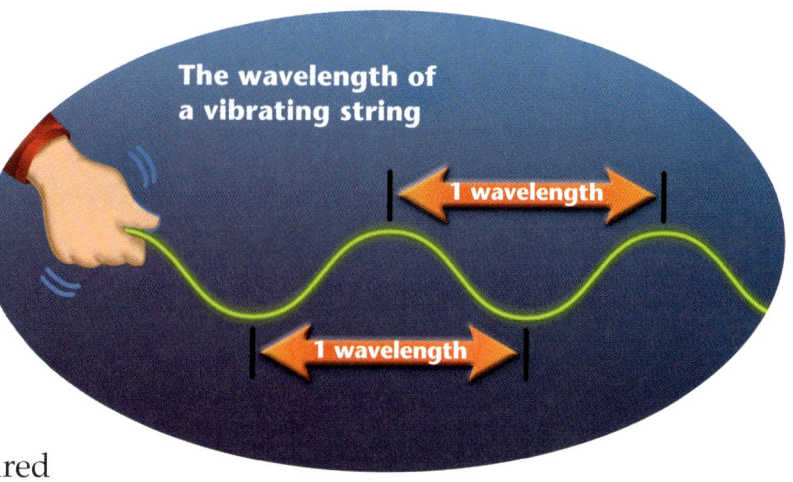

A model to help you visualize how a light wave travels is to shake a string. If you shake the end of a string continuously back and forth, a wave travels through the string, away from your hand. If we take a snapshot of the string, the string has a shape that repeats itself.

- The distance from one peak to the next on the wave is called a **wavelength**. Wavelength is measured in meters.

- If you tie a flag to the string at any point, that flag will vibrate as the wave passes through. The number of waves that pass through any point in a second is called the wave's **frequency**. Frequency is measured in cycles per second, or hertz.

In general the longer the wavelength of a wave, the lower the frequency. Each light wave has a wavelength and a frequency, just as a wave on a string does.

The Electromagnetic Spectrum

Many objects in the universe, such as stars, give off light at many wavelengths and frequencies. These waves vary from very long wavelengths (low frequencies) to short wavelengths (high frequencies).

This diagram shows waves of light in order of their wavelengths (and frequencies). It is called the **electromagnetic spectrum** (i lek′trō mag net′ik spek′trəm). Different ranges of wavelengths have special names and properties.

In order of long to short wavelength, wavelengths are radio, infrared, visible, ultraviolet, X-ray, and gamma ray.

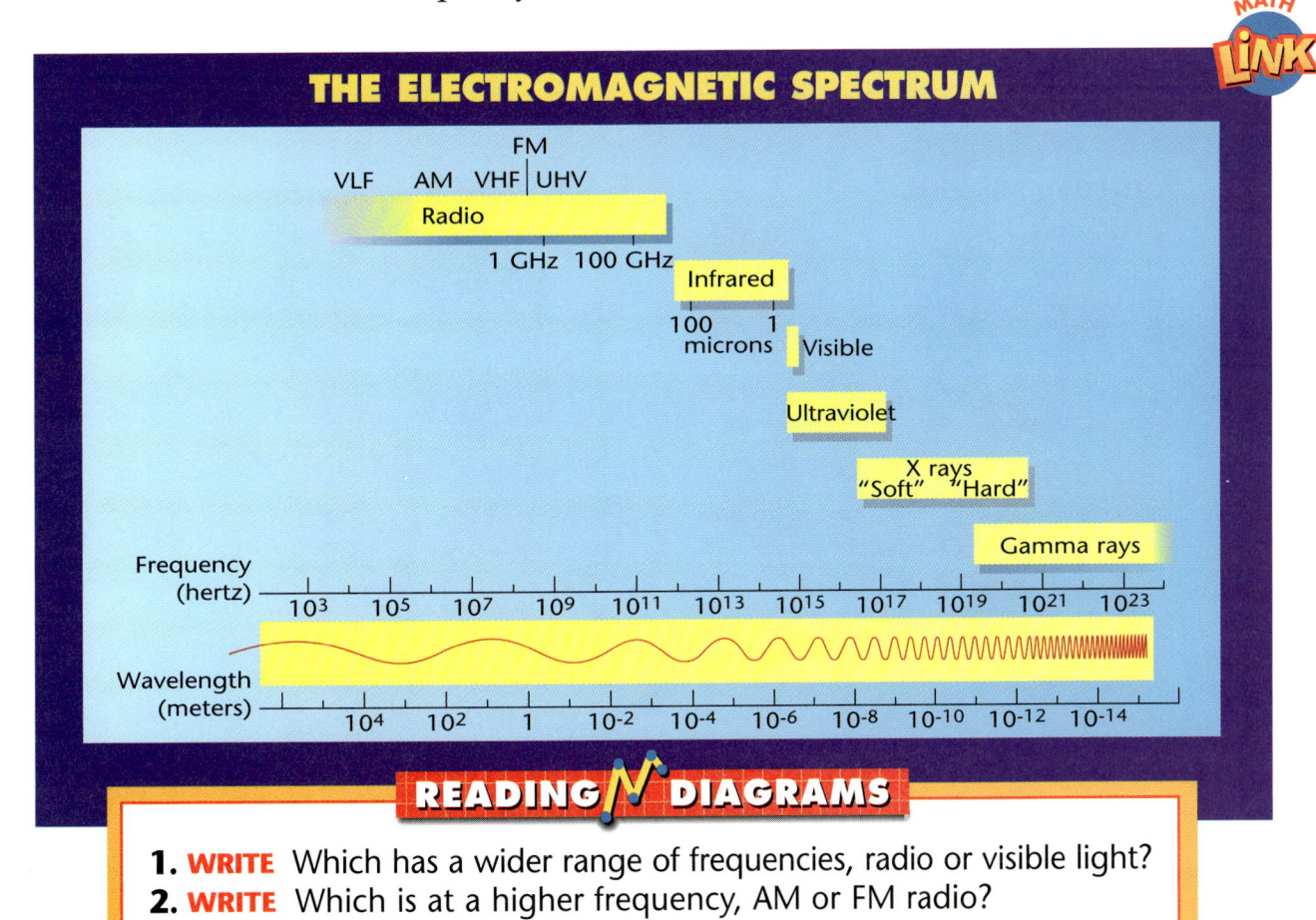

THE ELECTROMAGNETIC SPECTRUM

Radio: VLF, AM, VHF, FM, UHV — 1 GHz, 100 GHz
Infrared: 100 microns, 1 micron
Visible
Ultraviolet
X rays: "Soft", "Hard"
Gamma rays

Frequency (hertz): 10^3, 10^5, 10^7, 10^9, 10^{11}, 10^{13}, 10^{15}, 10^{17}, 10^{19}, 10^{21}, 10^{23}

Wavelength (meters): 10^4, 10^2, 1, 10^{-2}, 10^{-4}, 10^{-6}, 10^{-8}, 10^{-10}, 10^{-12}, 10^{-14}

READING DIAGRAMS

1. **WRITE** Which has a wider range of frequencies, radio or visible light?
2. **WRITE** Which is at a higher frequency, AM or FM radio?

How Do You Detect Visible Light from Space?

The first two pictures in this topic showed different views of the planet Mars. How were they different? The first image was viewed from Earth through a telescope. The second image was viewed by a *space probe*. A space probe is a vehicle sent beyond Earth to study planets and other objects within our solar system. This probe landed on Mars and sent the image to Earth.

These images were made by visible light. Remember, visible light is light that you can see. What are some other detectors of visible light? The eyes that you use to watch a movie are detectors of visible light. So is the pair of binoculars you use at a soccer game.

You cannot use just your eyes to see details of Mars. It's too far away. However, you can use a telescope. A telescope produces an enlarged image of something far away. Two kinds of telescopes are used to detect visible light.

- A reflecting telescope uses mirrors to form an image of a faraway object. Look at the diagram of a reflecting telescope. Describe the path that visible light follows as it travels from Mars to your eye. How is the image different from the object?

- A refracting telescope uses lenses to form an image of a faraway object. Look at the diagram of a refracting telescope. The refracting lens of this telescope bends the light passing through it. How is this image different from the object?

TWO TYPES OF TELESCOPES

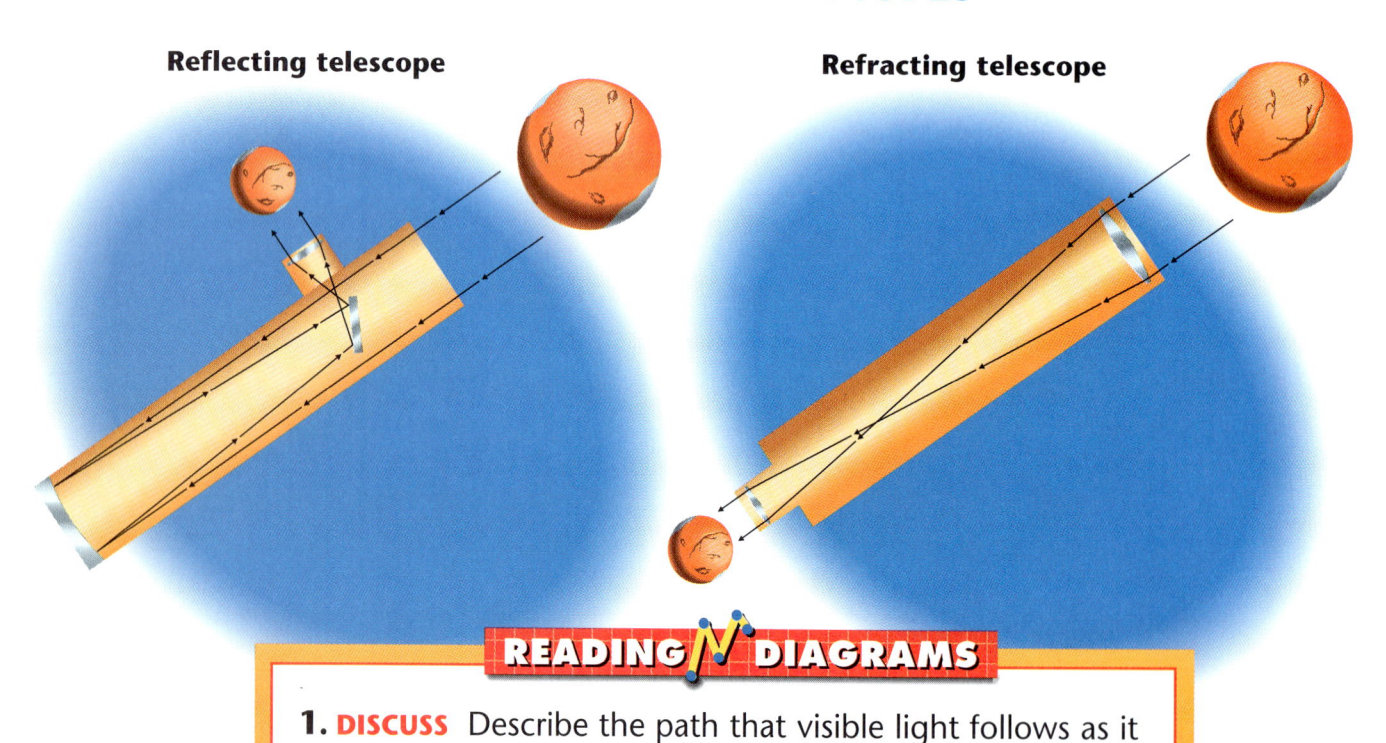

Reflecting telescope

Refracting telescope

READING DIAGRAMS

1. **DISCUSS** Describe the path that visible light follows as it travels from Mars through a refracting telescope to your eye. Do the same for a reflecting telescope.
2. **WRITE** Draw the path of light as described in 1.

How Do We Detect Invisible Light?

You learned that the electromagnetic spectrum includes from low-frequency radio waves to high-frequency gamma rays. Different parts of this spectrum can be detected by different instruments. Our eyes are instruments that can detect visible light. In fact, it is called visible because our eyes can detect it.

However, our eyes cannot detect most of the electromagnetic spectrum. Humans need special detectors, such as special telescopes, to detect the whole spectrum. Astronomers learn a lot from the invisible part of the spectrum. For example, by detecting microwaves in space, they learn about the history of the universe. You will learn about this in Topic 7.

Telescopes have been made to detect almost every kind of invisible light—radio, radar, infrared, ultraviolet, X-ray, and even gamma ray. Each kind of telescope gives people information not possible with just visible light.

Astronomers observe the universe using different parts of the spectrum. The part chosen depends on what information they wish to know.

Look at the three pictures below. Each shows the Milky Way, a huge group of stars that includes the Sun (and Earth). Each was taken with energy from a different part of the electromagnetic spectrum. In each case different information was obtained. However, the partial information given by each picture gives a more complete picture of the Milky Way.

The Milky Way as detected by . . .

① a visible light telescope

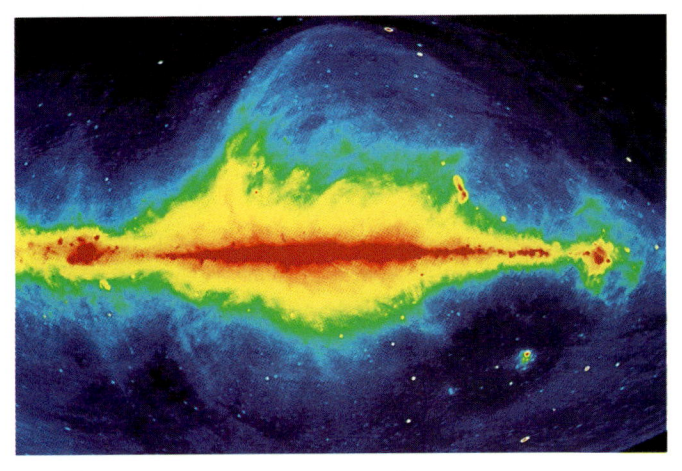

② a radio telescope

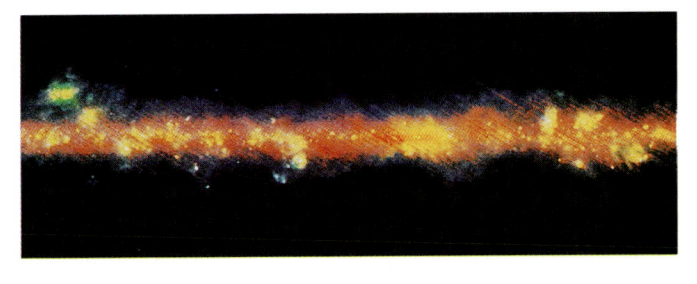

③ an infrared telescope

Brain Power

What advantage, if any, do you think there is in sending a robot to collect data on Mars instead of just observing Mars through a telescope?

What Information Do We Get from Space?

What would happen to your view if you were looking through a cloud of dust? When you see objects through a telescope, you are looking through Earth's atmosphere. The atmosphere blurs what you see. Can you think of a way to make the images better?

What if you took a photograph of a hurricane from the ground? This photograph would show the destruction the hurricane might have caused. However, it might not be able to provide other types of useful data. For this reason, scientists send *artificial satellites* into orbit high above Earth's atmosphere. The satellites transmit, or send back, data. These data reveal more detail of the clouds and the storm's center. However, they might not give much information about the destruction on the ground.

Look at these two pictures of Saturn. One of them was taken from Earth. The other was taken from *Voyager 2*, a space probe. Space probes travel away from Earth. They take photographs and perform experiments. They send the data back to Earth. Scientists put the data together, make observations, and draw conclusions.

TWO VIEWS OF SATURN

Saturn, as viewed from Earth

Saturn, as viewed from *Voyager 2*

READING CHARTS

DISCUSS How are these views different?

What Do Space Shuttles Do?

Satellites and space probes do not carry crew members. They get their instructions from the ground. Space probes such as *Voyager 2* have been launched to fly by and photograph distant planets. Others, such as *Mars Pathfinder*, actually land on other planets.

Earth-orbiting satellites serve many different functions. Weather satellites track hurricanes and other large storms. Commucations satellites allow us to see television pictures from around the world.

Satellites are sometimes sent up in a space shuttle. A space shuttle is a reusable spacecraft. It also carries astronauts. They do activities and experiments that could not be done by a machine. After the tasks and observations are completed, the shuttle lands and may be reused in the future.

Space shuttle astronauts launched a special telescope called the Hubble Space Telescope. This telescope has taken pictures of objects that could not be taken from the ground.

Space shuttle (above) lifting off

Space shuttle landing

What Would Life on a Space Flight Be Like?

What do you need to have to survive on Earth? What if you were an astronaut preparing to go to the Moon? What would you need to have to survive?

You need oxygen, water, and food to survive in space, as you do on Earth. Each day the average astronaut consumes about 0.9 kilograms (2 pounds) of oxygen, 3.2 kilograms (7 pounds) of water, and 1.4 kilograms (3 pounds) of food. How are you going to store all this material? Scientists have come up with some solutions, but they are always trying to improve on them.

Oxygen

When you breathe you inhale oxygen and exhale carbon dioxide. On the *Apollo* and *Skylab* spacecraft, exhaled gases were sent through canisters. These canisters removed the carbon dioxide. They also purified the oxygen in the spacecraft.

Water

In spacecraft water is also recycled. The water in the air is collected and then condensed into a liquid. It is then purified for reuse.

Food

As an astronaut you most likely would eat freeze-dried food cubes or powders to which you add water. Why do you think you would not be able to have fresh meat and fruit in a spacecraft?

Astronauts inside a spacecraft

A Martian Colony

The year is 2024. You are on the replacement team of the first colonists on Mars. You look out over the Martian landscape.

You are wearing a spacesuit with a supply of oxygen. The colony itself is enclosed in a dome. Why are these precautions necessary?

- The Martian atmosphere is mostly carbon dioxide, not breathable for humans.

- It's also very thin. Thin Martian atmosphere means the atmospheric pressure is very low. With a thin atmosphere and no magnetic field, there is very little to stop harmful radiation from outer space and the Sun from hitting the surface. Without protection you would not survive for long.

How does all this equipment help you and the colonists? What are some other reasons why the colony might look like this?

Martian landscape

QUICK LAB

Needs in Space

HYPOTHESIZE What would you need to have to survive if you were stranded on the Moon? Write a hypothesis in your *Science Journal*.

PROCEDURES

MATERIALS
- Science Journal

1. **COMPARE** Write in your *Science Journal* what you need to have to live on Earth. How do the conditions on the Moon differ from those on Earth?

2. **COMMUNICATE** Speak with your partner and other teams. What materials might be necessary? Useful?

3. **INFER** Decide what you would have to do to make sure you could survive.

CONCLUDE AND APPLY

1. **DRAW CONCLUSIONS** What did your team decide? What would you need to have to survive if you were stranded on the Moon?

2. **EVALUATE** What are the arguments for and against sending humans to the Moon? Consider cost and risks. Also consider what might be gained. Finally, consider whether robots could do what humans can.

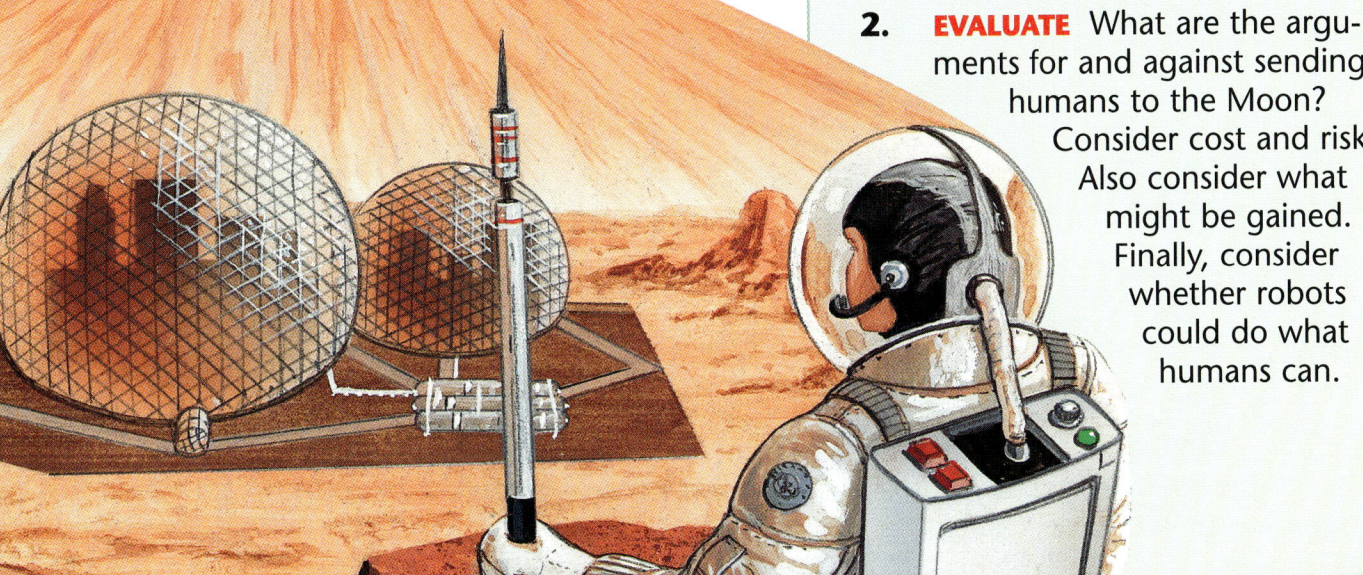

What Have We Done in Space So Far?

Some of the spacecraft sent into space contained crews. Some, such as the spacecraft to the right, did not. See the table below.

PAST SPACE MISSIONS

Year	Country	Spacecraft	Carrying Crew?	Mission/Achievement
1957	U.S.S.R.	Sputnik-1	No	First artificial satellite
1958	U.S.A.	Explorer III	No	Discovered Earth's radiation belt
1966	U.S.A.	Surveyor 1	No	First American soft landing on lunar surface
1968	U.S.A.	Apollo 8	Borman, Lovell, Anders	First lunar fly-around with humans aboard and return to Earth
1969	U.S.A.	Apollo 11	Armstrong, Aldrin, Collins	First landing by humans on the Moon
1972	U.S.A.	Pioneer 10	No	Flew by and took over 500 pictures of Jupiter; also collected magnetic data; crossed orbit of Pluto on June 13, 1983 and left solar system
1977	U.S.A.	Voyager	No	Spectacular photos of Jupiter, Saturn, Uranus, and Neptune between 1977 and 1989
1990	U.S.A. and Europe	Hubble Space Telescope	No	High resolution pictures of celestial objects; photographed collision of comet Shoemaker-Levy with Jupiter in 1994
1996	U.S.A.	Mars Pathfinder	No	Photographs of Martian surface taken by Sojourner rover
1997	U.S.A. and Europe	Cassini/Huygens	No	En route to study Saturn and Titan

READING TABLES

1. **DISCUSS** Describe the history of what we have learned through our explorations of space. Include information from this page and the next.
2. **WRITE** List what you think are the three most important discoveries shown in the table.

Where Do We Go from Here?

Have you seen the many wonders of space that space probes and astronauts have discovered? The table below lists just some of the many space missions planned for the beginning of the next millennium.

WHY IT MATTERS

Much of astronomy has no practical use. However, many people want to learn about it because of their curiosity. They want to know what this universe is made out of, where it came from, and where it's going.

A practical use of astronomy is that knowing the position of the stars helps navigators.

FUTURE SPACE MISSIONS

Year	Country	Spacecraft	Carrying Crew?	Mission
2001	U.S.A.	Pluto Express	No	Study Pluto and Charon
2002	U.S.A.	Columbia	Yes	Hubble service flight
2003	U.S.A.	Rosetta	No	Land on comet Wirtanen
2005	U.S.A.	Mars Surveyor	No	Return Martian soil samples to Earth

REVIEW

1. Why do you think people become astronomers?
2. What is meant by light? Is all light visible? Explain.
3. **COMPARE AND CONTRAST** What is the difference between a reflecting telescope and a refracting telescope? How are they alike?
4. What is needed for people to travel in space vehicles?
5. **CRITICAL THINKING** *Analyze* What are the advantages of space travel over using telescopes to explore the universe? What have we learned this way? What are some disadvantages of space travel?

WHY IT MATTERS THINK ABOUT IT
When you look at the stars at night, what questions come to mind? What things about the universe are you most curious about?

WHY IT MATTERS WRITE ABOUT IT
Write your questions down. Plan how you might find the answers. It could be by asking someone or looking in a book. It could also be by discovering the answers yourself.

NATIONAL GEOGRAPHIC
World of Science

Free FALLING

Astronaut in free fall

Mir space station in free fall around Earth

Physics Link

Would you be weightless in space? No, you would be in free fall, something Isaac Newton wrote about 300 years ago!

According to Newton a cannonball shot off parallel to the ground would orbit Earth. Two forces would create this orbit—the force pushing the cannonball forward and gravity. If the force launching the cannonball were great enough, gravity would pull the cannonball into orbit around Earth.

The same principle keeps the space shuttle and *Mir* space station in orbit. They are launched with enough power to keep them traveling forward, and the pull of gravity keeps them in free fall around Earth.

The astronauts inside the spacecraft are in free fall, too. They train for the experience at the Weightless Environment Training Facility (WET-F), a swimming pool that simulates working conditions in space. Astronauts wear weights so they have the same buoyancy as the water. However, in the pool, unlike space, the astronauts can push against the water and swim.

Because of the lack of gravity in free fall, astronauts can lose calcium and bone density. Their muscles weaken, and astronauts look about an inch taller because their spines aren't being pulled down.

Astronauts re-create free fall in WET-F training.

Discussion Starter

Explain why astronauts feel "weightless" in space.

interNET CONNECTION
To learn more about free fall, visit www.mhschool.com/science and enter the keyword **FREEFALL.**

Topic 2
EARTH SCIENCE

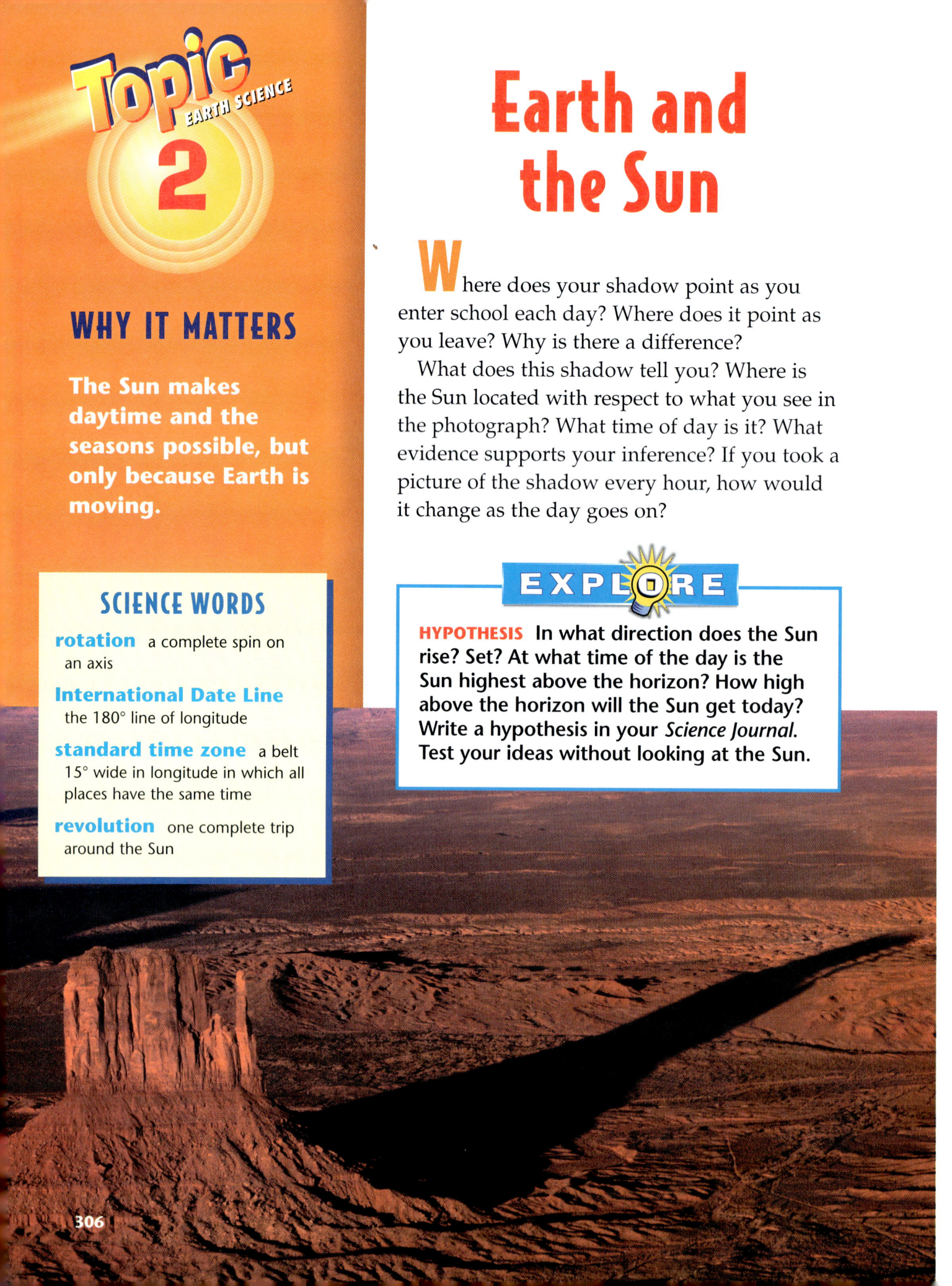

WHY IT MATTERS

The Sun makes daytime and the seasons possible, but only because Earth is moving.

SCIENCE WORDS

rotation a complete spin on an axis

International Date Line the 180° line of longitude

standard time zone a belt 15° wide in longitude in which all places have the same time

revolution one complete trip around the Sun

Earth and the Sun

Where does your shadow point as you enter school each day? Where does it point as you leave? Why is there a difference?

What does this shadow tell you? Where is the Sun located with respect to what you see in the photograph? What time of day is it? What evidence supports your inference? If you took a picture of the shadow every hour, how would it change as the day goes on?

EXPLORE

HYPOTHESIS In what direction does the Sun rise? Set? At what time of the day is the Sun highest above the horizon? How high above the horizon will the Sun get today? Write a hypothesis in your *Science Journal*. Test your ideas without looking at the Sun.

EXPLORE ACTIVITY

Investigate What We Learn from Shadows

Compare shadows throughout the day.

PROCEDURES

SAFETY Do not look directly at the Sun at any time.

1. Draw two lines on a sheet of paper (top to bottom and left to right) to make four quarters.

2. Label map directions on your sheet of paper: *N* at the top center, *S* at the bottom center, *W* at the center of the left side, and *E* in the center of the right side.

3. **MAKE A MODEL** Stand a pencil upright in a blob of clay. Place the clay in the center of your paper.

4. Place the paper on a flat surface where the Sun will shine on it all day. Place it so the *N* points north.

5. **OBSERVE** At 10 A.M. carefully trace the pencil's shadow. Put a heavy dot on the tip of the shadow tracing. Repeat at 11 A.M., 12 noon, 1 P.M., 2 P.M., and 3 P.M. Label your tracings with the times. Record your work in your *Science Journal*.

MATERIALS
- sheet of paper
- ruler
- blob of clay
- transparent tape
- piece of string
- protractor
- *Science Journal*

CONCLUDE AND APPLY

1. **INTERPRET DATA** What is the relationship between the shadow and the Sun's location?

2. **OBSERVE** When was the shadow longest? Shortest?

3. **INFER** When was the Sun highest? How could you tell from your shadow drawings?

4. **INFER** When was the Sun lowest? How could you tell from your shadow drawings?

GOING FURTHER: Problem Solving

5. **PREDICT** Make lines to predict the direction and length of the shadow at 9 A.M. and at 4 P.M.

What Do We Learn from Shadows?

Does the Sun move across the sky? The Explore Activity showed that shadows change as the Sun appears to move across the sky. However, is it really moving? The Sun only seems to move, because Earth is *rotating*, or spinning. It rotates on its axis, like a spinning top. The axis is an imaginary line through Earth from the North Pole to the South Pole.

One **rotation** is a complete spin on the axis. It takes just about 24 hours for Earth to make one rotation. What happens as a result of this motion? Any location on Earth experiences a cycle of day and night.

How do we know that Earth is spinning? One way is from data from satellites. Satellites can observe the rotation of Earth from space. Another piece of evidence was discovered by a Frenchman named Foucault (fü kō′).

A heavy ball was hung by a long string. It was made to sway back and forth in one direction. Pegs were arranged in a circle around the ball. As the ball swung back and forth, it should have knocked down only two pegs. However, during the course of the day, many pegs were knocked down! It seemed the direction of the ball's swing changed. The reason for this change was that Earth rotated under the ball.

The shape of Earth also tells us that Earth is rotating. Earth is not exactly a sphere. Earth is slightly flattened at the North and South Poles. It also bulges slightly at the equator. This is what happens to a sphere when it spins. It is similar to what happens in a washing machine. As the clothes spin around, they get thrown to the edge. As Earth spins, Earth's matter also gets thrown to the "edge." This creates the bulging equator.

In 1851 the Foucault pendulum showed that Earth rotated.

HISTORY LINK

The 24 hours for Earth to make one rotation results in one day.

Brain Power

If you are on a merry-go-round, how can you tell the merry-go-round is rotating? How is the motion like Earth's rotation?

What Path Does the Sun Follow Each Day?

You have learned that the Sun's position in the sky changes during the day. You also know that the cycle of day and night repeats every 24 hours. Why does all of this happen?

Think of the motion of a spinning top. As the top spins, a dot of paint on its equator is first lit up by a flashlight and then goes into the dark.

Earth's motion is similar to that of a top. It, too, rotates on its axis, making one rotation every 24 hours. It does this 365 times each year. Any location on Earth receives a certain amount of sunlight and a certain amount of darkness.

As a day progresses, what does the Sun appear to do? As the picture below shows, the Sun rises in the east. It seems to travel west, rising higher in the sky as the day passes. At noon the Sun reaches its highest point in the sky. After noon it appears to get lower in the sky, until it sets in the west.

THE SUN'S PATH IN THE SKY

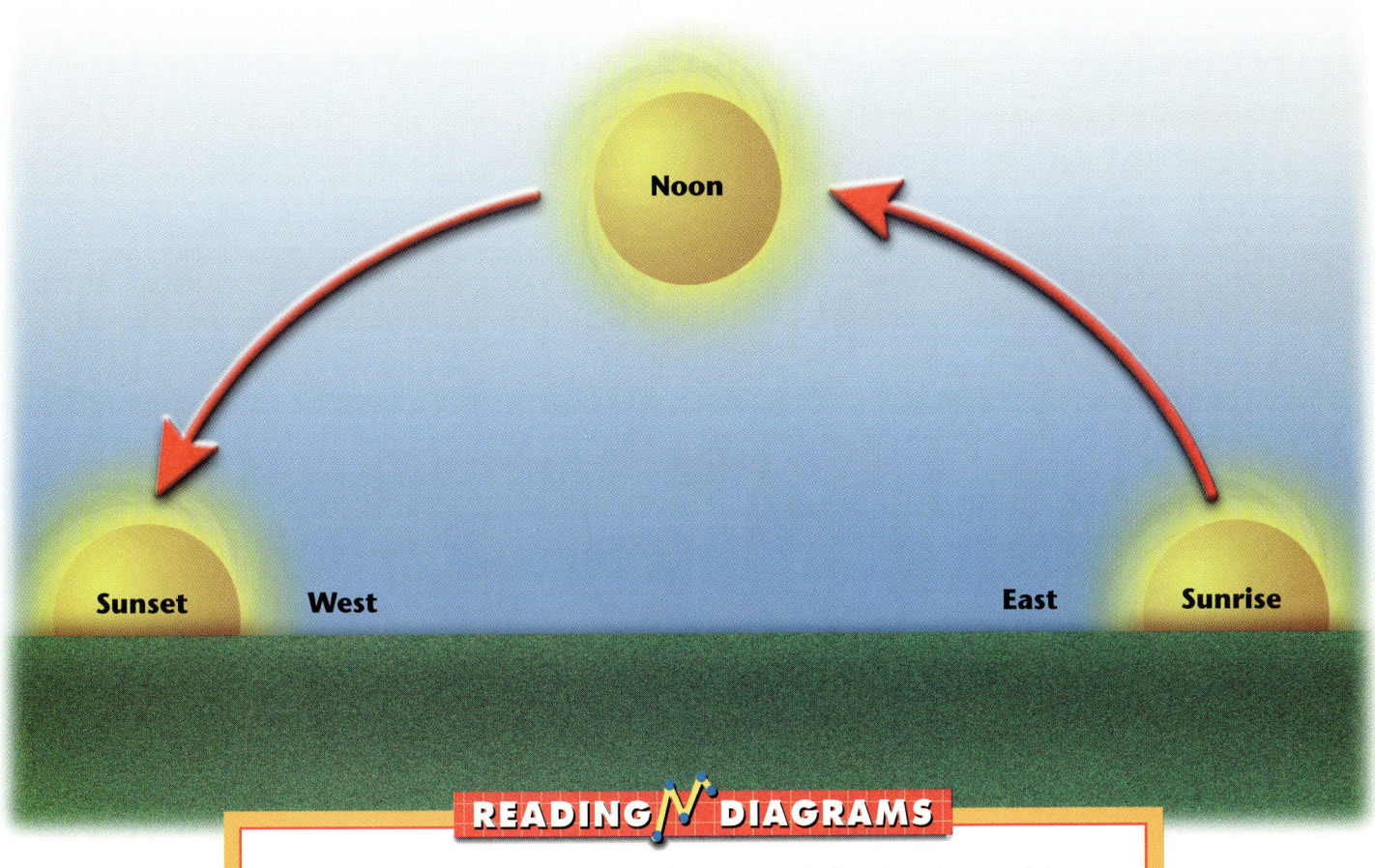

Noon

Sunset   West   East   Sunrise

READING DIAGRAMS

1. **WRITE** How can you tell the time of day by the position of the Sun in the sky? Write a description.
2. **DISCUSS** Why can't you tell the Sun's position by looking at the Sun directly?

QUICK LAB

What Time Is It?

HYPOTHESIZE How can you tell the time at any place in this country? Write a hypothesis in your *Science Journal*.

MATERIALS
- United States wall map (optional) or encyclopedia showing a map of the United States
- Science Journal

PROCEDURES

1. **OBSERVE** Use a map of the United States to locate as many towns or cities as you like. List the names in your *Science Journal*.

2. **CLASSIFY** Use the time zone map on this page to give the time zone of each town or city you named.

CONCLUDE AND APPLY

1. **INFER** Which town or city on your list has the earliest time at any moment? The latest time?

2. **INFER** If it is 4 P.M. in Houston, Texas, what time is it in each town or city on your list?

What Is the International Date Line?

What if you are traveling west in a jet? You set your watch back one hour each time zone you cross. After 24 hours you are back home. However, the date on your watch is the same! What happened?

The **International Date Line** was created as the location where a new day begins. It is universally recognized. The International Date Line is the 180° line of longitude. If you cross the date line going west, you add a day. What would you do if you crossed the date line going east?

SOME U.S. TIME ZONES

(PST) (MST) (CST) (EST)

PACIFIC STANDARD TIME (PST) — San Francisco, CA
MOUNTAIN STANDARD TIME (MST) — Phoenix, AZ
CENTRAL STANDARD TIME (CST) — Green Bay, WI; Houston, TX
EASTERN STANDARD TIME (EST) — Boston, MA; Charlotte, NC; Miami, FL

How Do We Tell Time Around the Globe?

When and where is it noon? When the Sun is at its highest over your town, it is noon for your town. But it is not noon everywhere in the world. What time is it in other places of the world?

You can tell the time by knowing how many times Earth spins each day. Earth spins toward the east. It rotates 360° (one complete turn) in 24 hours. In one hour Earth turns $\frac{360°}{24}$, or 15°. This angle defines a time zone. A **standard time zone** is a belt, 15° wide in longitude, in which all places have the same time. There is a one-hour difference between time zones that are next to each other.

When you cross time zones, you have to change your clock time. If you travel west, you must turn your clock back (subtract) one hour for each time zone you cross. If you travel east, you must set your clock ahead (add) an hour for each time zone you cross.

STANDARD TIME ZONES

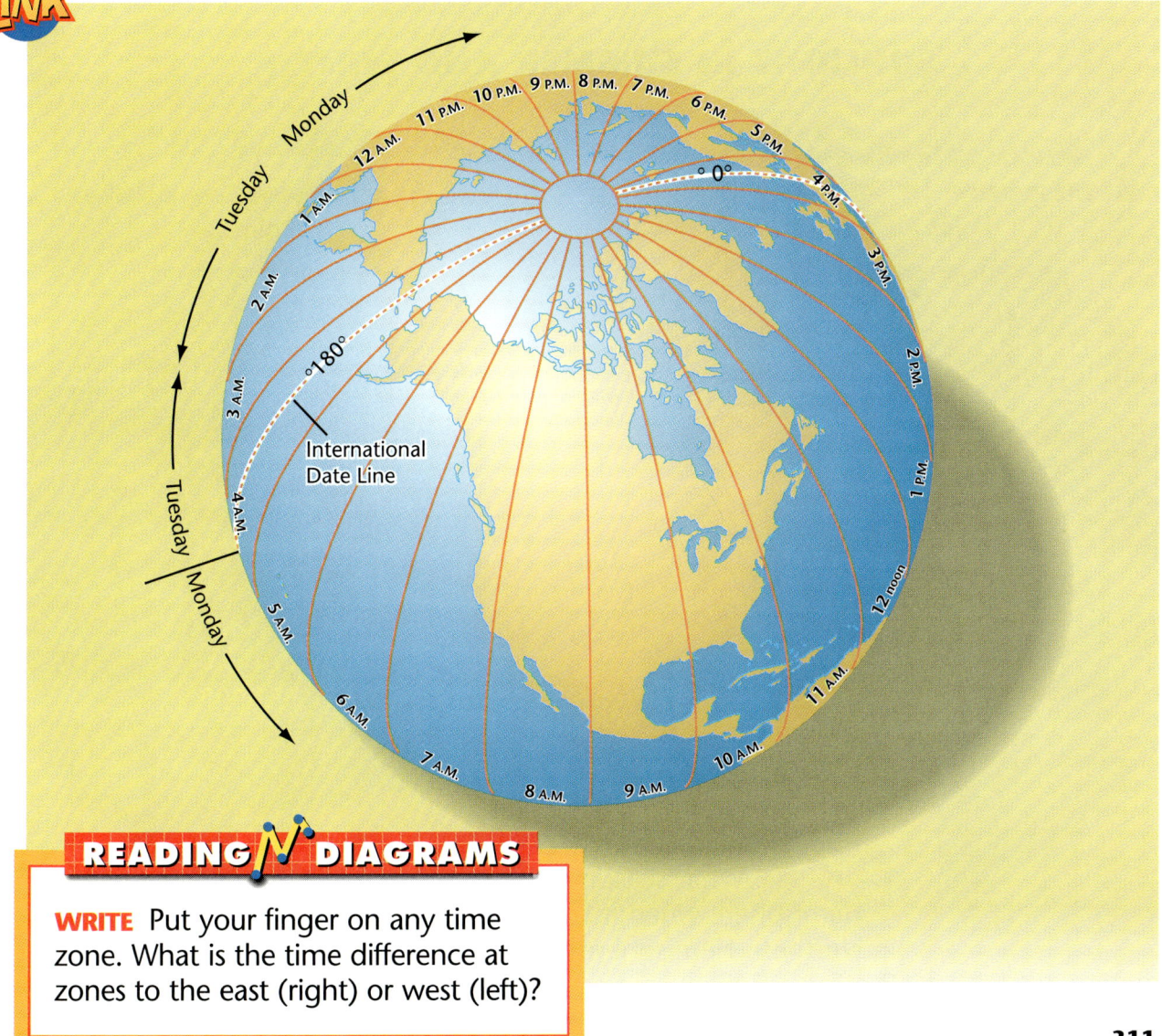

READING DIAGRAMS

WRITE Put your finger on any time zone. What is the time difference at zones to the east (right) or west (left)?

311

Why Are There Seasons?

How is summer different from winter? Why is there a difference? As a year progresses, you observe the seasons change. You most easily notice this seasonal change as the average temperature rises and falls. This change is not caused by the change in distance between Earth and the Sun through the year. What then causes this change?

Earth takes $365\frac{1}{4}$ days to revolve, or travel in its orbit, once around the Sun. One complete trip around the Sun is called a **revolution** (rev′ə lü′shən).

Remember that while it is revolving, Earth is also rotating on its axis. However, the axis is not vertical. It is tilted at an angle of $23\frac{1}{2}°$. What happens as a result of this tilt?

The effect of this tilt is the cycle of seasons. As the diagram shows, when Earth is at point A of its orbit, the Northern Hemisphere is getting the direct sunlight. At this time the Northern Hemisphere has summer. Six months later, Earth is now at point B of its orbit. Now the Northern Hemisphere is not getting the direct sunlight. It is now winter in the Northern Hemisphere.

SUNLIGHT IN SUMMER AND WINTER

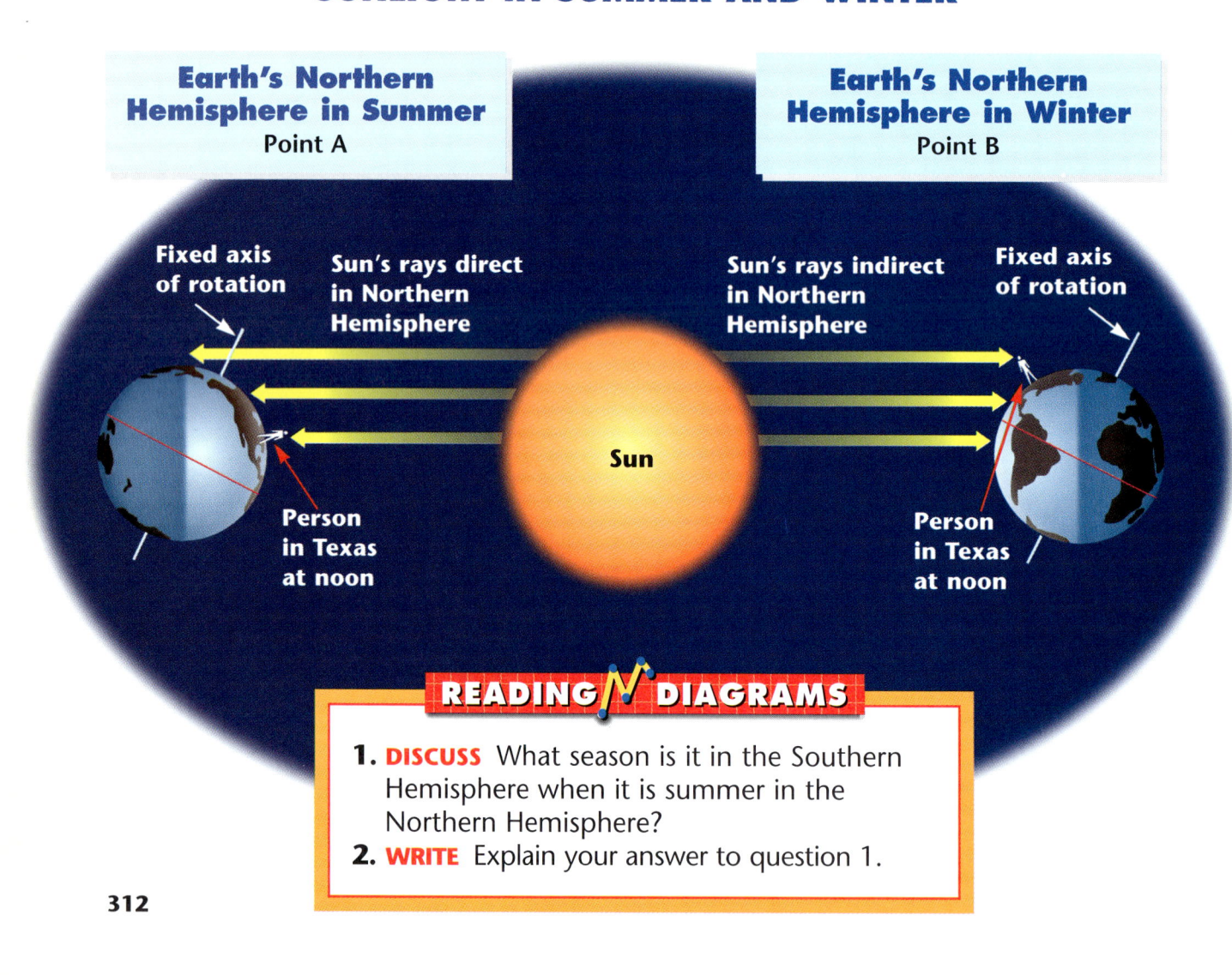

Earth's Northern Hemisphere in Summer
Point A

Earth's Northern Hemisphere in Winter
Point B

- Fixed axis of rotation
- Sun's rays direct in Northern Hemisphere
- Sun's rays indirect in Northern Hemisphere
- Fixed axis of rotation
- Person in Texas at noon
- Sun
- Person in Texas at noon

READING DIAGRAMS

1. **DISCUSS** What season is it in the Southern Hemisphere when it is summer in the Northern Hemisphere?
2. **WRITE** Explain your answer to question 1.

Where Is the Sun in Summer and in Winter?

We learned that in the summer, the Sun's rays hit Earth most directly. In the winter the Sun's rays hit Earth less directly. In spring and fall, the directness of the rays falls somewhere in between.

From the picture you might see that the more directly the Sun's rays hit Earth, the higher in the sky the Sun will appear. This means that the Sun is higher at noon in the summer than it is in the winter.

The Sun's path in the sky is different in winter and in summer.

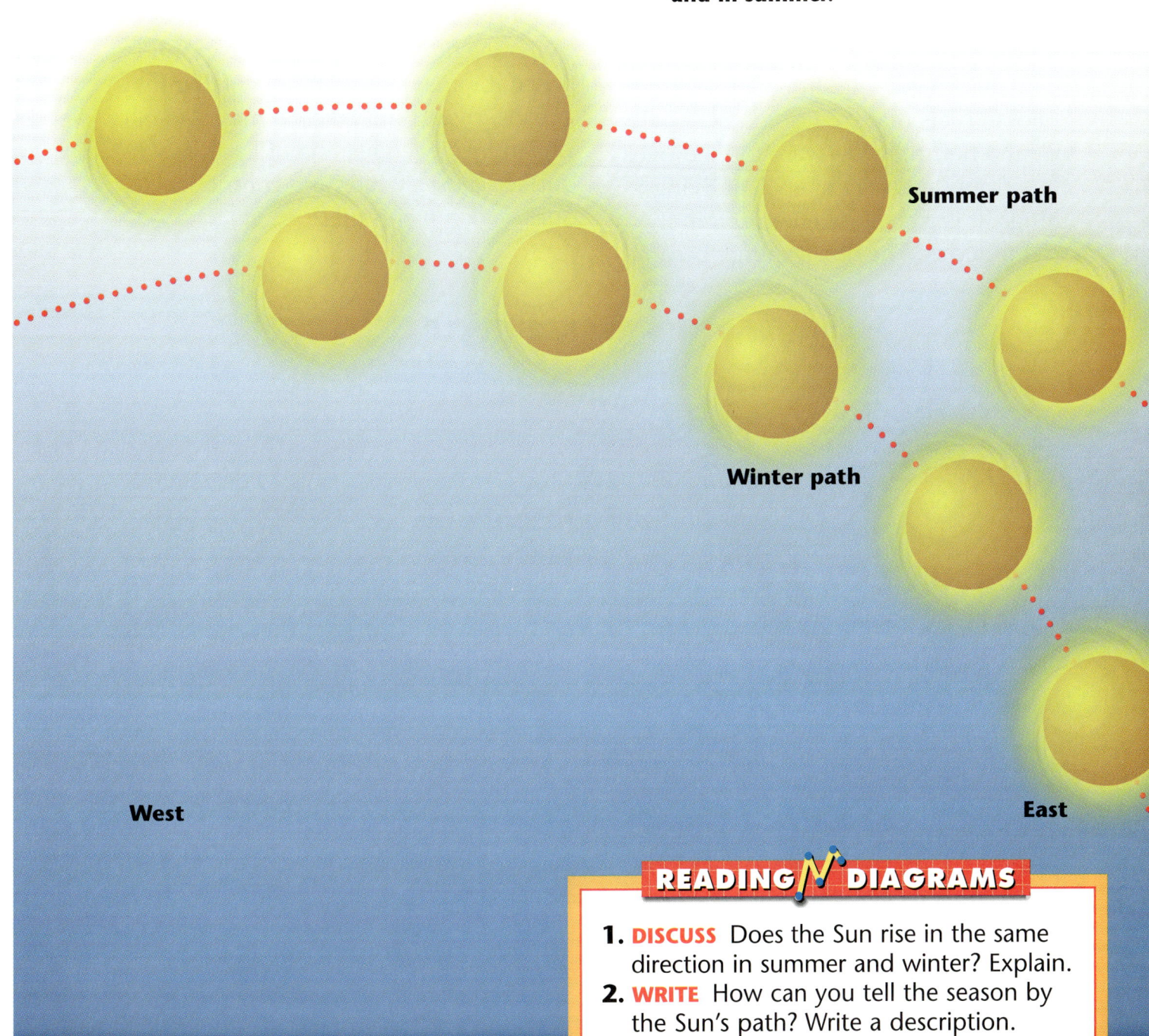

Summer path

Winter path

West

East

READING DIAGRAMS

1. **DISCUSS** Does the Sun rise in the same direction in summer and winter? Explain.
2. **WRITE** How can you tell the season by the Sun's path? Write a description.

How Is the Sun an Important Energy Source?

The Sun is the energy source for life on Earth. Light from the Sun is necessary for the growth of plants. Plants and other of Earth's producers trap the Sun's energy and use it in their food-making process. Food made by producers is necessary to pass energy on to all other living things.

Fossil fuels that we use today—coal, oil, and natural gas—were formed over time from the decay of ancient living things. It is a chain of energy from the past to today. The Sun's energy became trapped in ancient producers, which became food for other living things. The energy was stored in the fuels that formed over time.

The Sun also provides energy for events involving nonliving things. For example, the Sun is the source of energy for the water cycle. The Sun's energy causes ocean water to evaporate. As the evaporated water rises, it forms clouds. Water eventually returns to the ground when it rains. This water may fall into oceans, rivers, and lakes. It may also fall on land. Uneven heating of Earth's surface causes winds and contributes to surface ocean currents.

EARTH'S WATER CYCLE

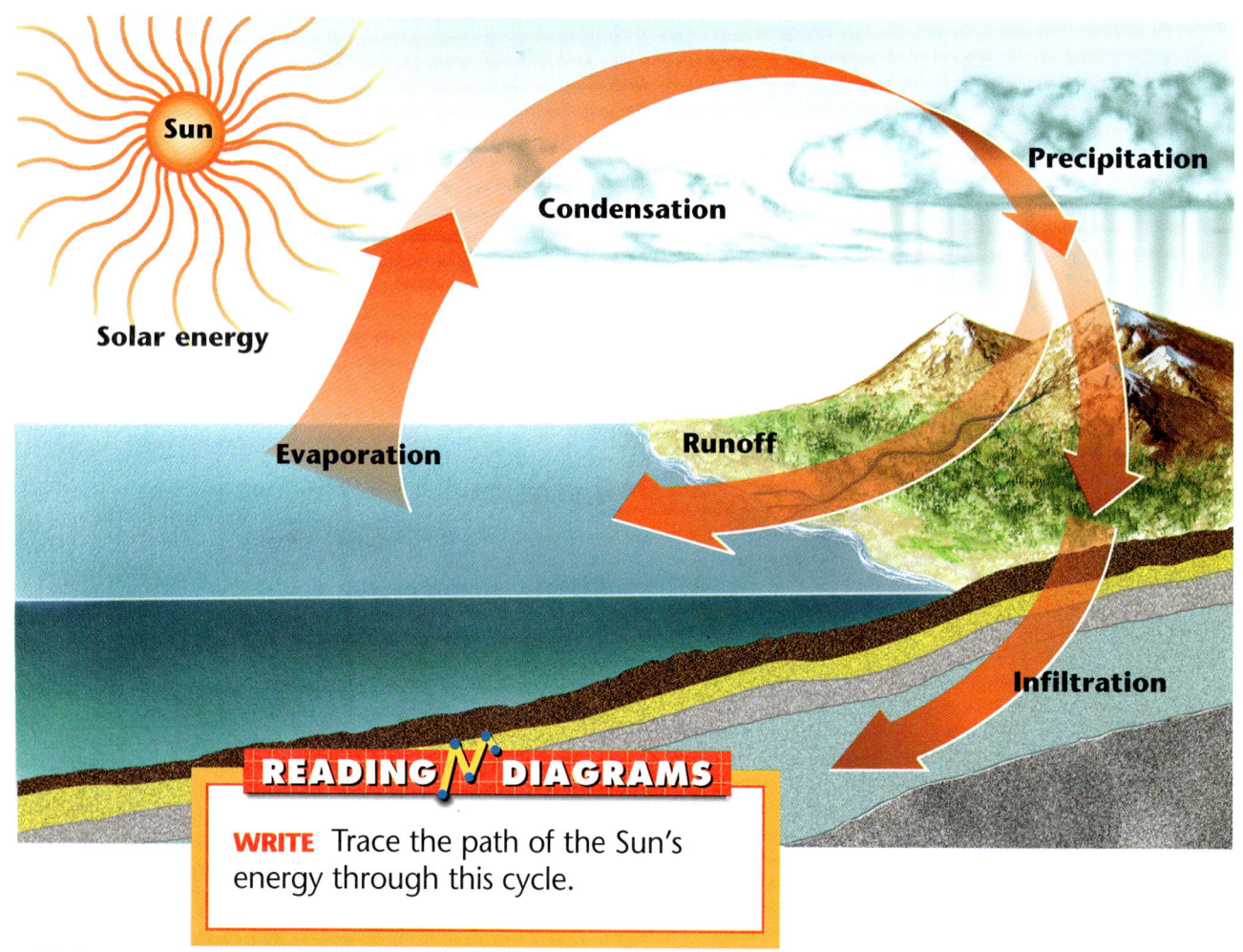

Sun
Solar energy
Condensation
Precipitation
Evaporation
Runoff
Infiltration

READING DIAGRAMS

WRITE Trace the path of the Sun's energy through this cycle.

What Is the Midnight Sun?

You know about day and night. You learned that the length of the day depends on the season. It also depends on the latitude of the person on Earth.

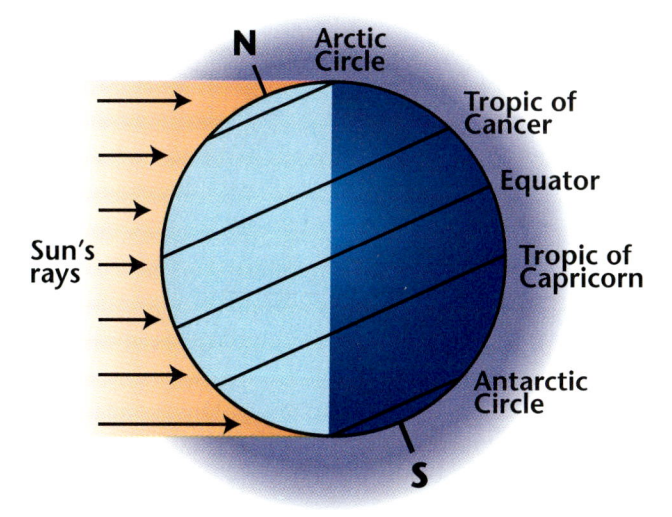

Near the North Pole, the Sun does not set from the first day of spring to the first day of autumn.

WHY IT MATTERS

The amount of sunlight has a great effect on life on Earth. For example, you know that some animals go to sleep for extended periods of time, or hibernate. Why do people want to know so much about day and night and the seasons?

People study the day/night cycle to keep calendars up to date. That is why an extra day is added once every four years—a leap year.

Also, scientists have discovered that some people become depressed and feel ill during the winter. Sometimes the reason is because the people are not getting enough sunlight. When these people turn on their lights for longer periods of time, they often feel better.

REVIEW

1. What causes day and night?
2. How are the time zones organized to help us know times around Earth?
3. **COMPARE AND CONTRAST** How can you tell the difference between summer and winter by the Sun?
4. How is the Sun a source of energy for Earth?
5. **CRITICAL THINKING** *Analyze* How does having different time zones help people live their daily lives?

WHY IT MATTERS THINK ABOUT IT
How does the Sun affect your daily life? Do you depend on it to tell you the time of day? Does the cycle of day and night affect your sleep? What other ways do you depend on the Sun's cycles?

WHY IT MATTERS WRITE ABOUT IT
What if you moved to a part of the world where a day was several months long? List the changes you would have to make in your life to adjust to this new condition.

READING SKILL
Write about some examples of cause and effect you read about in this topic.

SCIENCE MAGAZINE

The Chain of Life

Life is a never-ending circle of links in a food chain. Plants and other producers such as algae convert the Sun's light into stored chemical energy. Plant eaters, or herbivores, eat plants and use that energy for their own survival. In turn meat eaters, or carnivores, eat the herbivores, and after they die, they're eaten by worms, fungi, and bacteria.

Every food chain starts with green plants or algae. They are producers, because they make food with the Sun's energy. Imagine a food chain starting with prairie grass. A rabbit that eats the grass is a primary consumer. The snake that eats the rabbit is a secondary consumer. The eagle that eats the snake is a tertiary (third) consumer. The eagle dies. The worms and bacteria that eat the eagle are decomposers. Each link on this chain is called a trophic level.

Of course nothing in nature is quite that simple. For example, both rabbits and mice eat the grass. Both snakes and owls eat the mice and rabbits. Luckily this food chain is part of a food web.

Life Science Link

A complex food web assures that if one species dies out, another can take its place in the food chain. For example, what if a virus kills off all the rabbits in our sample chain. The snakes will become extinct, too, if rabbits are the only food they eat. The eagles will also die off, if they depend solely on snakes for food. However, if the chain is part of a rich and varied food web, the flow of energy can remain unbroken.

Only about ten percent of the energy is transferred between each level from producers to tertiary consumers.

Why? Each organism uses energy while working and doesn't completely digest all the food it eats. Picture this process as an energy pyramid, with plants at the bottom and animals that eat other animals, such as lions and humans, at the top. To get all the energy they need to survive, the top dogs are dependent on all the organisms below them.

DISCUSSION STARTER

1. Explain the flow of energy in a food chain.

2. Why is a food web more stable than a food chain?

To learn more about the food chain, visit *www.mhschool.com/science* and select the keyword LINKS.

interNET CONNECTION

Topic 3 — EARTH SCIENCE

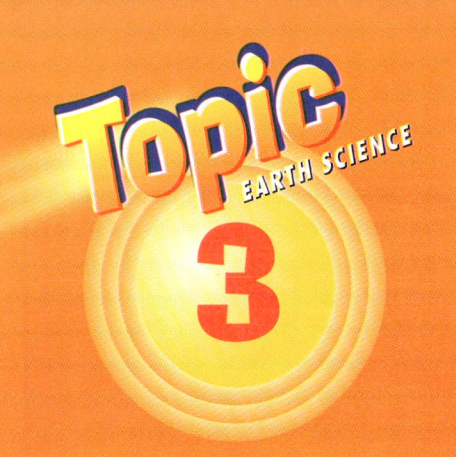

WHY IT MATTERS

Watch the Moon over a month and you'll find some interesting patterns.

SCIENCE WORDS

phase of the Moon the shape of the lighted part of the Moon seen from Earth at any time

lunar eclipse a blocking of a view of the full Moon when the Moon passes into Earth's shadow

solar eclipse a blocking out of a view of the Sun when Earth passes through the Moon's shadow

tide the regular rise and fall of the water level along a shoreline

The Moon in Motion

What shape did the Moon seem to have the last time you saw it? Describe other shapes the Moon has had. In what order did these shapes occur?

Why do people say that for part of a month, the Moon is waxing, or growing?

EXPLORE

HYPOTHESIZE Why does the Moon seem to change shape? Is Earth casting a shadow on it? Do the shapes result from the positions of the Moon, Earth, and the Sun? Write a hypothesis in your *Science Journal.* Test your ideas.

EXPLORE ACTIVITY

Investigate Why the Moon Changes Its Appearance

Use a model to explore how a ball can appear to change shape.

MATERIALS
- 3 balls (one for Earth, one for the Sun, one for the Moon)
- black tape
- crayon or felt-tipped pen (to label each ball)
- *Science Journal*

PROCEDURES

1. **MAKE A MODEL** The Sun, Earth, and the Moon are each represented by a ball. The half-dark/half-light ball represents the Moon. The light side always faces the Sun. The dark side always faces away from it.

2. **MAKE A MODEL** Arrange your model of Earth, the Sun, and the Moon so that someone on Earth would see the lighted portion of the Moon as a circle, as shown on page 318. Remember to keep the lighted side of the ball facing the Sun.

3. **COMMUNICATE** Draw a diagram in your *Science Journal* to show the location of Earth, the Sun, and the Moon in your model. Show where Earth's shadow falls.

4. **EXPERIMENT** Move the Moon around Earth in the model system so that you can match the other pictures on page 318.

CONCLUDE AND APPLY

1. **OBSERVE** How are Earth, the Sun, and the Moon arranged in order to see the views of the Moon on page 318?

2. **DRAW CONCLUSIONS** Do you think the monthly cycle of light and dark on the Moon is caused by Earth's shadow on the Moon? Explain your answer.

GOING FURTHER: Problem Solving

3. **ANALYZE** In which direction must the Moon move around Earth to produce the shapes in the proper order?

Why Does the Moon Change Its Appearance?

How can we summarize the motion of Earth and the Moon? The Moon revolves around Earth and Earth revolves around the Sun. You also know that the Moon changes its appearance in monthly cycles. The amount of the bright part of the Moon changes shape. The **phase of the Moon** is the shape of the lighted part of the Moon at any given time. What causes these shapes? The Explore Activity provided a model to help answer this question.

Remember, half of the Moon is always lighted by the Sun. However, you can't always see all of that half. Sometimes you can see only small amounts of this portion of the Moon. Sometimes you can see a lot. Sometimes you can't see any of the lighted half of the Moon at all!

The phase, or shape, of the Moon that you see depends on the position of the Sun, the Moon, and Earth with respect to each other.

- *New Moon* **Phase:** At New Moon the Moon is between Earth and the Sun. The half of the Moon lit by the Sun is opposite the half that faces Earth. As a result, you cannot see any of the Moon's sunlit half.

- **Waxing Phases:** As the Moon orbits Earth, more of its sunlit half becomes visible. When half of the sunlit side is visible, the Moon is at *First Quarter phase.* As you see it, the right half of the Moon is visible. If all of its sunlit half is visible, the Moon is at the phase called *Second Quarter*, or the *Full Moon*.
When the phase that is visible is more than New Moon but less than First Quarter, the phase is called a *Waxing Crescent. Waxing* means "growing larger." When the phase visible is more than First Quarter but less than Full Moon, the phase is a *Waxing Gibbous* Moon.

Half of the Moon visible from Earth

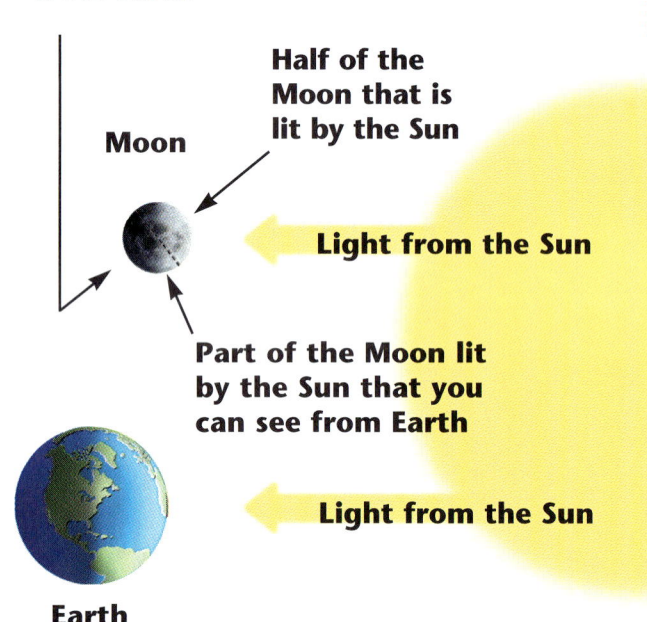

Moon

Half of the Moon that is lit by the Sun

Light from the Sun

Part of the Moon lit by the Sun that you can see from Earth

Light from the Sun

Earth

Note the positions of the Sun, the Moon, and Earth during the Waxing Crescent phase.

- **Waning Phases:** After Full Moon the part of the sunlit half of the Moon you can see gets smaller. The phases you see are the same as from new to full, only in reverse.

When the left half of the Moon is visible, the phase of the Moon is the *Third Quarter*, or *Last Quarter*. The phase of the Moon that is less than Full Moon phase but more than Third Quarter is called a *Waning Gibbous* Moon. *Waning* means "growing smaller." When the phase you see is less than Third Quarter but more than New Moon, the phase is called a *Waning Crescent*.

PHASES OF THE MOON

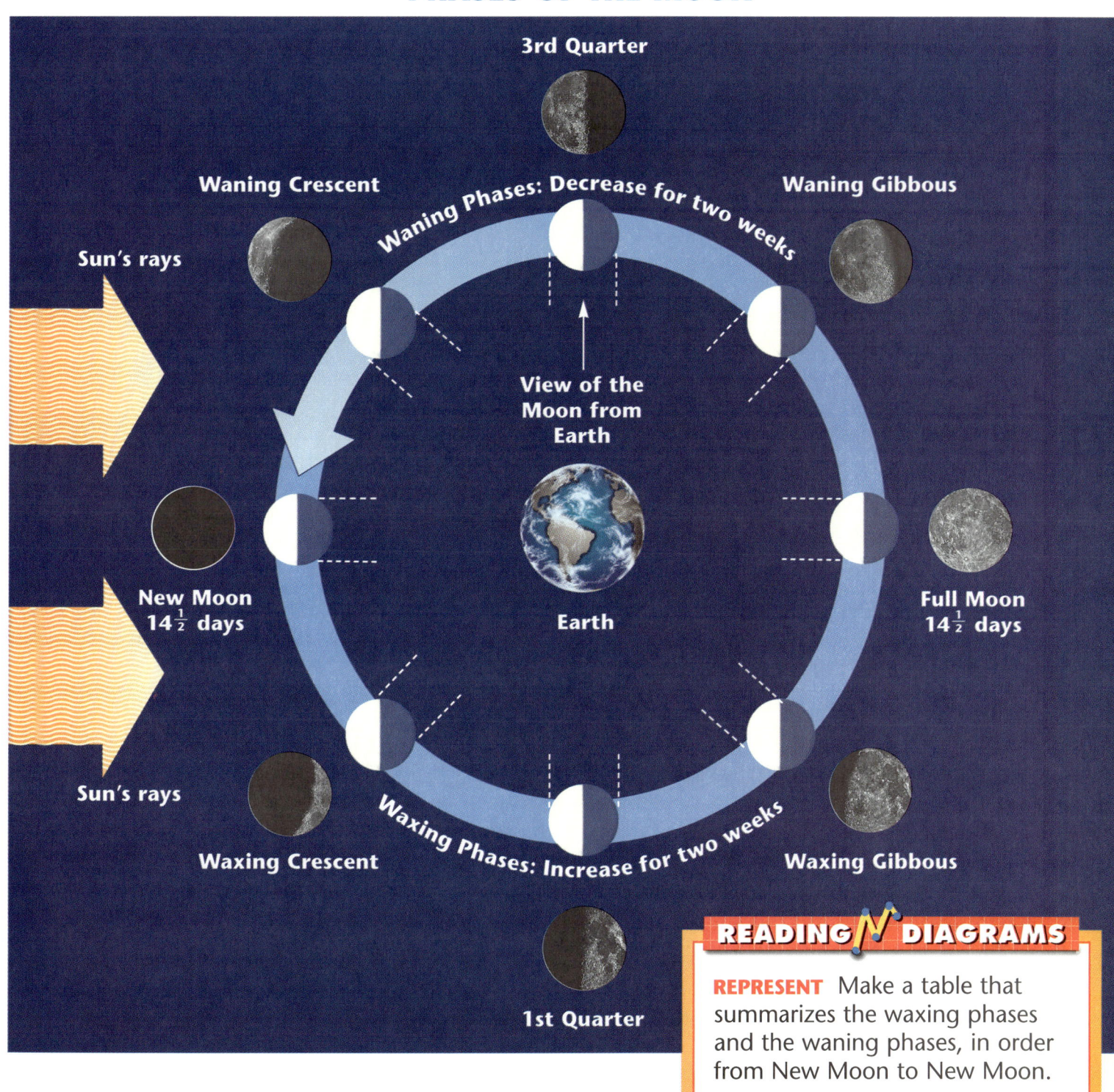

- 3rd Quarter
- Waning Crescent
- Waning Phases: Decrease for two weeks
- Waning Gibbous
- Sun's rays
- View of the Moon from Earth
- New Moon 14½ days
- Earth
- Full Moon 14½ days
- Sun's rays
- Waxing Crescent
- Waxing Phases: Increase for two weeks
- Waxing Gibbous
- 1st Quarter

READING DIAGRAMS

REPRESENT Make a table that summarizes the waxing phases and the waning phases, in order from New Moon to New Moon.

LUNAR ECLIPSE

Partial lunar eclipse

The path of light in a total lunar eclipse

Sun — Sunlight — Earth — Umbra — Moon — Penumbra

The umbra is the dark part of the shadow where the Sun is completely blocked. The penumbra is the lighter part of the shadow where the Sun is only partially blocked.

Brain Power
What does the Moon look like as it passes into Earth's shadow? Would you see phases of the Moon? Explain.

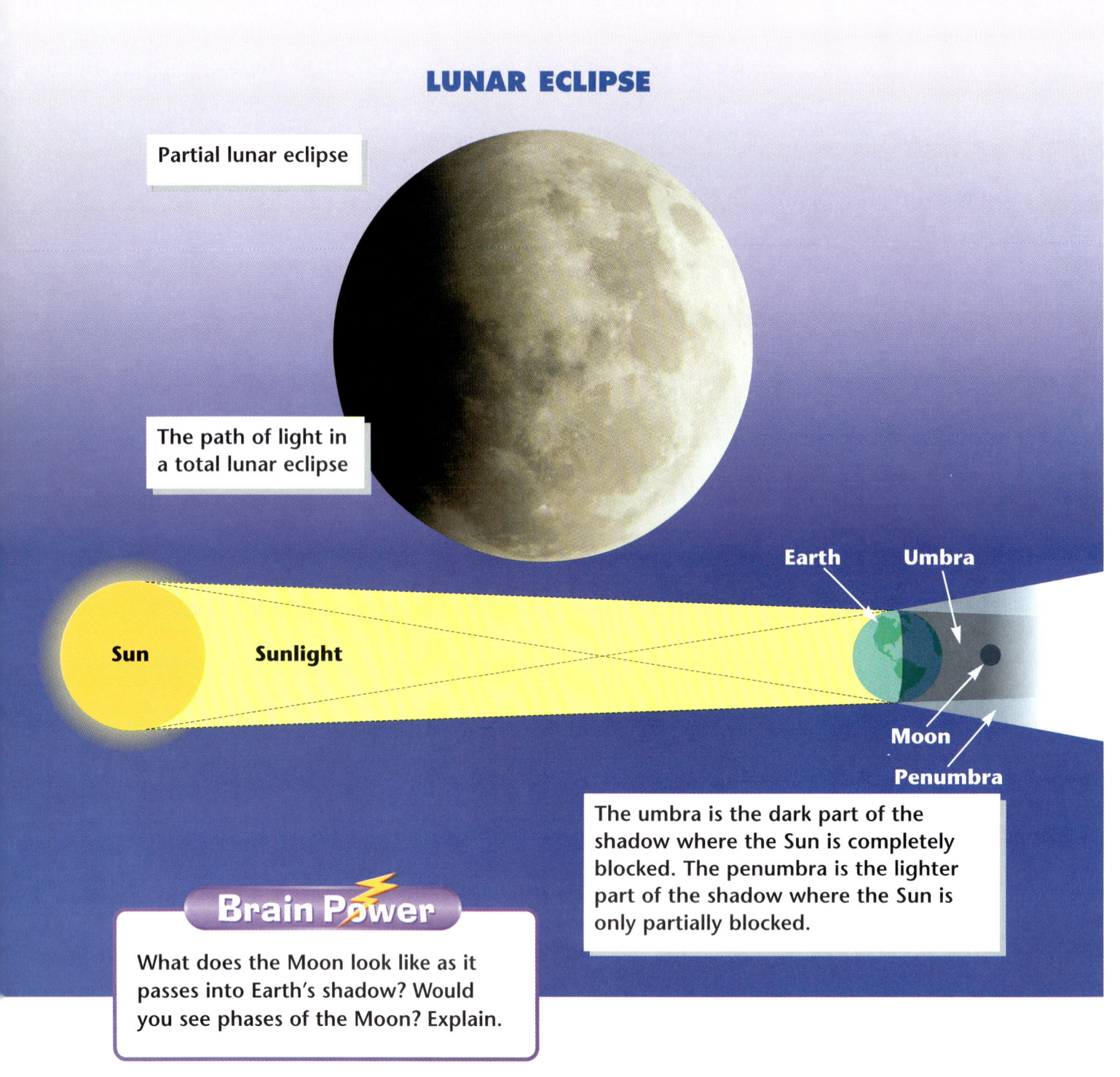

Can Earth's Shadow Hide the Moon?

Recall that the Moon revolves around Earth. Recall also that at the same time, Earth revolves around the Sun.

The plane of the Moon's orbit is tilted to the plane of Earth's orbit around the Sun. As a result the Moon is usually above or below Earth's orbit. Twice a month the Moon crosses the plane of Earth's orbit. When this takes place at full Moon, the Moon might pass through Earth's shadow. When this happens a **lunar eclipse** occurs. Our view of the full Moon is blocked.

322

What Is an Eclipse of the Sun?

When Earth passes through the Moon's shadow, a solar eclipse occurs. At what phase must a **solar eclipse** occur?

For a solar eclipse to occur, the Moon must be in a straight line between the Sun and Earth. This arrangement happens at New Moon phase. A solar eclipse can occur when the Moon crosses the plane of Earth's orbit at New Moon phase.

Have you ever seen a total solar eclipse? It is a fascinating sight. At the greatest part of the eclipse, the Moon completely hides the Sun. All you can see is the gases in the outer atmosphere surrounding the Sun.

Earth-orbiting satellites have actually been able to photograph an eclipse! See the picture below. Where do you think the eclipse of the Sun is occurring at this moment?

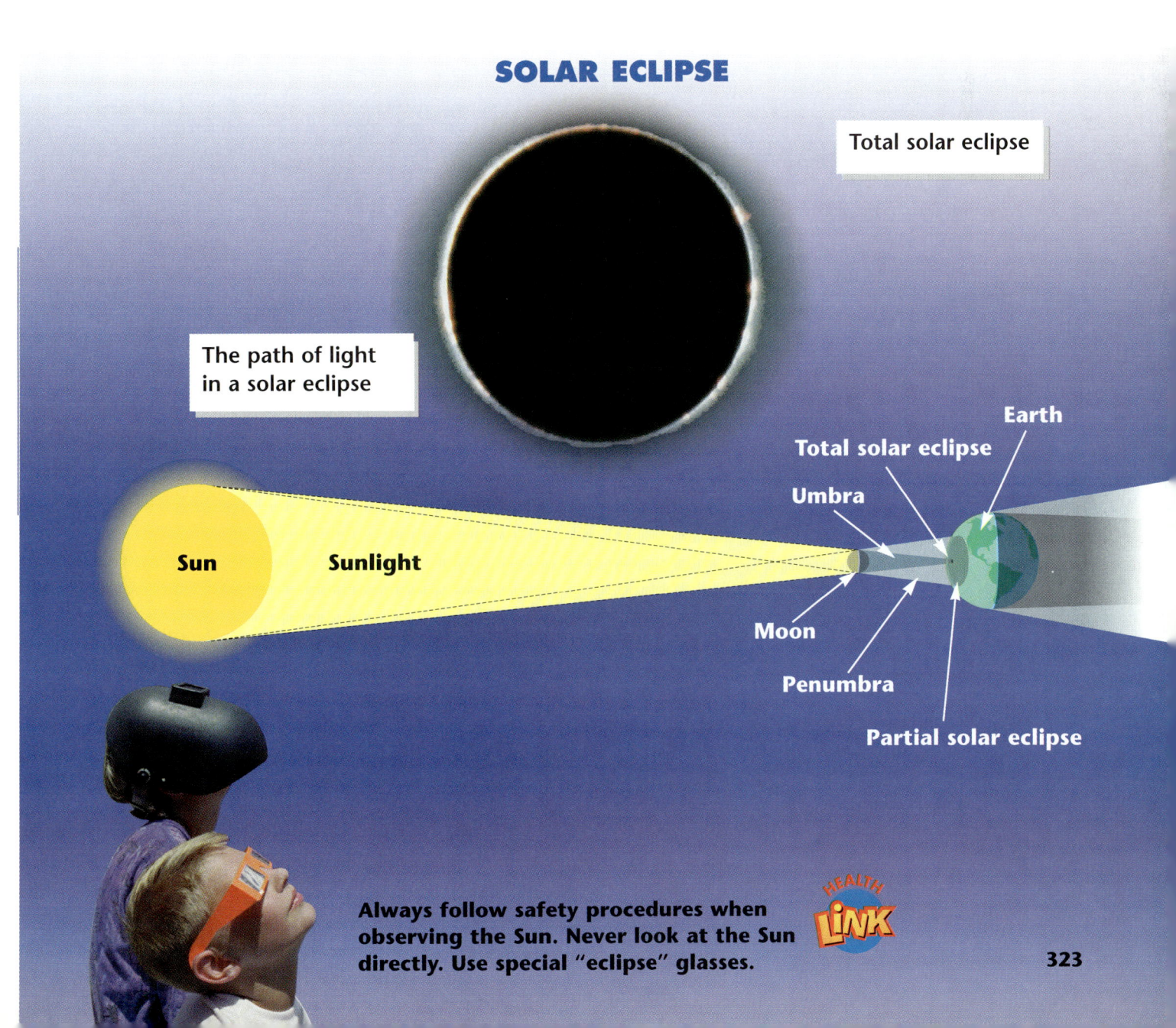

SOLAR ECLIPSE

Total solar eclipse

The path of light in a solar eclipse

Sun — Sunlight — Moon — Umbra — Total solar eclipse — Earth — Penumbra — Partial solar eclipse

Always follow safety procedures when observing the Sun. Never look at the Sun directly. Use special "eclipse" glasses.

HEALTH LINK

323

What Are Tides?

Have you ever been at the seashore and watched the ocean waves? If you have, you may have noticed that as time passed the waves came higher up on the shore. You were looking at the **tide** coming in. Tides are the regular rise and fall of the water level along a shore.

The tides are caused by the pull of the Moon's gravity on Earth. The Moon's gravity is stonger on the side of Earth that is facing the Moon. This causes the water to bulge on this side of Earth. A bulge also forms on the side facing away from the Moon.

At certain times of the year, the alignment of the Sun, the Moon, and Earth causes what are called *spring tides* and *neap tides*.

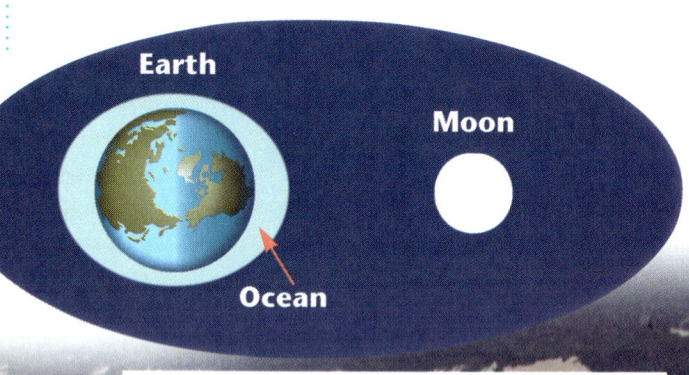

These tides are caused by the Moon. The same effect occurs with the Sun.

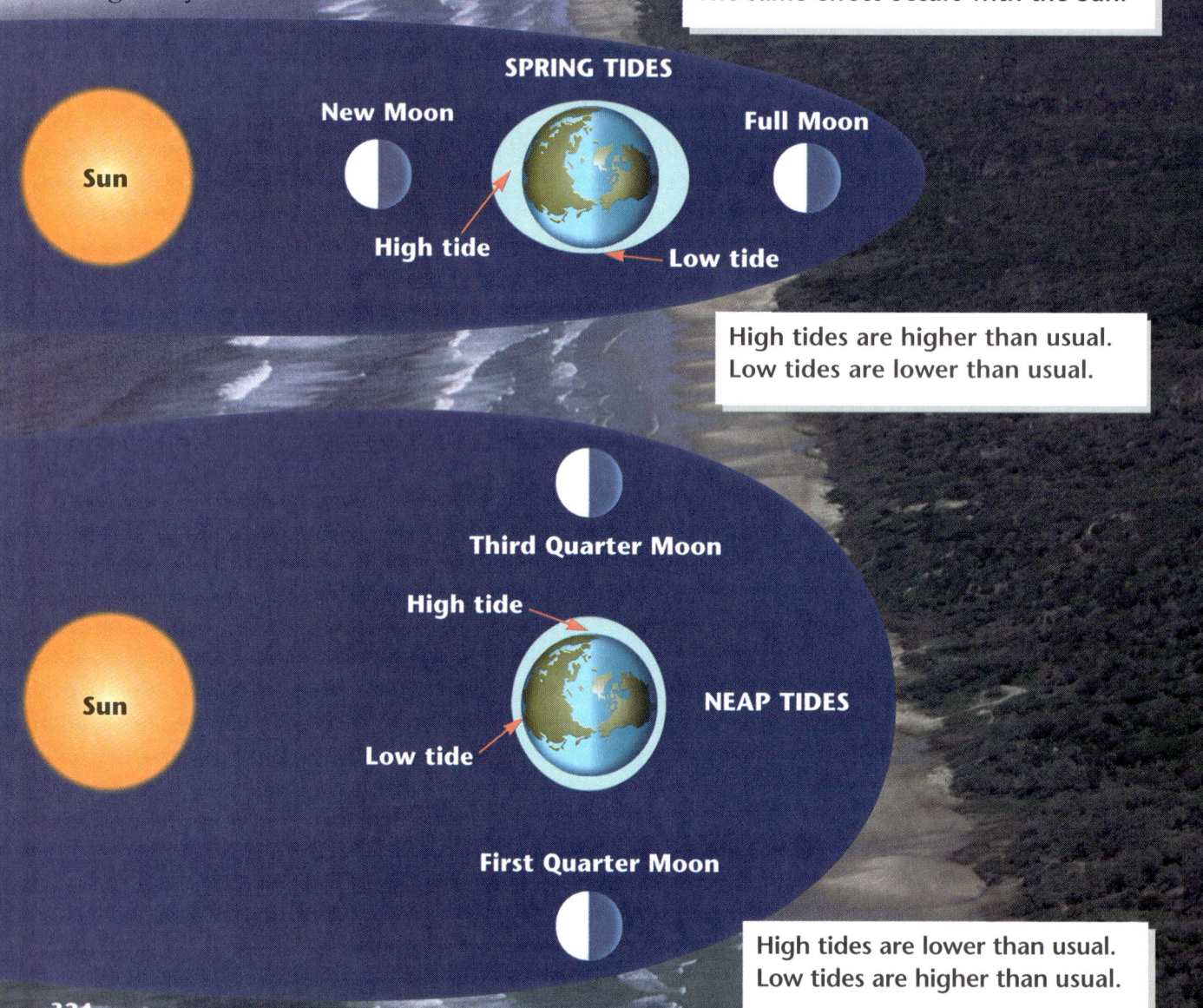

SPRING TIDES

High tides are higher than usual. Low tides are lower than usual.

NEAP TIDES

High tides are lower than usual. Low tides are higher than usual.

SKILL BUILDER

Skill: Making a Model

MODEL OF THE TIDES
Now that you have read about spring and neap tides, you and a partner are going to practice making a model of a spring tide. How good a model can you make?

MATERIALS
- large ball (the Sun)
- balloon, not fully inflated (Earth)
- small ball (the Moon)
- *Science Journal*

PROCEDURES

1. **MAKE A MODEL** How are you going to arrange the materials to model a spring tide? A neap tide? How are you going to model the pull on Earth due to the Moon and the Sun? Talk with your partner. Record your ideas in your *Science Journal*.

2. **EXPERIMENT** Test your model. Repeat your test, switching roles with your partner.

3. **COMMUNICATE** In your *Science Journal*, sketch your model. Write or draw the results of your test.

CONCLUDE AND APPLY

1. **OBSERVE** How did you model the pull of the Moon and the Sun on Earth? What results did you obtain?

2. **ANALYZE** How well did your model work? What went right with your model? What things did you have difficulty with in your model?

3. **COMPARE AND CONTRAST** Share your model and your results with your classmates. Did other teams have similar successes or difficulties? How would you change your model to make it work better?

What Does the Moon's Surface Look Like?

When you look at the Moon from Earth, it shows features that can be easily seen. When the *Apollo* astronauts visited the Moon in the 1960s and 1970s, they took close-up pictures of many of these same features. Some of the features looked the same way they looked from Earth. Some of them looked very different. What do we know about these features?

- **Craters** were formed by the impact of objects from space. Craters are in many sizes and shapes. Some have peaks in the center. Some craters also seem to have rings that make them look like bull's-eye targets. When the meteorites hit the surface, the impact sent out waves, just like when you throw a rock into a pond. The waves formed rings, or rims, around the craters. Even though the Moon and Earth are hit by space objects at about the same rate, there are more craters on the Moon. This is because erosion on Earth wears away Earth craters. There is no erosion on the Moon.

- **Maria** (singular, *mare*) are large, dark, flat areas. They were the "seas" seen by the people of long ago. You can still see them if you look now. However, the maria are not really seas. They were formed by huge lava flows that covered low-lying areas, including the craters, billions of years ago.

- **Highlands** are light-colored, heavily cratered regions at higher elevations than maria.

- **Mountains** are named after mountain ranges on Earth. These features were formed as a result of violent impacts of debris from space that created the maria.

- **Valleys** are cigar-shaped depressions. The most famous is the Alpine Valley. It is located in the mountain range known as the Alps. The Alpine Valley is on the northeastern edge of Mare Imbrium.

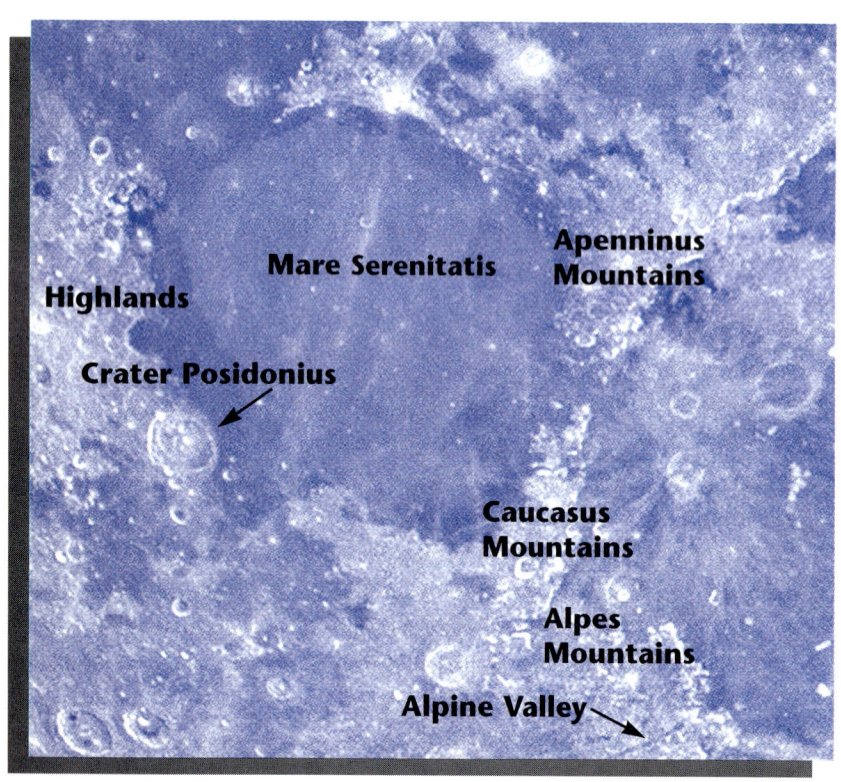

Various features of the moon's surface as observed from Ringgold, Georgia.

What Have We Learned About the Moon?

HISTORY Link

The *Apollo* missions to the Moon have given us much data about the Moon. We have also learned a lot from telescopes and probes sent to the Moon.

What Was Learned

- The Moon has no magnetic field today. However, it had a weak one in the past.
- Seismometers show that the Moon is still being hit by meteors.
- Heat-flow experiments show that the Moon is losing heat.
- Rock samples brought back to Earth have provided clues to the early history of the Earth and Moon system.

Apollo changed our ideas about the Moon.

WHY IT MATTERS

Human beings get great satisfaction when a simple idea can explain many different observations. We can take pleasure then in the simple idea of this lesson. The Moon moves around Earth as Earth goes around the Sun. This simple model explains Moon phases, eclipses, and tides.

REVIEW

1. Why do we see the phases of the Moon?
2. How is a lunar eclipse different from a solar eclipse?
3. **MAKE A MODEL** Where are the Sun, the Moon, and Earth during a neap tide? During a spring tide?
4. How does the Moon's surface compare with Earth's?
5. **CRITICAL THINKING** *Apply* During a total lunar eclipse, the Moon looks completely dark as seen from Earth. When this happens what do you think Earth looks like from the Moon? To answer this draw a model of a lunar eclipse.

WHY IT MATTERS THINK ABOUT IT
What if you receive an E-mail message from your friend? Your friend writes that the phases of the Moon are caused by Earth's shadow cast on the Moon. Why is this not correct?

WHY IT MATTERS WRITE ABOUT IT
Write a reply to your friend that explains why Moon phases cannot be caused by shadows. Then give the correct explanation.

SCIENCE MAGAZINE

Straddling Worlds

Imagine living in a place where waves continually pound you, a place that is dry one minute and submerged the next. That's what it's like for the creatures of the tidal zone. Within each distinct area, animals and plants make the most of what's available.

THE LOW-TIDE ZONE
Sea urchins dig holes in the rocks to assure that even at low tide, water will fill their homes. Sea urchins graze on algae. They scrape algae off surfaces with teeth around their mouth.

THE MIDTIDE ZONE
The spiny starfish, or sea star, uses its suction-cup feet to stay put even when the waves are rough. To eat, this critter sticks its feet to either side of a mussel shell, pries it open, inserts its own stomach, and digests the mussel!

Life Science Link

THE HIGH-TIDE ZONE
The barnacle has a hard shell to bear the crushing weight of pounding surf. It also has a gluey substance on its head. It sticks to rocks so it won't wash away. To eat, a barnacle kicks its featherlike feet into the water and moves plankton into its shell.

THE SPLASH ZONE
Animals in the splash zone don't need much moisture. Periwinkle snails scrape algae off splash-zone rocks with their sharp tongues. However, a dogwinkle snail can drill through a periwinkle's shell and eat the animal inside!

DISCUSSION STARTER

1. What makes life difficult for animals and plants in the tidal zone?

2. How have animals adapted to life in the tidal zone?

To learn more about life in the tidal zones, visit *www.mhschool.com/science* and select the keyword TIDES.

interNET CONNECTION

CHAPTER 7 REVIEW

SCIENCE WORDS

frequency p. 295
lunar eclipse p. 322
reflection p. 294
refraction p. 294
revolution p. 312
rotation p. 308
solar eclipse p. 323
telescope p. 293
tide p. 324
universe p. 292

USING SCIENCE WORDS

Number a paper from 1 to 10. Fill in 1 to 5 with words from the list above.

1. When the Moon blocks our view of the Sun, it is called a __?__.

2. The regular rise and fall of the water level along a shore is called the __?__.

3. The bending of waves when they go from one substance to another is called __?__.

4. Earth makes one __?__ each year.

5. __?__ is the bouncing of waves off a surface.

6–10. Pick five words from the list above that were not used in 1 to 5, and use each in a sentence.

UNDERSTANDING SCIENCE IDEAS

11. What properties distinguish radio waves from visible light?

12. Telescopes can be designed based on which two properties of light?

13. The flattening of Earth at the poles and the bulging at the equator is evidence for what?

14. Describe what astronomers study.

15. What can make the Moon look completely dark as seen from Earth?

USING IDEAS AND SKILLS

16. **READING SKILL: CAUSE AND EFFECT** How do astronomers find out about the universe if they cannot leave Earth?

17. Is the cycle of seasons due to a change in the tilt of Earth's axis?

18. Why are there more craters on the Moon than on Earth?

19. **MAKE A MODEL** How does the arrangement of Earth, the Sun, and the Moon affect the tides on Earth?

20. **THINKING LIKE A SCIENTIST** The force of gravity depends on your distance from Earth's center. How would you test this hypothesis?

PROBLEMS and PUZZLES

Lunar Month For one month observe the Moon at the same time of the day. Draw its shape, and label it with the date and time you observed it. Label the drawings with the phases you observe. Is the Moon always in the same part of the sky? How did the Moon's shape change from day to day?

CHAPTER 8
THE SOLAR SYSTEM AND BEYOND

When you think of a cloud, what comes to mind? A storm? A sunny day? How about a nursery?

This is a kind of cloud in outer space. In a way it is a nursery. In this cloud stars will eventually be born. Revolving around some of these stars might even be planets!

In this chapter you will compare and contrast many things. To *compare* means to tell how things are alike. To *contrast* means to tell how things are different.

Topic 4 EARTH SCIENCE

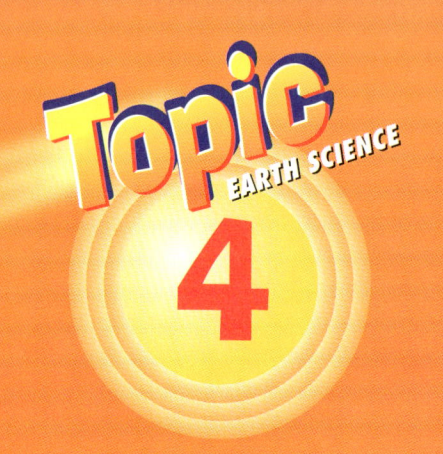

WHY IT MATTERS

Earth is only one of many objects in orbit around the Sun.

SCIENCE WORDS

planet a large body orbiting a star, such as the Sun

solar system a star, such as the Sun, and all the objects orbiting it

asteroid a rocky, metallic object that orbits the Sun

Kepler's laws laws that summarize the movement of the planets

The Inner Solar System

How are planets and stars different? On clear nights, away from city lights, stars appear to be points of light. However, some of these points of light are not stars. Some are planets—such as Jupiter and Venus. How can you tell them from stars?

The arrows in these pictures point to a planet at two different times of the year. What has changed between the two pictures?

EXPLORE

HYPOTHESIZE How does the sky change from night to night? How do these changes allow you to tell stars from planets? Write a hypothesis in your *Science Journal*. Test your ideas.

EXPLORE ACTIVITY

Investigate How to Tell Planets from Stars

Use a map to search for planets.

MATERIALS
- 6 marbles
- 4 lumps of clay
- *Science Journal*

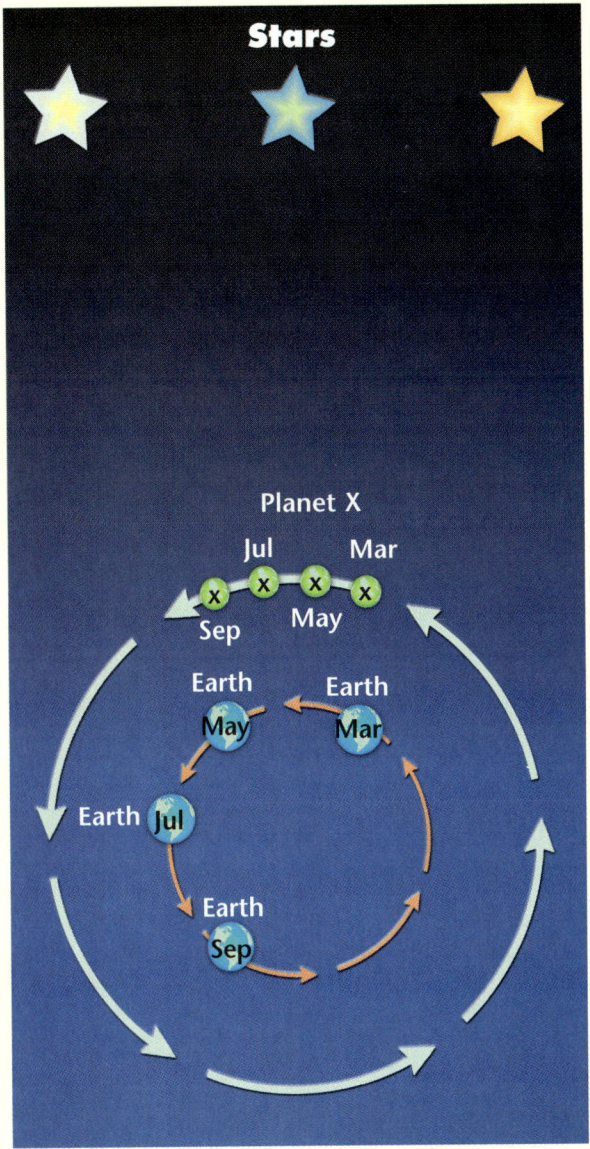

PROCEDURES

This "map" shows the locations of three different stars and the orbits of Earth and Planet X. It also shows the positions of both planets for four observations. The observations are made every two months.

1. **EXPERIMENT** Work with a copy of this drawing in your *Science Journal*. Use clay to fix a marble in each of the three star locations. Fix a marble on Planet X for the March observation. Look at Planet X from Earth's March position. Note its position with respect to the stars. Write a 1 to mark where Planet X appears between the stars.

2. **EXPERIMENT** Repeat step 1 for May, July, and September. Write a 2, 3, or 4 in the field of stars for these monthly observations.

3. **OBSERVE** Study the pattern of numbers showing the changing position of Planet X.

CONCLUDE AND APPLY

1. **MEASURE** Compare the distance Earth and Planet X seem to move in one month. Which seems to be traveling faster?

2. **ANALYZE** In what direction does Planet X appear to move from March to July with respect to the stars?

3. **COMMUNICATE** Did the stars seem to move? If so, describe what you saw.

GOING FURTHER: Problem Solving

4. **MAKE CONCLUSIONS** How can you tell the stars from the planets? What would you have to do to check your answer? What kind of information would you have to collect?

333

READING DIAGRAMS

1. DISCUSS What is the order of planets from the closest to the farthest?

2. WRITE Is the same planet always the farthest?

The solar system

How Can We Tell Planets from Stars?

Long ago, before telescopes, astronomers noticed stars (balls of glowing hot gas). They also noticed objects that changed position from night to night against the background of stars. These objects are the **planets**. Planets are large bodies orbiting a star. In this case the star is the Sun. We detect planets from the sunlight reflected off them.

The ancient astronomers did not know what the planets were. However, they used observations much like those in the Explore Activity to follow the motion of these objects.

They tried to explain how these moving objects could change position. Early ideas of how objects in the universe were organized put Earth at the center of everything. It did not move. The Sun, the Moon, and the stars revolved around Earth.

However, this organization had some problems. What about the planets? (*Planet* comes from the Greek word meaning "wanderer.") The planets seemed to wander among the stars. This, in fact, was how ancient astronomers could recognize planets. Sometimes the planets seemed to be moving backward.

Some astronomers said the Sun was at the center. Earth and everything else revolved around it.

At the time it was introduced, this model was very unpopular. Many people did not like to know about things that would challenge their ideas about the order of things. However, this new model explained the motions of the planets. It explained them more simply than the Earth-centered idea.

Astronomers today are still interested in the motion of planets. They are also interested in their properties. The planets are part of the solar system. The **solar system** is the Sun and all of the planets, moons, and other bodies traveling around it.

334

SKILL BUILDER

Skill: Experimenting

PATHS IN SPACE

How do planets and other objects in the solar system move? Does the path depend on how fast the object moves? Is the path affected by gravity? Write a hypothesis in your *Science Journal*.

In this activity you are going to use observations of a model to test your hypothesis.

MATERIALS
- rubber ball
- 2 different-colored pencils
- paper
- *Science Journal*

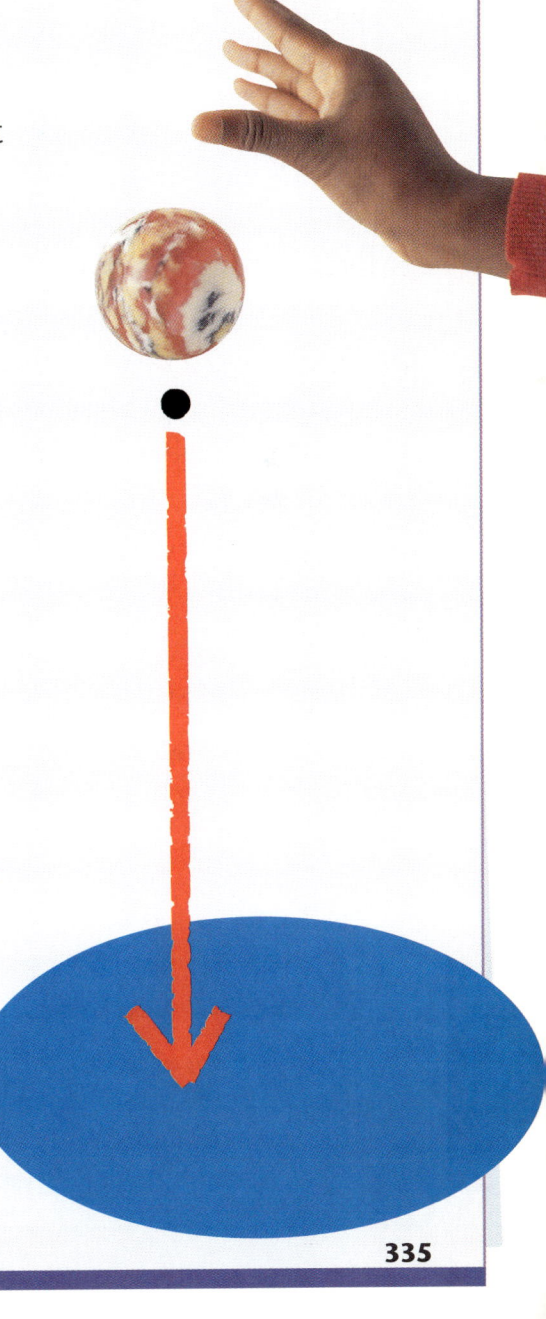

PROCEDURES

1. **MAKE A MODEL** In your *Science Journal*, draw a large circle on your paper. This circle is Earth. Draw a dot about 10 cm above Earth's surface. The dot represents a ball.

2. **EXPERIMENT** Drop a ball from 1 meter above the ground (that is, above Earth's surface). Observe its path. Draw this path above the circle in your *Science Journal*.

3. **USE VARIABLES** Now hold the ball the same height as in step 2, but toss it sideways with just a little speed. Observe the ball's path. Draw the path in your *Science Journal*.

4. **USE VARIABLES** Repeat step 3 three more times. Each time throw the ball sideways a little faster.

CONCLUDE AND APPLY

1. **OBSERVE** What did you observe about the path of the ball as you increased the sideways speed?

2. **INFER** Suppose a cannon can fire the ball faster and faster. Using the second colored pencil, draw the path you think the ball would take.

3. **ANALYZE** Is there a speed the cannon could fire the ball at so that it circles Earth but never lands again? If so, draw the path the ball would take.

4. **DRAW CONCLUSIONS** Do you think there is a speed at which the ball would escape Earth, that is, never come back? If so, draw its path.

What Do We Know About Mercury and Venus?

Mercury

Mercury is the closest planet to the Sun and the second-smallest planet.

The *Mariner 10* space probe sent back most of the data on Mercury. Here is some of the information collected by *Mariner 10*:

- Mercury has cliffs, craters, and lava flows.
- Mercury revolves around the Sun in 88 Earth days. It rotates once every 59 Earth days.
- Temperatures on Mercury range from –173°C (that is, 173° below 0°C) to 427°C.
- Mercury has a very weak magnetic field.
- Mercury's density is about the same as Earth's density.
- Deep inside craters where the Sun's light never reaches, there may be water ice.

Venus

Venus has been visited by space probes. *Pioneer Venus* (U.S.A. 1978), the *Venera 15* and *16* probes (U.S.S.R. 1983–1984), and *Magellan* (U.S.A. 1990–1994) all visited the planet. They sent back much fascinating data:

- Venus has a surface covered with vast plains, lava flows, thousands of volcanoes, huge mountains, and craters.
- A day on Venus is longer than its year. Venus rotates once every 243 Earth days. It revolves around the Sun in 225 Earth days. Venus also rotates in a direction opposite that of Earth's rotation.
- Temperatures on Venus hover around 480°C (900°F). This high temperature is mostly due to a runaway greenhouse effect. Sunlight hits the surface and atmosphere. The surface and atmosphere then reemit the light in the infrared range. Infrared light cannot get through the atmosphere. That is, it becomes "trapped" by the atmosphere.
- Pressure at the surface is 92 times atmospheric pressure at Earth's surface.

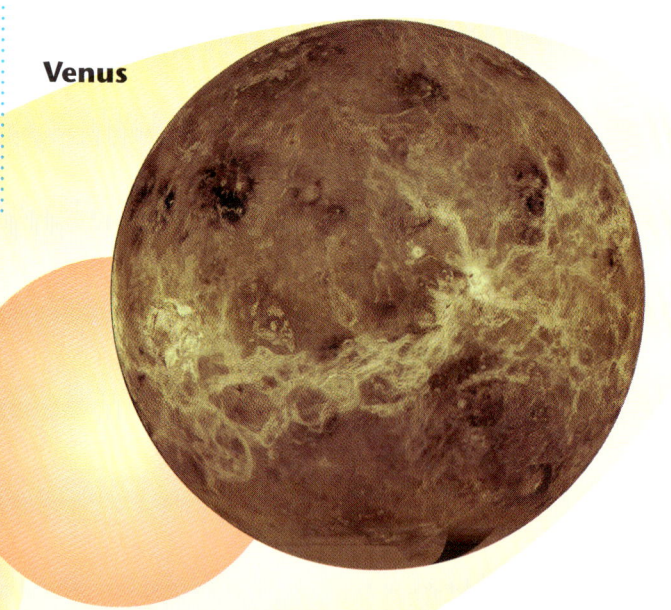

Brain Power

What would a space vehicle from Earth have to withstand in order to land on Venus's surface? How would that be different from Mercury's surface?

What is Earth Like?

Earth is the third planet from the Sun. Its day is 23.9 hours long, and its year is 365.26 days long. Its diameter is only a few hundred kilometers larger than that of Venus. It is also the only planet in the solar system known to support life.

Many space satellites have been launched to study Earth. They have sent back much valuable information:

- Earth has a strong magnetic field. It is distorted into a teardrop shape because of the solar wind.
- The first American satellite, *Explorer 1*, discovered what are now called the Van Allen radiation belts. These belts are areas around Earth where particles from the Sun are trapped, much as a bar magnet traps paper clips.
- Earth is an active planet, with earthquakes, volcanoes, and building and wearing of land masses.
- Temperatures on Earth average 15°C on the surface.
- The atmosphere protects us only from small debris from space. It does not protect us from large objects. There are as many craters on Earth as on the Moon. However, erosion on Earth causes these craters to disappear.

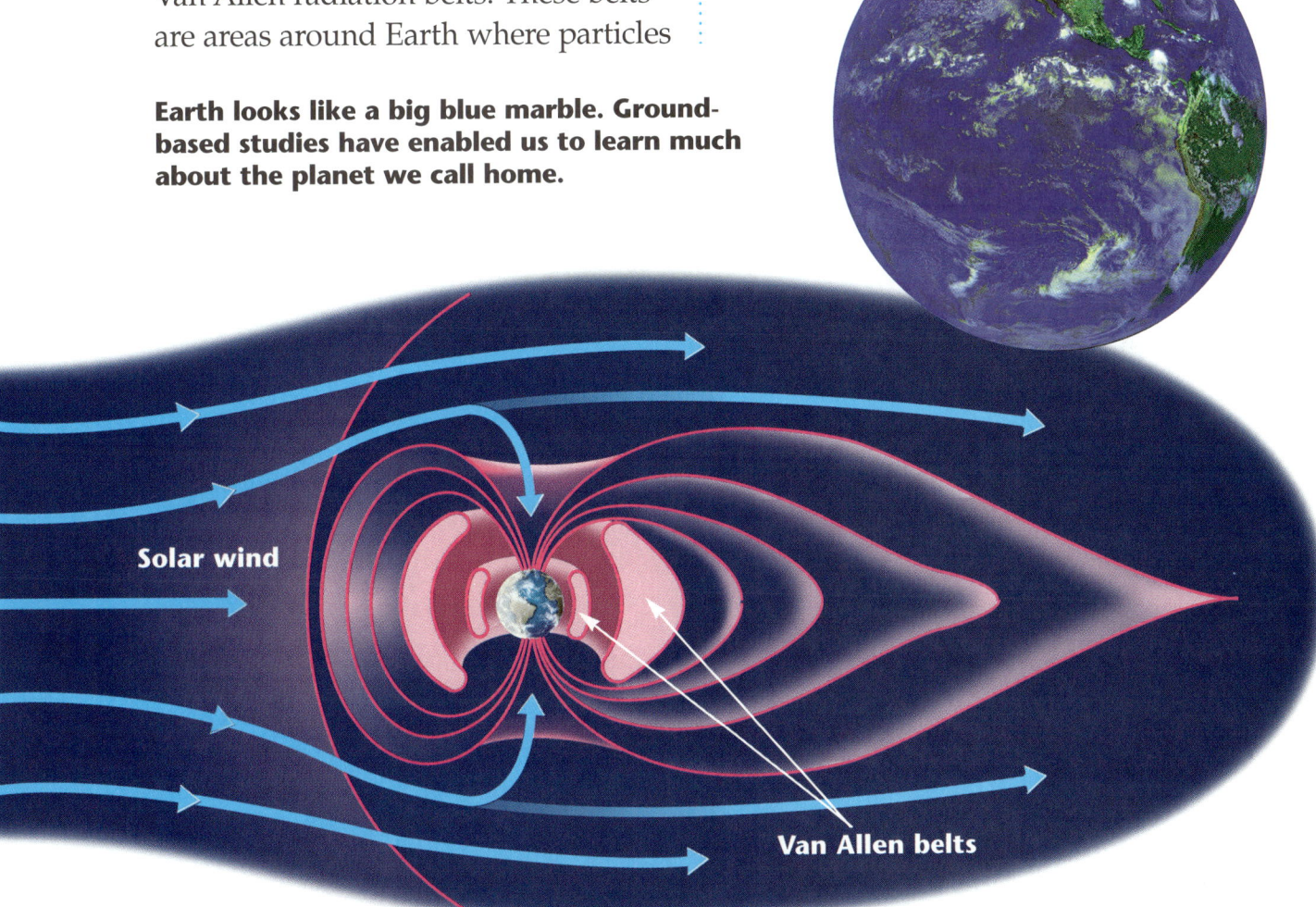

Earth looks like a big blue marble. Ground-based studies have enabled us to learn much about the planet we call home.

Magnetic effects around Earth

What is Mars Like?

Here are some facts about Mars.

- The planet Mars is 6,786 kilometers (4,218 miles) in diameter. At 228 million kilometers (142 million miles) from the Sun, it is the fourth planet. It has a rotation period of 24.6 hours, almost the same as Earth's. Its year is twice as long as ours, and its axis is tilted 24°. This means Mars also has seasons.

- The *Mariner 4* space probe showed many craters on Mars, especially in the southern hemisphere. *Mariner 9* discovered huge volcanoes in the northern hemisphere. One of them, Olympus Mons, rises 24 kilometers (15 miles) above the surrounding plain. That's almost three times as high as Mount Everest! Mountains can "grow" higher on Mars because its gravity is less than Earth's.

- *Mariner 9* also photographed a vast canyon. It was named the Mariner Valley. If this canyon were on Earth, it would stretch from New York City to Los Angeles! Scientists believe it was formed by running water.

- In 1997 the *Mars Pathfinder* landed on Mars. It sent out the six-wheeled rover Sojourner to study the area near the lander. Scientists are still studying the data.

Mars from Hubble Space Telescope

Tharsis volcanoes

Mariner Valley

Olympus Mons at the upper right is about as wide as the state of Missouri. The Mariner Valley can be seen to the right.

Why is Earth's Atmosphere Special?

How do the atmospheres of the inner planets compare?

- Mercury has no true atmosphere, but hydrogen, helium, argon, oxygen, sodium, and potassium have been detected.
- Venus's atmosphere consists primarily of carbon dioxide (96%) and nitrogen (3%), with traces of sulfur dioxide and other gases.
- Mars has a very thin atmosphere. Its primary compounds include carbon dioxide (95%), nitrogen (2.7%), and argon (1.6%). The sky appears to be pink. This is because much reddish dust is suspended in the atmosphere.
- Earth has an atmosphere made up of nitrogen (77%) and oxygen (21%). Why is Earth's atmosphere so different from that of its neighbors? Why is there so much oxygen? Oxygen has been building up on Earth for billions of years! Green plants and other producers release oxygen into the atmosphere as part of photosynthesis, the food-making process.

Earth's atmosphere is very complex. It is divided into several layers.

The troposphere is the part of the atmosphere nearest Earth's surface. All weather occurs in this layer. The stratosphere is the layer just above the troposphere. Ozone in the stratosphere helps absorb harmful ultraviolet radiation from the Sun. Above the stratosphere is the mesosphere, and above it the thermosphere.

ATMOSPHERIC LAYERS

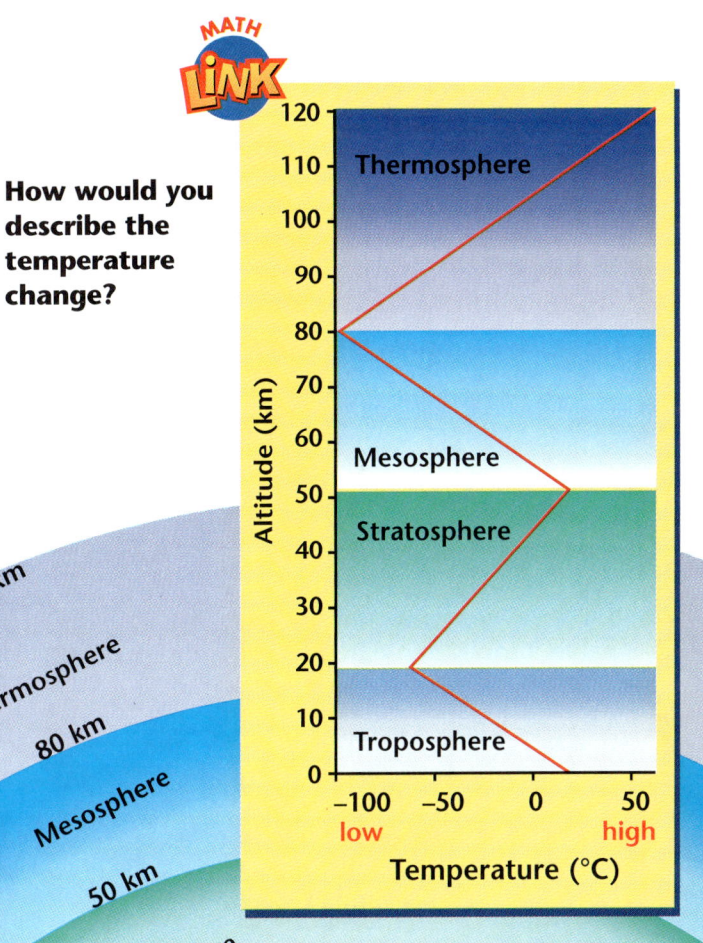

MATH LINK

How would you describe the temperature change?

READING DIAGRAMS

WRITE Write a description of the layers of Earth's atmosphere. Write it as if you were entering the atmosphere from space or rising up from Earth.

What Are Asteroids?

What is the life of a dinosaur like? It is early morning, but already the air is hot. The *Tyrannosaurus rex* doesn't seem to mind. She's busy eating her food. Suddenly she stops eating. She sniffs the air. Then she hears something. At first it was just a hissing, but now it is a sizzling sound, very menacing. The dinosaur begins to run. Then there's a blinding flash, and she's blown away by terrific winds.

Is this science fiction, or is it real? Near Winslow, Arizona, there is a crater. It may have been caused by an **asteroid**. Asteroids are rocky and metallic objects that orbit the Sun. They are too small to be considered planets. That crater was formed by a small asteroid. If the asteroid had been large, who knows what might have happened?

Some astronomers suggest that asteroids are material that never combined to become a planet. They are found mostly in a belt between the orbits of Mars and Jupiter. Some asteroids, however, travel out as far as Saturn's orbit or farther. Others have orbits that cross Earth's path.

Space probes have passed by asteroids and obtained much information. On June 27, 1997, the spacecraft *NEAR* encountered the asteroid Mathilde. *NEAR* is scheduled to orbit the asteroid Eros in February of 2000. These and other flybys by space probes are giving a good picture of the nature of these smaller members of the solar system. The spacecraft *Galileo* has already flown by the asteroids Gaspra and Ida.

Brain Power

What if you tie a ball to a string and twirl it around? The string keeps the ball from flying away from you. The planets move around the Sun. What keeps the planets from flying away from the Sun? What would happen if you let the string go? Explain.

Gaspra

Many scientists think an asteroid made the dinosaurs go extinct.

What Keeps the Planets in Orbit?

The planets and asteroids all travel in orbits around the Sun. An orbit is the path the object travels on. Gravity keeps these objects in their orbits. Without the Sun's gravity, a planet would keep moving in a straight line because of Newton's first law.

The astronomer Johannes Kepler stated three laws that summarize the motion of the planets. The first of **Kepler's laws** as they are called states that planets move on a special path, an ellipse. Law two says that planets move more quickly when they are nearer the Sun. Law three says that the farther away a planet is from the Sun, the longer its year is.

The orbit of a planet is an ellipse.

WHY IT MATTERS

Why is it important to study the inner planets? Looking at one of Earth's closest neighbors may provide an answer.

Venus has what is known as a runaway greenhouse effect. Infrared light given off by Venus cannot escape its atmosphere. This "trapped" infrared light causes the high temperature on Venus. By studying what happens on Venus, scientists hope to learn how to keep Earth's own greenhouse effect under control.

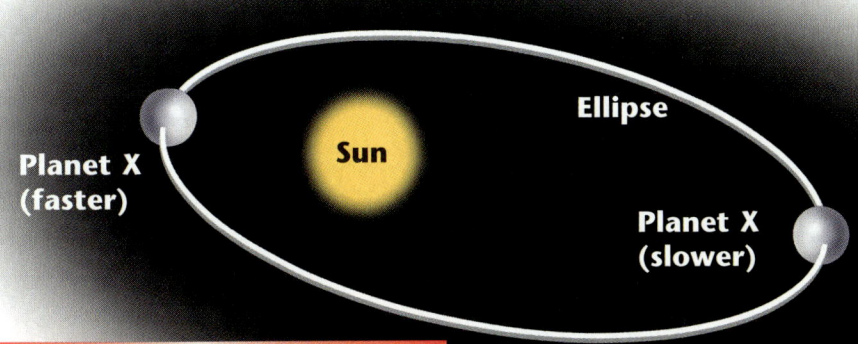

REVIEW

1. How can we distinguish a planet from a star by looking at its motion?
2. **EXPERIMENT** In the activity on page 335, what is changing from step to step? What effect can this change have?
3. How are the inner planets alike? Different? Include atmospheres in your answer.
4. What is an asteroid?
5. **CRITICAL THINKING** *Apply* What would happen to the planets' orbits if gravity were suddenly shut off?

WHY IT MATTERS THINK ABOUT IT
How might the greenhouse effect cause changes on Earth?

WHY IT MATTERS WRITE ABOUT IT
List the similarities between Earth and Venus. Consider distance from Earth and size. Also consider the presence of atmosphere.

READING SKILL
Compare and contrast any two planets you read about.

SCIENCE MAGAZINE

Be Your Own Weather Forecaster

"What's the temperature going to be today?" That's the question we most often ask about the weather.

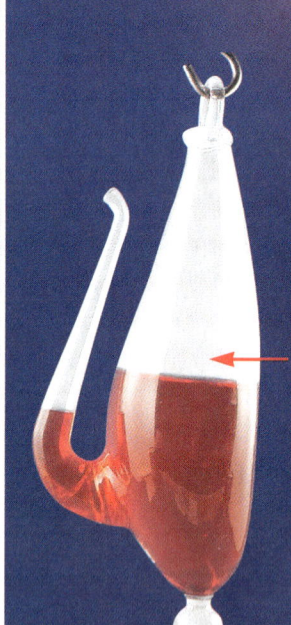

THERMOMETER
Air temperature is measured by a thermometer. The glass tube contains mercury or colored alcohol that expands (rises) or contracts (falls) with temperature changes.

BAROMETER
A barometer measures air pressure—the force on a given area by the weight of air. In one type of barometer, not shown here, mercury in a glass tube is inverted into a reservoir of more mercury. Changes in air pressure cause the mercury to rise and fall.

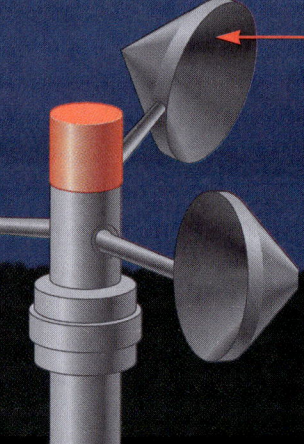

ANEMOMETER
Winds are described by the direction from which they blow—a north wind comes from the north. Wind vanes show wind direction. An anemometer measures wind speed by counting the revolutions of the cups in a given amount of time.

Science, Technology, and Society

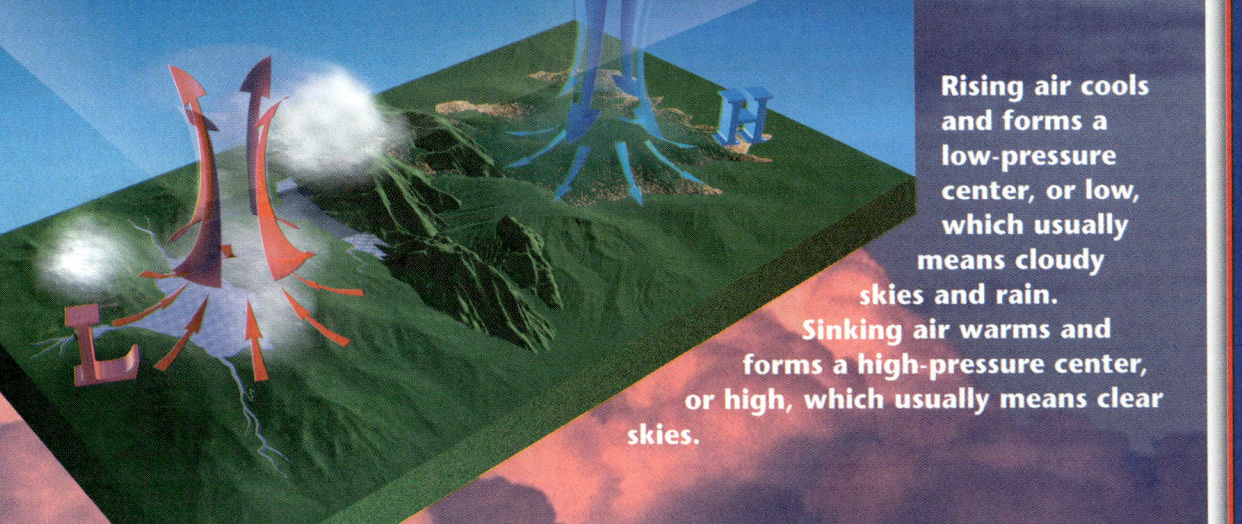

Rising air cools and forms a low-pressure center, or low, which usually means cloudy skies and rain. Sinking air warms and forms a high-pressure center, or high, which usually means clear skies.

HYGROMETER

A hygrometer measures humidity, or the amount of water vapor in the air. It consists of two thermometers, one dry and one covered by a wet sack. The instrument is whirled in the air, and the wet thermometer records a lower temperature. Meteorologists use a chart to convert the difference in temperatures to relative humidity.

Different shapes and patterns of clouds can predict a cold front, a warm front, or even a thunderstorm! You can use a cup and ruler to measure precipitation!

DISCUSSION STARTER

1. Collect weather data from any instruments you have at home, and listen to weather reports on TV for five days. Record changes. Are there any patterns to these changes?

2. What are some of the reasons weather prediction is so important?

To learn more about weather forecasting, visit *www.mhschool.com/science* and select the keyword FORECAST.

interNET CONNECTION

Topic 5 EARTH SCIENCE

The Outer Solar System

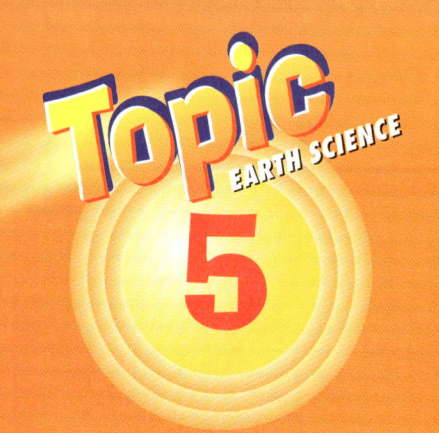

WHY IT MATTERS

Some members of the solar system can get very close to Earth.

Have you ever seen a time line? A time line is a way of showing a sequence of events. Here is an example.

Which planet was the first to be discovered in modern times? What does the ragged line just to the left of 1700 mean? Why do you think it took so long to discover the planet Neptune?

SCIENCE WORDS

comet a ball of rock and ice that orbits the Sun

meteoroid a small asteroid (rocky object that orbits the Sun), which may be far out in the solar system or close to the inner planets

meteor a meteoroid that enters Earth's atmosphere and burns with a streak of light

meteorite any part of a meteoroid that reaches Earth's surface

HISTORY LINK

EXPLORE

HYPOTHESIZE How are the planets arranged in the solar system? Does the arrangement help explain why it took so long to discover some of them? Write a hypothesis in your *Science Journal*. Test your ideas.

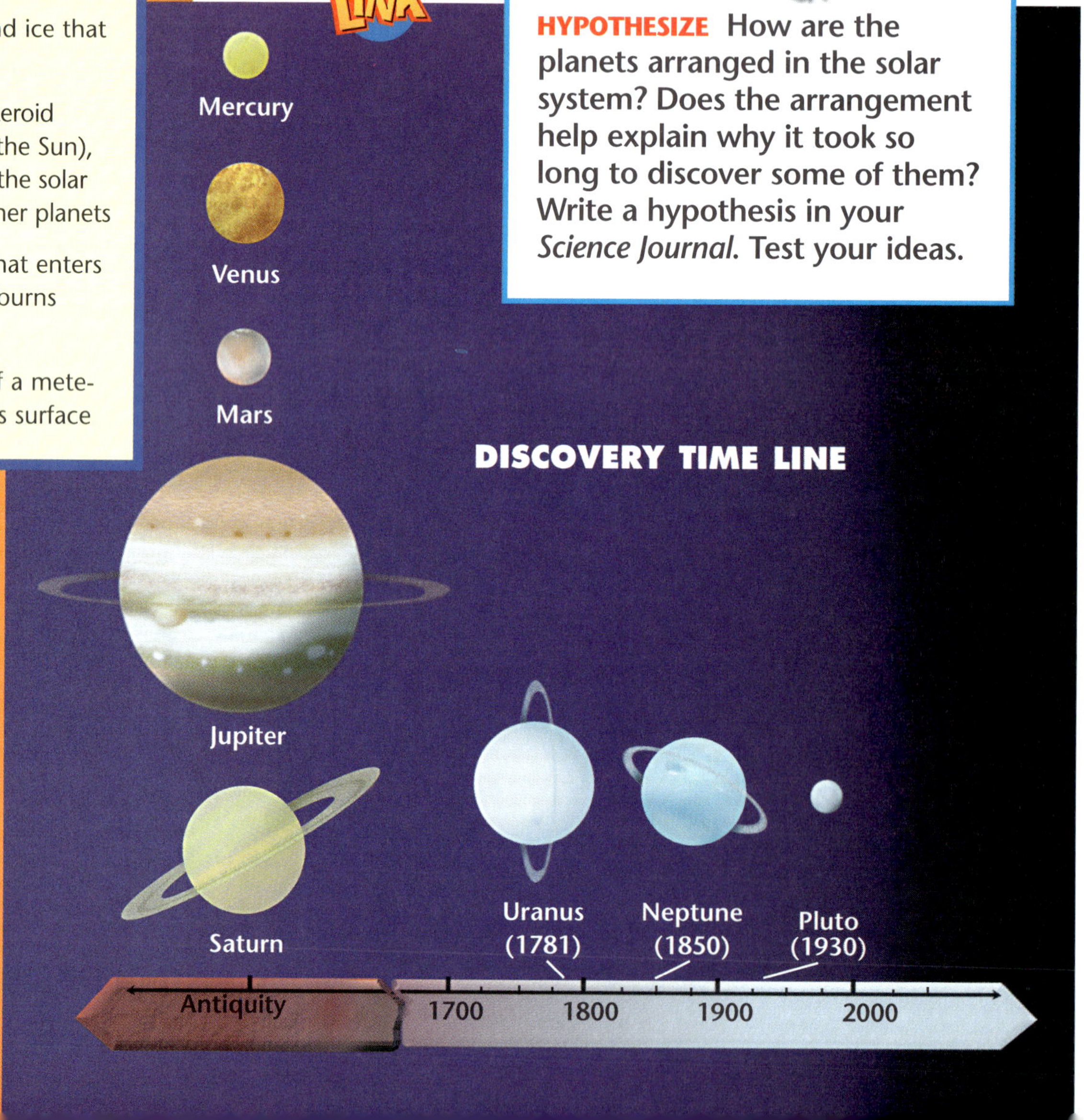

DISCOVERY TIME LINE

Mercury
Venus
Mars
Jupiter
Saturn
Uranus (1781)
Neptune (1850)
Pluto (1930)

Antiquity — 1700 — 1800 — 1900 — 2000

344

EXPLORE ACTIVITY

Investigate How the Planets Are Arranged

Make a model to compare how far planets are from the Sun.

MATERIALS
- cellophane tape
- roll of waxed paper
- meterstick
- crayon (or blobs of modeling compound)
- *Science Journal*

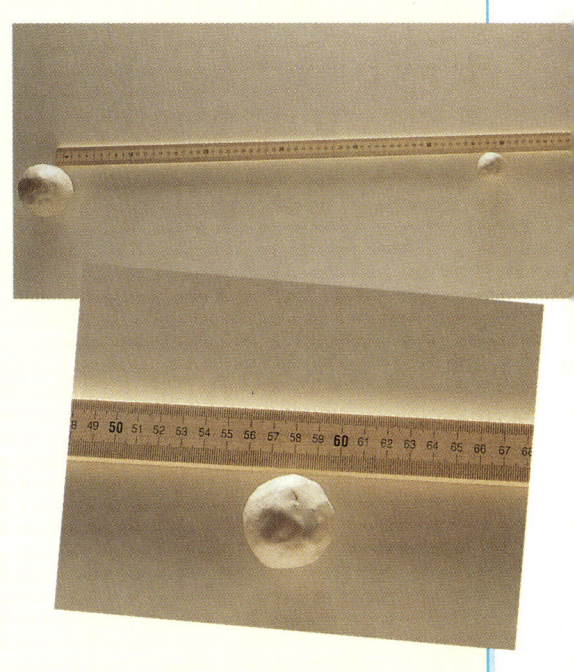

PROCEDURES

1. **MAKE A MODEL** Set up a scale of the average distance of each planet from the Sun. To do so divide by 10 the distance in millions of kilometers from the Sun to each planet. Record this data in your *Science Journal*.

Planet Distance to the Sun (millions of kilometers)		
Mercury 58	Mars 230	Uranus 2,900
Venus 110	Jupiter 780	Neptune 4,500
Earth 150	Saturn 1,400	Pluto 6,000

2. **USE NUMBERS** Change the units from kilometers to millimeters.

3. **MEASURE** Based on your scale of distances, use the meterstick to plot on the waxed paper each planet at the correct distance from the Sun.

CONCLUDE AND APPLY

1. **COMPARE AND CONTRAST** How does the spacing of the inner planets contrast with the spacing of the outer planets?

2. **ANALYZE** Between which two neighboring planets is there the greatest gap in space?

GOING FURTHER: Problem Solving

3. **CLASSIFY** Use your answers to 1 and 2 to classify the planets into at least two groups. Explain your reasoning.

4. **USE NUMBERS** In your scale how many kilometers are represented by one millimeter?

345

QUICK LAB

A Planet Model

HYPOTHESIZE Is the atmosphere of an outer planet larger than the solid interior? Write a hypothesis in your *Science Journal*.

MATERIALS
- data table
- pencil
- sheet of paper
- crayons or markers
- *Science Journal*

PROCEDURES

1. **INTERPRET DATA** Use the data in the table. What scale will you use: 1 cm = 10,000 km? You need to pick a scale to show the total depth of the planet.

2. **MAKE A MODEL** Draw a large circle, using the scale you described in step 1. This circle will represent the planet.

3. **MAKE A MODEL** Calculate how deep each layer of the planet's atmosphere will be in your model. Color each layer on your scale model. Be sure to include a color key.

CONCLUDE AND APPLY

1. **COMPARE AND CONTRAST** Which layer is largest? Which is smallest?

2. **INFER** How do you think the interiors of the other outer gas planets would look?

3. **DRAW CONCLUSIONS** Do you think the interior of Pluto would be similar to that of Jupiter? Explain.

346

How Are the Planets Arranged?

Where are the different planets located? The planets Jupiter, Saturn, Uranus, Neptune, and Pluto are called the *outer planets*. Scientists distinguish these from the inner planets you learned about in Topic 4 (Mercury, Venus, Earth, and Mars). The Explore Activity shows how both the inner and outer planets are arranged.

The outer planets share many properties. They tend to be much larger than the inner planets. There is a gap—the asteroid belt—that separates the inner planets from the outer planets. The outer planets also tend to rotate very rapidly. Finally, their interior structure is different from the inner planets. With the exception of Pluto, the outer planets tend to have a small solid core, surrounded by a thick gaseous atmosphere.

Data on Jupiter and Saturn

Planet	Distance from Center of Planet	Chemical Composition
Jupiter	71,000–54,000 km 54,000–10,000 km 10,000–0 km	hydrogen gas liquid hydrogen solid rocky core
Saturn	60,000–28,000 km 28,000–16,000 km 16,000–0 km	hydrogen gas liquid hydrogen solid rocky core

What is Jupiter Like?

Imagine a ball of gas so big that 1,000 Earths could fit inside it. Imagine a "storm" that has lasted almost 300 years! What name would you give to this ball of gas? If you could imagine such a planet, it would be Jupiter.

Jupiter is the largest planet in the solar system. Its diameter is 142,000 kilometers, 11 times Earth's diameter. At 778 million kilometers from the Sun, it is 5 times more distant from the Sun than Earth. It also has more mass than all the other planets combined.

When the *Voyager* space probes visited Jupiter back in 1979, scientists learned a tremendous amount of information about the largest of the planets.

- Ground-based observations of Jupiter have shown cloud belts. These cloud belts are made primarily of hydrogen and helium, with smaller amounts of methane, ammonia, and water vapor.

- Ground-based observations of Jupiter have also shown the Great Red Spot. This ranges from about one to three Earths in diameter. This feature has lasted for about 300 years. Some years it is more visible than others.

Look at the picture above. Do you see the round satellite over the clouds of the planet? That moon is one of the four satellites, or moons, of Jupiter first seen by Galileo in 1610. In all, Jupiter has 16 satellites.

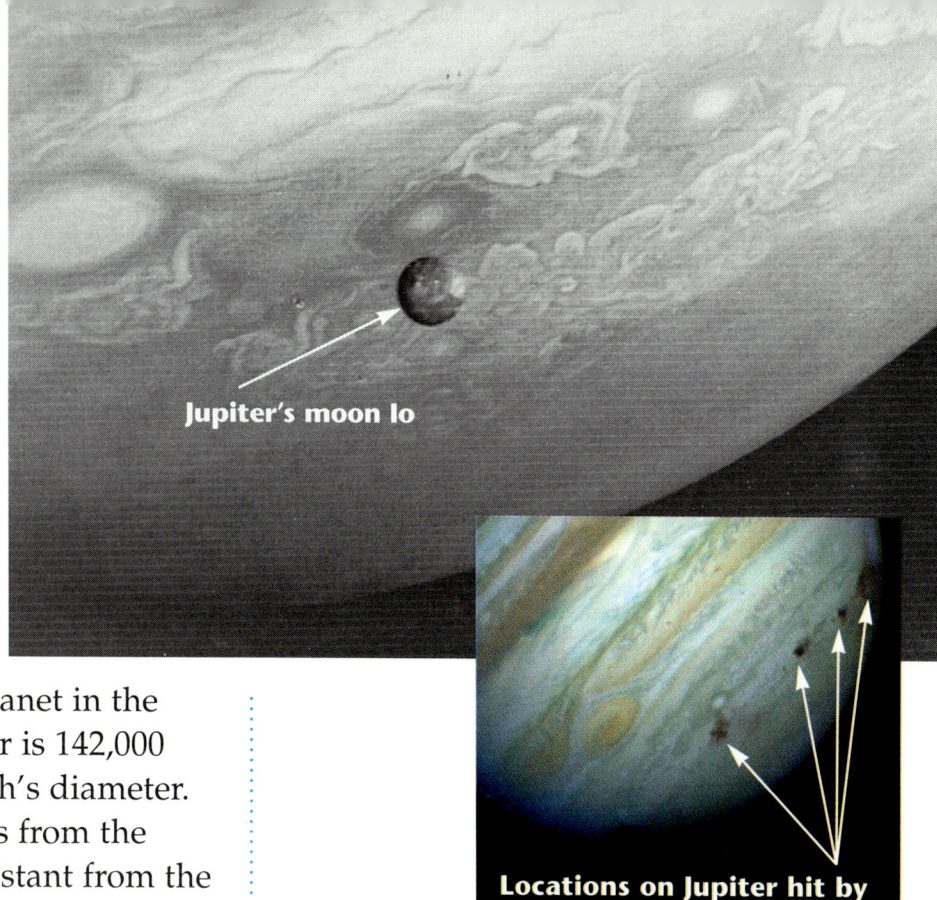

Jupiter's moon Io

Locations on Jupiter hit by the comet Shoemaker-Levy

In July 1994 people on Earth witnessed a very spectacular and very unusual event. A comet, Shoemaker-Levy, plunged into the atmosphere of Jupiter. The actual impact occurred when the collision site was on the part of Jupiter not yet facing Earth. Soon after the impact, the collision site rotated into Earth's view. The result was spectacular! The Hubble Space Telescope made an image of the places that were hit. The picture above shows these places. There are several locations because the comet broke into about 20 pieces before it hit Jupiter.

Brain Power

How would it be best to explore Jupiter? Are there any problems with landing a space probe on Jupiter?

How Do They Compare?

Saturn

Saturn is the second-largest planet. It is about 1.4 billion kilometers from the Sun. It takes almost 29.5 years for Saturn to make one complete trip around the Sun. Much of what we know about Saturn is due to the *Voyager* flybys of 1980–1981.

- Saturn is noticeably flattened at the poles. This is because of its very fast rotation (1 day = 10 hours 39 minutes).

- The atmosphere is composed mostly of hydrogen, with small amounts of helium and methane. It has broad cloud belts similar to Jupiter's, but not as distinct.

- Winds on Saturn move at about 500 meters per second near the equator. Saturn is also less dense than water.

- There are seven major rings. Some of the rings are made of thinner rings. These are called ringlets. The rings are made of particles ranging from a few centimeters to a few meters in size and are about 2 kilometers thick. They contain a significant amount of water.

Uranus

Uranus is the seventh planet from the Sun. It lies at a mean distance of 2.9 billion kilometers from the Sun and orbits it once every 84 Earth years. Its diameter of 51,800 kilometers makes it the third-largest planet.

- The atmosphere of Uranus is composed of 83% hydrogen, 15% helium, and 2% methane, with small amounts of acetylene and other hydrocarbons. The blue-green color of Uranus is due to methane in the planet's upper atmosphere.

- Winds in the Uranian atmosphere move between 40 and 160 meters per second.

- Like Saturn, Uranus has a ring system. Eleven rings have been discovered. The rings are much dimmer than Saturn's.

- Uranus is unusual because it looks as though it was knocked on its "side." Its axis of rotation is tilted about 98° to its orbit. Because of this, summer at the north pole of Uranus lasts for 42 years. The same is true at its south pole.

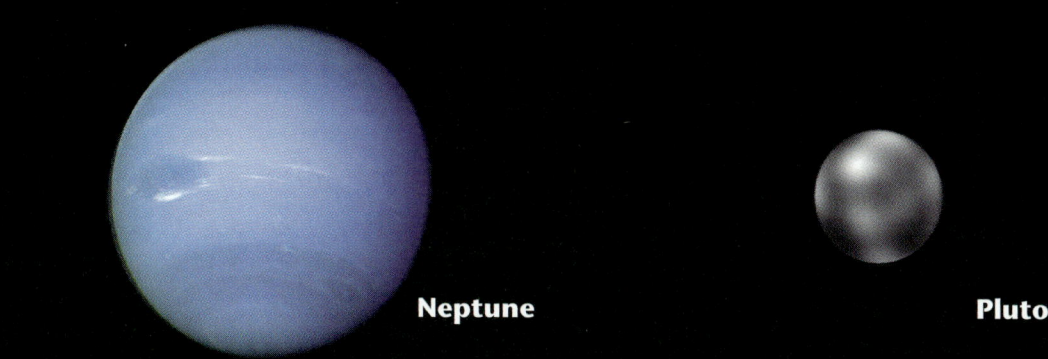

Neptune

Out here the light from the Sun is 900 times fainter than it is on Earth.

Neptune is the last of the gas giants. Its radius is 24,746 kilometers. It lies at a mean distance of 4.5 billion kilometers from the Sun. Its orbital period is 165 years. It has at least five rings, none of which are very bright.

- The atmosphere is composed of hydrogen, helium, water, and methane. Methane gives Neptune its blue color.

- Neptune has the strongest winds of any planet. In some spots the winds were measured by *Voyager* to blow at speeds up to 2,000 kilometers per hour.

- Many storms on Neptune have been detected by *Voyager*.

- Neptune has eight moons. One moon, Triton, is larger than Pluto. Triton has similarities to Earth. It has geysers, and it also has seasons. This shows that we can learn about Earth by studying other planets and their moons. It also shows that in many ways Earth is not unique.

Pluto

Pluto is the smallest planet. At a mean distance from the Sun of almost 6 billion kilometers, Pluto's sky would show the Sun only $\frac{1}{1,600}$ as bright as from Earth.

The orbits of Neptune and Pluto overlap. Pluto is usually farther from the Sun than Neptune.

- Astronomers have discovered that Pluto's surface is covered with methane ice. There is also a thin methane/nitrogen atmosphere.

- Because Pluto is so far from the Sun, scientists think the atmosphere may freeze out as the planet moves back beyond Neptune's orbit.

- Pluto has one satellite, Charon. Charon is almost half the size of Pluto. The two revolve around each other about once every six days. Also, Pluto and Charon always keep the same side facing each other.

- Before Pluto was discovered, the astronomer Percival Lowell predicted that a ninth planet must exist. The ninth planet was named Pluto after a mythological Roman god, and also because the first two letters are Lowell's initials.

What Is a Comet?

Were you one of the millions of people who were treated to a fantastic light show from March to May of 1997? If you missed it, you'll have to wait 2,400 years for the rerun! What was it? It was comet Hale-Bopp.

A **comet** is a ball of ice and rock that orbits the Sun. Comets come from the outer fringes of the solar system. One place where comets originate is a region stretching from just outside Pluto's orbit to about 45 billion kilometers out. This region is called the *Kuiper* (kwīp′ər) *Belt*. The Kuiper Belt probably contains about 40,000 to 70,000 objects with diameters of more than 100 kilometers. The asteroid belt, by comparison, has about 230 objects of more than 100 kilometers in diameter.

How long do comets take to orbit the Sun? Some comets have orbits that take less than 200 years. The most famous of these comets is Halley's comet. Its orbit brings it past Earth every 76 years.

However, some comets have much larger orbits, which take more than 200 years. Comet Hyakutake (hī′ ä kū tä′kē) went past Earth in 1996. It will not return for 16,000 years! These comets come from a region called the *Oort* (ôrt) *Cloud*. This is a cloud that surrounds the solar system at about 15 trillion kilometers from the Sun.

What makes a comet visible? As the chunk of rock and ice approaches the Sun, sunlight begins to warm it. The comet's ice begins to thaw and forms a cloud surrounding the nucleus, or core, of the comet. As the comet gets closer to the Sun, the sunlight exerts pressure on the cloud. The pressure from the sunlight drives this cloud material away from the nucleus, forming the comet's tail. Part of the tail always points away from the Sun.

Comet Hale-Bopp showed features that are not unusual for comets. It was first seen when it was near Saturn's orbit. It was also discovered to rotate like a lawn sprinkler, about once a week. The most interesting discovery concerned its tail. Comets have one or two tails. Hale-Bopp was the first comet to be found that has three tails. It has a dust and an ion tail like most comets. It also has a tail made of sodium atoms. Scientists are trying to figure out the source of the sodium tail.

Comet Hale-Bopp

COMET IN MOTION

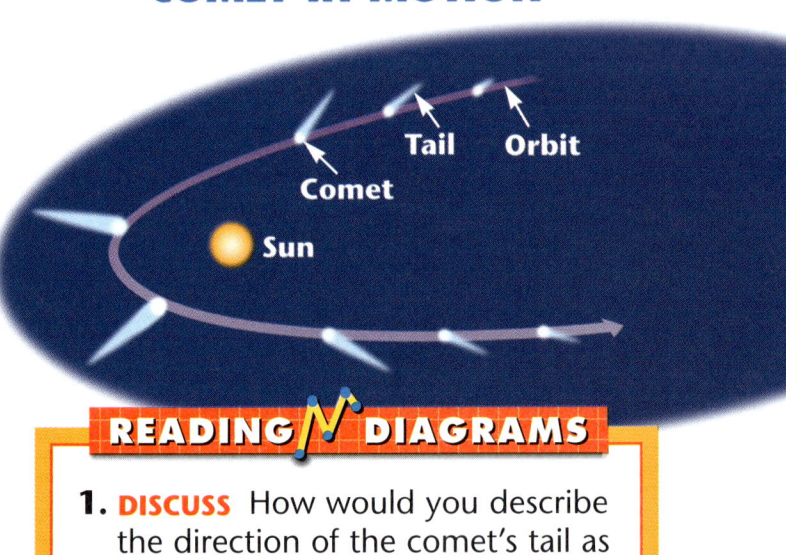

READING DIAGRAMS

1. **DISCUSS** How would you describe the direction of the comet's tail as it travels around the Sun?
2. **WRITE** What happens to the size of the tail during the comet's orbit?

Where Can We Find Small Asteroids?

In Topic 4 you learned that the solar system has many asteroids. They are rocky, metallic objects in orbit around the Sun. Larger asteroids are in a belt between Mars and Jupiter. There are also small asteroids, which are often called **meteoroids** (mē′tē ə roidz′). Some travel to the edge of the solar system. Others spend their time within the orbits of the inner planets. Sometimes a meteoroid collides with the atmosphere of a planet, such as Earth. What happens?

To get an idea of what happens, rub your hands together. The rubbing produces heat. When a meteoroid hits Earth's atmosphere, the rubbing, or friction, causes the meteoroid to burn. At this stage the meteoroid is sometimes called a **meteor**. We usually see the meteor as a bright streak of light.

Most times a meteor burns up completely. Any part of a meteoroid that reaches Earth's surface is called a **meteorite**.

Some meteoroids come from material ejected by a passing comet. Other meteoroids are believed to have come from the asteroid belt.

Meteorites are usually classified into three types. Stony meteorites are made of rock. Metallic meteorites are made of metals (nickel and iron) or a mixture of metals and rock. Carbonaceous meteorites are carbon rich.

Sometimes many meteoroids hit Earth's atmosphere at the same time. This often happens after a comet has recently traveled past Earth. The sudden occurrence of many meteors is called a meteor shower. Some meteor showers occur year after year.

The Perseid meteor shower is an example. Each year around August 11, if you look at the sky, you may see as many as 60 meteors an hour.

A meteorite

A meteor

Brain Power

Meteor showers occur each year around January 3, August 12, October 21, and December 14. Why do they happen around these dates?

What's Special About Jupiter's Moons?

When Galileo discovered the four largest moons of Jupiter in 1610, he showed that other planets had moons. They were named the *Galilean* (gal′ə lē′ən) *satellites* in his honor. Their names are Ganymede, Io, Europa, and Callisto. Over the centuries that followed, 12 more moons have been found.

Ganymede

Ganymede is the largest satellite in the solar system. At one time Saturn's moon Titan was thought to be largest. The *Voyager* flybys, however, showed that Ganymede is the title-holder. *Voyager* measurements showed that Ganymede has two kinds of land features.

The surface has many craters on it. It also has curious features called grooves. They look like someone scraped parts of the surface with a rake! Scientists think these surface features mean that Ganymede's icy crust may be undergoing some kind of tectonic activity.

Io

Io may be the most interesting of the Galilean satellites. When *Voyager* swept past Io, it discovered that Io had active volcanoes. The spacecraft detected nine volcanoes. Many more are suspected. The volcanoes may be caused by gravitational forces from Jupiter and the other Galilean satellites. What do you think is erupting from Io's volcanoes? Lava. Probably not the kind you're thinking, though. This lava is composed mainly of sulfur, oxygen, and sodium.

Jupiter and its four Galilean satellites

Europa

Europa is a smooth world. Voyager showed it to have lots of cracks on its surface. They reminded scientists of how ice looks when it has been broken and then refreezes. Europa may have an ice crust about 5 kilometers thick. Below this crust may be an ocean as deep as 50 kilometers.

Because Europa may have an ocean, scientists wonder if life may be present there. In 1996 the *Galileo* spacecraft arrived at Jupiter. It collected data on the planet and its moons. Scientists hope *Galileo* will help them find answers to some of their questions.

Callisto

The last of the Galilean satellites is Callisto. Callisto has a very old surface, with many craters. Long ago several large meteorites or other bodies must have hit the surface. Remnants of these impacts have been found.

Why Is Saturn's Moon Titan Special?

Titan is the largest of Saturn's 22 satellites. It is also the only satellite known to have a dense atmosphere. Scientists are very interested in Titan because its atmosphere may be similar to Earth's atmosphere several billion years ago.

Titan's surface cannot be seen because of the composition of its atmosphere. Its atmosphere is mostly nitrogen, but it also contains methane. Scientists think Titan's surface is made of rock and ice.

The *Cassini/Huygens* (kä sē′nē hig′gənz) space probe, launched in 1997, will study Titan.

WHY IT MATTERS

We learned that one of Neptune's moons, Triton, is in some ways similar to Earth. In this sense Earth is not unique. It is also evidence that the same laws of science operate everywhere in the universe. Finding out these things is important to satisfy our curiosity.

Titan, a moon of Saturn, is about half the size of Earth. The reddish color indicates that it has an atmosphere made up of nitrogen, argon, and methane.

REVIEW

1. How far apart are the outer planets compared to the inner planets?

2. **COMPARE AND CONTRAST** Describe the similarities and differences between the outer planets.

3. What are comets? How may they cause meteor showers?

4. Describe the moons of Jupiter and Saturn.

5. **CRITICAL THINKING** *Analyze* What if you were a scientist directing the Galileo space probe around Europa? You want to know if life exists on Europa. What data would you tell the space probe to collect?

WHY IT MATTERS THINK ABOUT IT
Which planet, other than Earth, are you most curious about?

WHY IT MATTERS WRITE ABOUT IT
What if you could travel to the planet you are most curious about? Write a plan of exploration. What observations would you make?

SCIENCE MAGAZINE

Looking Skyward

Ever look up at the sky and wonder what's really going on out there? Science and religion have often disagreed about it, but the need to know has always been strong.

Ancient people studied the skies to figure out when the seasons began and when they should plant their food. They saw that objects in the sky were in patterns. They saw changes in the sky that corresponded to the seasons. That was the beginning of astronomy.

Aristarchus theorized that Earth orbited the Sun. This "radical" idea was rejected by almost everyone. People believed that Earth was the center of the universe. This theory held for almost 2,000 years and was the basis of many religious beliefs.

Around 400 B.C. the Babylonians created the first calendar based on the movements of the Sun and the Moon.

History of Science

In the second century A.D., Ptolemy described in detail the math behind the theory that the planets moved around Earth. Hypatia, the first female astronomer, was born in A.D. 370. She invented the plane astrolabe that measured the position of stars, planets, and the Sun. An outraged mob killed her because of her beliefs.

Aryabhata the First (476–550) determined that Earth rotates on its axis. In the 700s Turk Al-Battani calculated the lengths of a year and of the seasons with great accuracy.

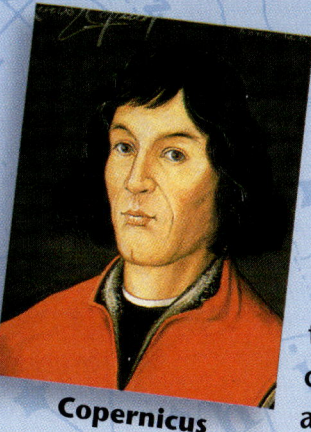

In the 16th century, Copernicus upset the scientific world by suggesting that Aristarchus was correct—that Earth and the other planets orbit the Sun.

A hundred years later, Galileo made one of the first telescopes and used it to prove Copernicus was right. Galileo was imprisoned for his beliefs, making him one of the first heroes of science.

Ptolemy

Copernicus

Hypatia

Galileo

DISCUSSION STARTER

1. Compare Aristarchus's theory with Ptolemy's.
2. Why did Copernicus's theory upset the scientific world?

To learn more about astronomy, visit www.mhschool.com/science and select the keyword ASTRONOMY.

interNET CONNECTION

Topic 6
EARTH SCIENCE

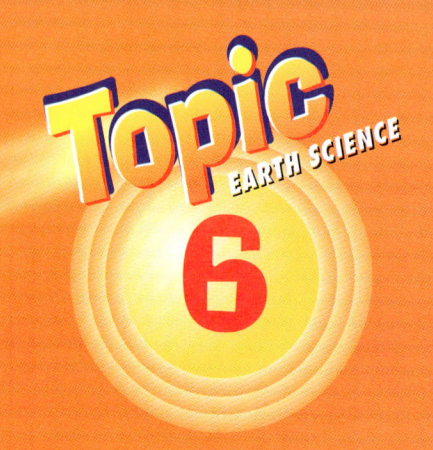

WHY IT MATTERS

The Sun is one of billions of stars, the closest to Earth.

SCIENCE WORDS

star a large, hot ball of gases, which is held together by gravity and gives off its own light

parallax the apparent shift in an object's location when viewed from two positions

light-year the distance light travels in a year

constellation a number of stars that appears to form a pattern

magnitude the brightness of a star

nebula a cloud of gas and dust in space

supernova a star that explodes

black hole an object whose gravity is so strong that light cannot escape it

Stars

What are stars? Why do they look like points of light in the night sky?

In the past people saw stars arranged in groups tracing pictures of heroes or other characters. In a star "picture," the stars appear to be side by side against a flat background. That would mean they are all the same distance away from the observer.

Do you think stars really come in groups? Are they all the same distance away?

EXPLORE

HYPOTHESIZE Can stars be different distances away and still appear to be side by side? Write a hypothesis in your *Science Journal*. Test your ideas.

EXPLORE ACTIVITY

Investigate if Stars Are at Different Distances from Earth

Make a model to show that stars can be at different distances yet appear to be side by side.

MATERIALS
- art supplies
- flashlights (optional)
- *Science Journal*

PROCEDURES

1. Work with four other group members to design a model "star outline" with a simple shape, such as a square with one "star" at each corner. The stars are group members holding flashlights or some visible objects.

2. **OBSERVE** Arrange the model with all stars the same distance away from you at one end of a long room or hallway. You stand at the opposite end and draw in your *Science Journal* the pattern you see.

3. **USE VARIABLES** Close your eyes. Ask one star to step forward and another to step backward. Open your eyes, and draw the outline as you see it.

4. Repeat steps 1–3 so that each person gets a chance to be the observer.

CONCLUDE AND APPLY

1. **COMPARE AND CONTRAST** Does the outline appear to change when the stars are not all the same distance away? Explain your answer.

2. **EVALUATE** Do the results of this activity support your hypothesis? Explain your answer.

GOING FURTHER: Problem Solving

3. **OBSERVE** From your vantage point at the opposite end of the room, can you identify the stars that are farthest and nearest? What do you have to do to be sure?

357

QUICK LAB

How Parallax Works

HYPOTHESIZE Can an object change position when you look at it from two different locations? Write a hypothesis in your *Science Journal*. Test your ideas.

MATERIALS
- Science Journal

PROCEDURES

1. **MAKE A MODEL** Sight on a distant object with your left eye. Hold your thumb about 10 cm in front of your face. Hide the object with your thumb. Look at the object with your left eye. Note the position of your thumb.

2. **USE VARIABLES** Close your left eye, and now look at the object with your right eye. What has changed? Write your observations in your *Science Journal*.

3. **USE VARIABLES** Now repeat the activity, holding the thumb farther away each time. Record your observations.

CONCLUDE AND APPLY

1. **MAKE A MODEL** What does your thumb represent in this model?

2. **DRAW CONCLUSIONS** How does parallax work? Explain.

3. **ANALYZE** What happens as your thumb is farther and farther in front of your face?

358

Are Stars at Different Distances from Earth?

You may know what a star is, but how would you define it? A **star** is a large, hot ball of gas, which is held together by gravity and gives off its own light. The Explore Activity showed how objects at different distances can appear to be the same distance away. Stars are actually at different distances from Earth.

How do scientists know a star's distance? If the star is close, they view it from different points in Earth's orbit. The star appears to shift its location compared with other stars farther away. This apparent shift of an object's location when viewed from two positions is called **parallax** (par′ə laks′). The closer a star is, the greater the shift. By measuring the shift, scientists can tell how far the star is.

Astronomers use a unit called the **light-year** (ly) to describe distances in space. A light-year is the distance light travels in a year, or about 9 trillion kilometers. The star Alpha Centauri is 4.3 light-years from Earth. Light leaving that star now will reach Earth in 4.3 years.

PARALLAX

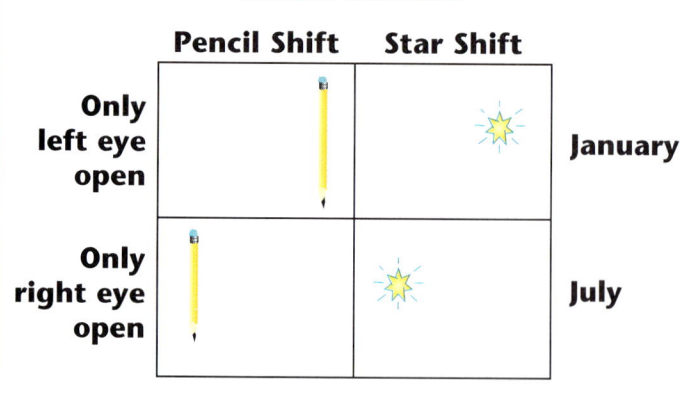

	Pencil Shift	Star Shift	
Only left eye open			January
Only right eye open			July

Both pencil and star shift because of parallax.

How Can You Recognize a Star?

How can you find Rigel (rī′jəl) or other stars in the night sky? The easiest way to find a star is by looking for its **constellation**. A constellation is a number of stars that appears to form a pattern. For example, Rigel is a star in the constellation Orion, the hunter.

As Earth travels in its orbit around the Sun, its night side faces different directions. You see only the constellations that are in that direction. The constellation Orion, for example, is a winter constellation. We see it from the Northern Hemisphere in the winter months during our orbit around the Sun.

Many people notice that some stars are brighter than others. Sirius (sir′ē əs), in the constellation Canis Major, is the brightest star in the winter sky. It appears brighter than Rigel.

However, Rigel is actually a brighter star than Sirius. The reason Sirius appears brighter is that it is closer to us than Rigel. For example, if a very bright flashlight is side by side with a dimmer one, you can tell the difference. If the brighter flashlight is moved far behind the dimmer one, the brighter one seems to get dimmer and dimmer.

The word **magnitude** is used to describe the brightness of a star. The word is used in two ways. It can describe actual brightness of a star, the *absolute* magnitude. The brightness of a star as you see it in the night sky is its *apparent* magnitude. That depends on how much light it gives off and how far away it is.

CONSTELLATIONS

READING DIAGRAMS

1. **REPRESENT** Make a table of the four seasons. Identify one or more constellations for each season.
2. **WRITE** Describe why we see different constellations at different seasons.

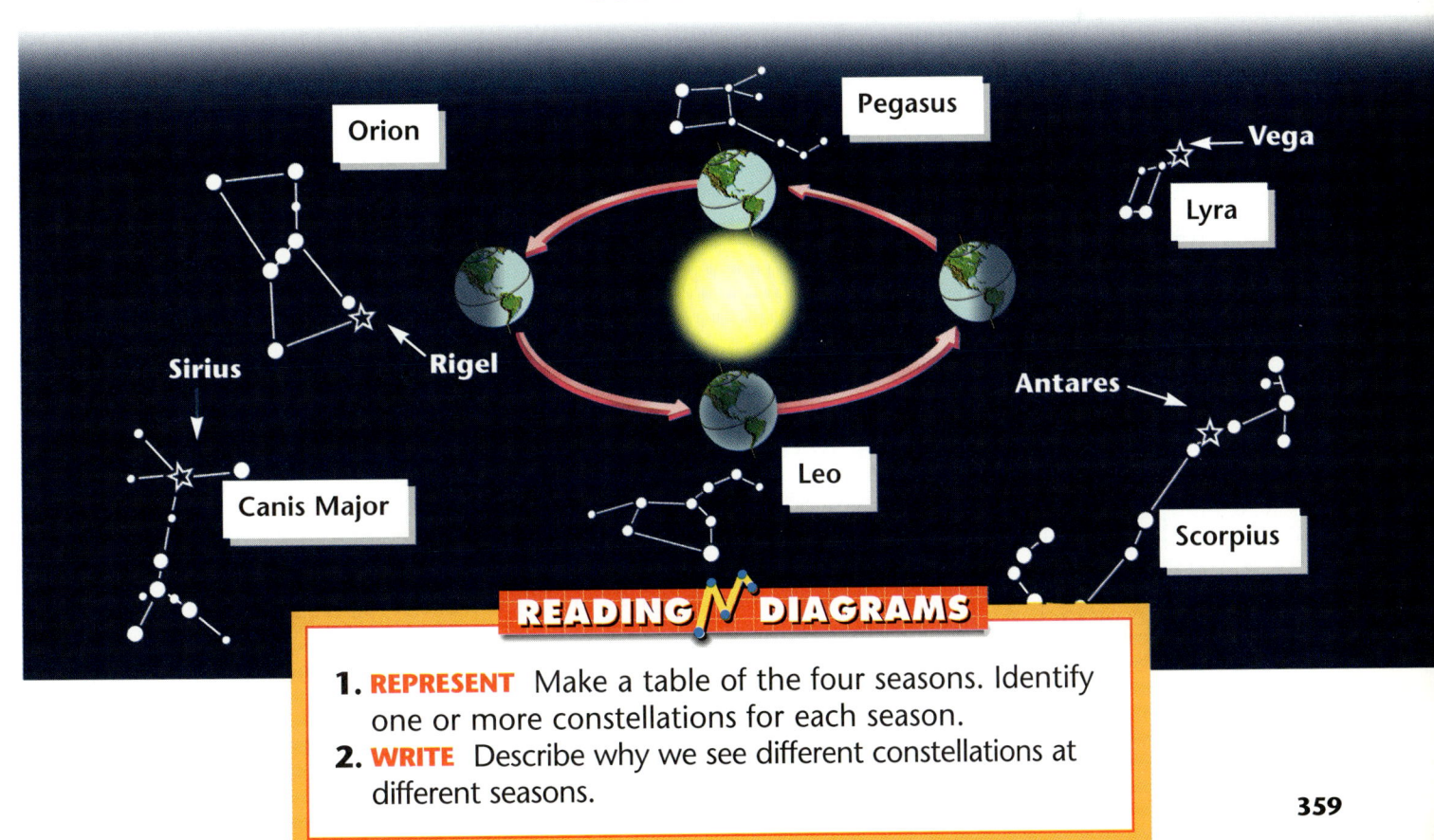

| 3,000° | 4,000° | 6,000° | 10,000° | 20,000° or more |

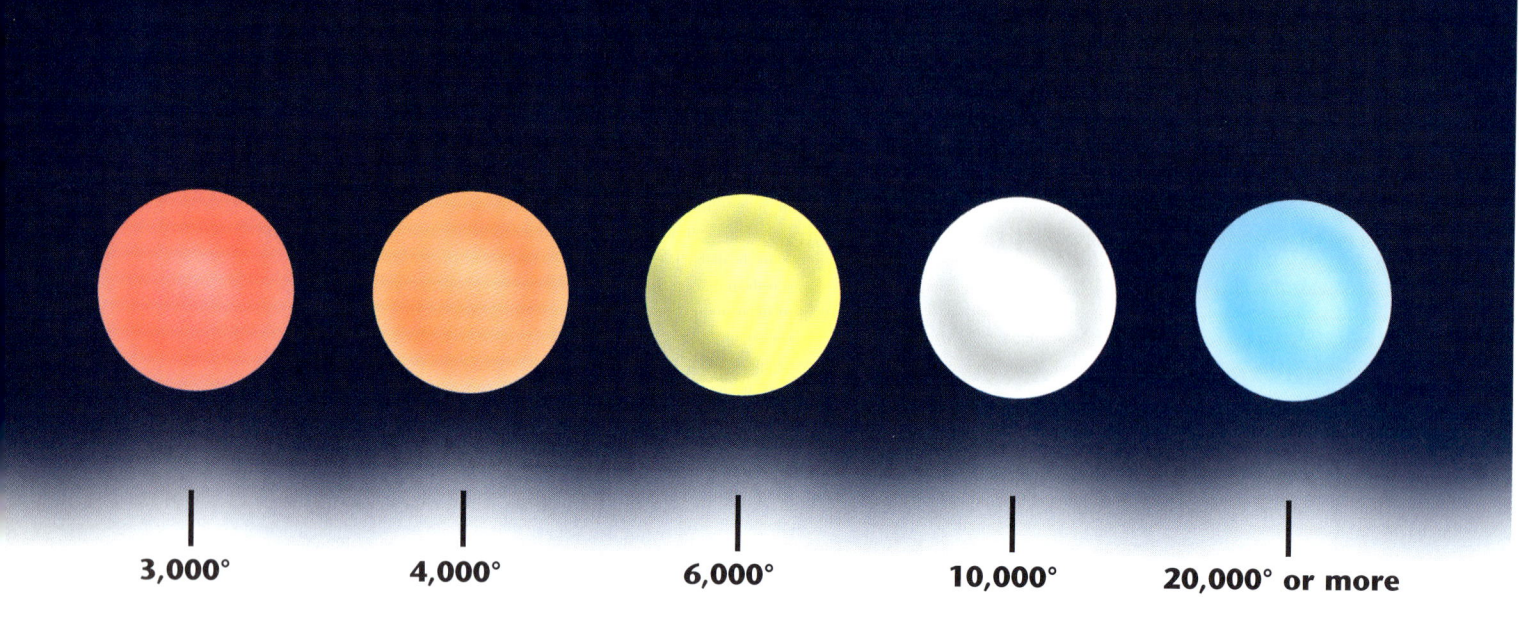

What Properties Does a Star Have?

What color are stars? Sirius is blue-white. Antares (an târ′ēz), a bright summer star, is reddish.

A star's color is related to its surface temperature. Think of a coil of a toaster getting hotter. As the coil heats up, it turns to bright red, then orange, and then orange-yellow. In stars this same relationship applies. The coolest stars are red and orange. Hotter stars are yellow, and the hottest are blue-white.

In the center of a star, nuclear reactions are occurring. These reactions make the star shine by releasing large amounts of energy. The light we see from a star is the energy released by the nuclear reactions. The high temperature produced tends to make the star expand. At the same time, gravity pulls in on the star's gases. Gravity tends to make the star contract. As long as these two forces balance, the star stays the way it is.

Surface temperature, size, and the distance from Earth are what determine the star's brightness. The higher the temperature is, the brighter the star. The larger the size is, in general, the brighter the star. The closer a star is to Earth, the brighter it appears to be.

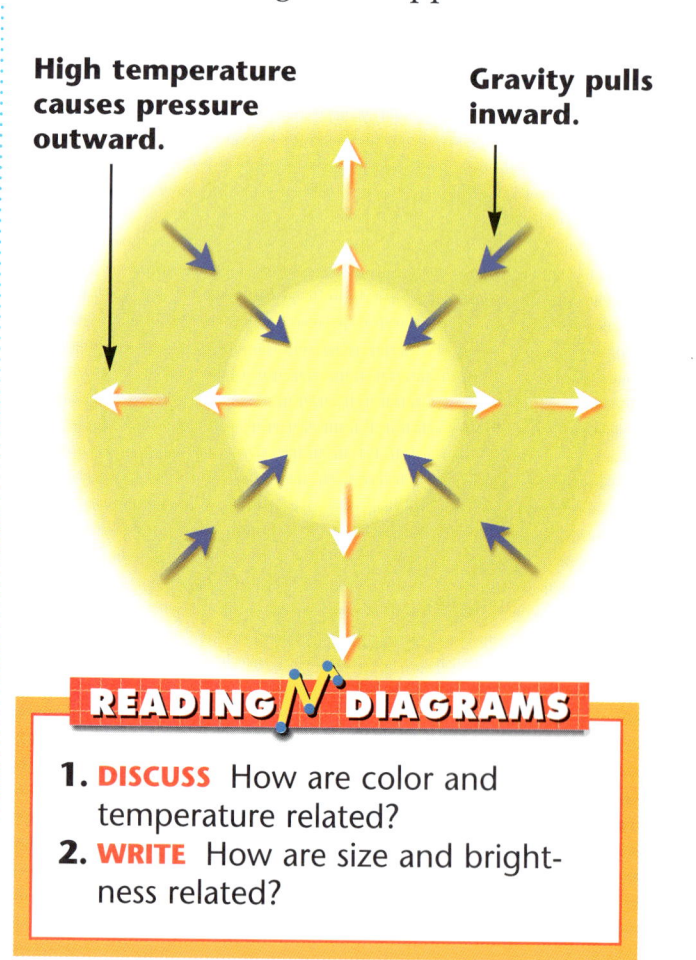

High temperature causes pressure outward.

Gravity pulls inward.

READING DIAGRAMS

1. **DISCUSS** How are color and temperature related?
2. **WRITE** How are size and brightness related?

Are Brightness and Temperature Related?

Two scientists, Ejnar Hertzsprung and Henry Norris Russell, tried to see if brightness and temperature were related. The diagram below shows the results of their work. It is called the Hertzsprung-Russell (H-R) diagram. An H-R diagram compares the temperatures and absolute magnitudes of stars.

To read the diagram, start at the bottom of the absolute magnitude scale. Move out to where the stars are plotted. Stars at the bottom are dim. They are called white dwarfs. White dwarfs are small, dim stars that are neither the hottest nor the coolest.

The coolest dim stars are the red stars at the end of the group called main-sequence stars. Most stars are found in the band called the main sequence. In the main sequence, the hotter a star is, the brighter it is.

Now move to the top of the absolute magnitude scale. Run your finger across to the supergiants. These are extremely large stars. Some are hotter than others. The remaining group, the giants, are large stars. They are just below the supergiants in the chart. That means they are dimmer than the supergiants.

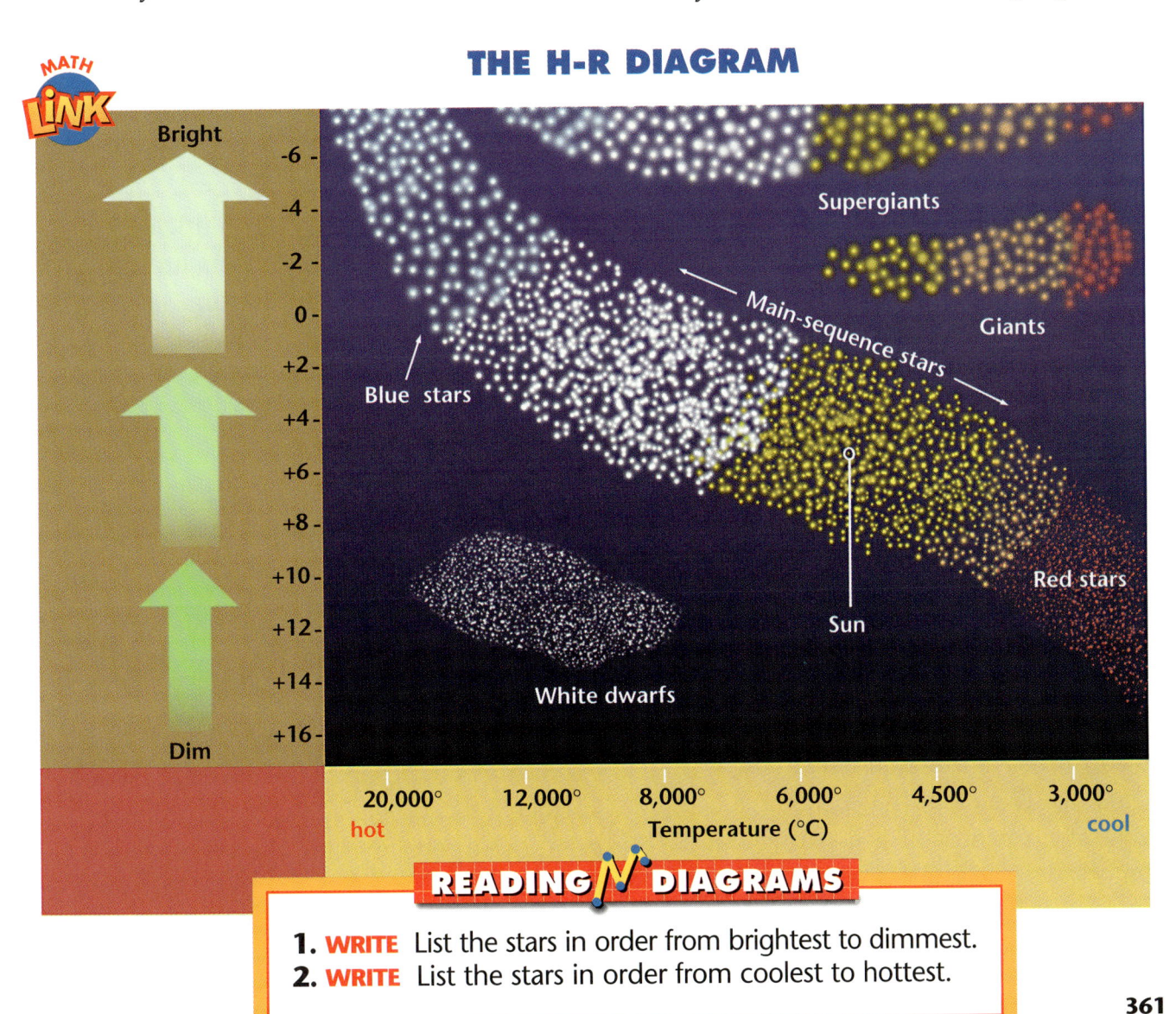

THE H-R DIAGRAM

READING DIAGRAMS

1. **WRITE** List the stars in order from brightest to dimmest.
2. **WRITE** List the stars in order from coolest to hottest.

Eagle Nebula

What Is the Life Cycle of a Star?

What can we learn from an H-R diagram? The stars that are plotted on the H-R diagram are groups of stars classified by their temperature and brightness. They are also stars at different points or stages in the life cycle of stars. Stars have a life cycle. They are born. They mature, grow old, and eventually die.

Beginning

A star begins its life as an enormous cloud of gas and dust in space, a **nebula** (neb′yə lə) (plural, *nebulae*). As time goes by, gravity causes the nebula to contract. As the cloud shrinks, it heats up. The cloud has become a *protostar*. A protostar is a young star that glows as gravity makes it collapse.

Main-Sequence Stars

Eventually the center of the protostar reaches a temperature of several million degrees. At this point nuclear reactions occur. Four hydrogen atoms fuse and form one helium atom. Energy and electrons are released in this reaction. The energy moves outward, balancing against the force of gravity. The protostar is now a *main-sequence star*. A main-sequence star is a star that is fusing hydrogen into helium. A star spends most of its life on the main sequence.

Giants and Supergiants

As a star uses up the supply of hydrogen at its core, the star begins to expand. As it expands the star's surface gets cooler. The star becomes a giant or supergiant star, depending on its mass.

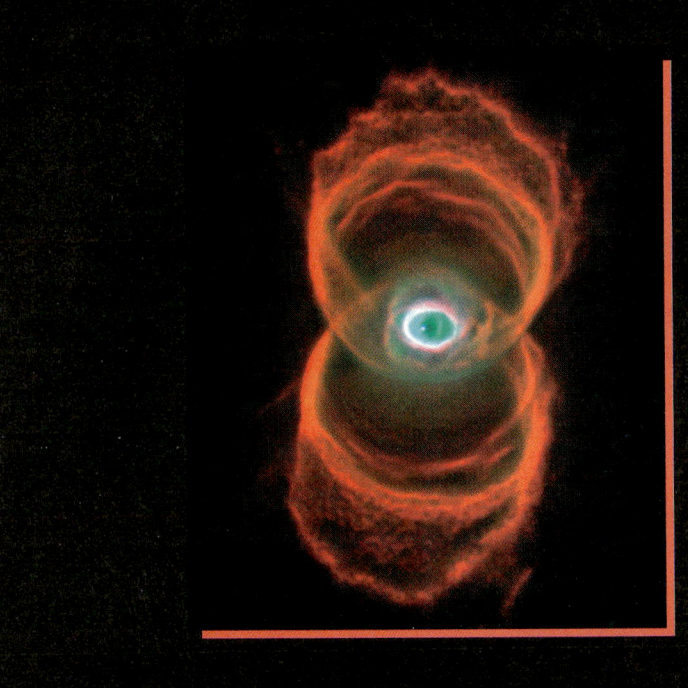

Colliding stellar
winds in Helix Nebula

The remains of
supernova SN 1987A

Final Stage: Lower-Mass Stars

Stars up to about ten times the mass of the Sun become red giant stars. In a red giant's core, both hydrogen and helium are changed into heavier elements. Energy is also released. As a red giant, its gravity is not strong enough to hold on to its outer layer of gas. This expanding layer of gas, called a *planetary nebula*, slowly spreads out into space.

Meanwhile the star's core continues to shrink. Its surface heats up, becoming white hot. The star has become a white dwarf. Stars produce a wind. Wind from a white dwarf often travels very fast. It catches up with the planetary nebula formed thousands of years earlier. As the wind hits the nebula, the wind makes the nebula shine. The wind also tears the nebula apart.

Final Stage: More-Massive Stars

More-massive stars, stars greater than ten times the mass of the Sun, become supergiants. These stars use up energy at a fantastic rate. As a result the star becomes unstable. It may become a **supernova** (sü′pər nō′və). A supernova is a star that explodes.

What happens next depends on the star's mass. Most supernova remnants become *neutron stars*, extremely dense stars made entirely of tightly packed neutrons. Neutron stars rotate very rapidly. Sometimes the neutron star seems to be blinking on and off, in a way, like light from a lighthouse. When this happens the star is called a *pulsar*.

When a star is very massive, something different occurs. It becomes a supernova. However, the remaining star does not become a neutron star. The star's core collapses. The star becomes a **black hole**. A black hole is an object whose gravity is so strong that even light cannot escape from it.

Can We See a Star Explode?

Would you like to go back in time? The place: China. The time: 1054. Some Chinese astronomers were observing the sky. Their focus was on the region known now as Taurus. Suddenly a new, bright star appeared. It was brighter than any other star in the sky. The astronomers called it a "guest star." They didn't know it, but the Chinese astronomers had just witnessed a supernova.

A *supernova* is an extremely powerful explosion in the universe. Some supernovas are so bright that they have been seen during the daytime, when the Sun was shining! What conditions are needed for a star to become a supernova?

Stars more massive than ten Suns become supergiant stars. These stars make heavier and heavier elements as they burn. Eventually the element iron is formed. Elements heavier than iron require more energy to be produced than is available.

No heavier elements are made, the reaction stops, and no more energy is sent out. No more energy is available to balance the pull of gravity. Suddenly the star collapses. This collapse makes the star explode in a supernova. Depending on the original mass of the star, the core, or center, of the supernova will become a neutron star or a black hole.

DID YOU KNOW?

Most of the elements in the universe are "cooked" inside of stars. These elements are then spread over the universe by supernovas.

Pulsar in the heart of the Crab Nebula

Brain Power

The elements that make up a star that exists today may be from another star. Explain how that might be true.

Where Does Even Light Disappear?

If the core of a supernova is very, very massive, it may not become a neutron star. It may become a black hole instead. How does a star become a black hole?

Companion star

After a supernova explosion, the leftover star collapses. Sometimes a star has too much mass to stop collapsing at the neutron star stage. Its gravity is too strong. As a result the star continues to collapse. Eventually it becomes so small that it warps, or changes, the space around it. The star's gravity becomes so powerful that not even light escapes it. The star has become a black hole.

Black holes don't give off light. They cannot be seen directly. The only way they can be seen is by observing their effects. Let's take a trip on an imaginary spacecraft to see what's happening around a black hole.

As you approach the black hole, you see that it has a companion star. (Many black holes may have companions, in fact.) Gas from the star is streaming toward the black hole. The gas spirals toward it in an orbit that keeps getting smaller. As the material spirals inward, it heats up. It gets hotter as it gets closer to the black hole. Just before the gas enters the black hole, it emits X rays.

Presently the most promising black-hole candidate is an X-ray source in the constellation Cygnus (sig′nəs), the Swan. It has a blue supergiant companion with the unusual-sounding name HDE226868. The X-ray source is called Cygnus X-1. It is 8,000 light-years from Earth.

Black hole

This is Cygnus X-1. Gas streaming off the blue supergiant is pulled into the black hole, giving off X rays.

What Kind of Star Is the Sun?

The Sun has 99.8 percent of all the mass in the solar system.

- The outermost part of the Sun, the *corona*, can be seen from Earth only during a total solar eclipse. Temperatures in the corona can reach 100 million degrees Celsius.

- The next layer in is the *chromosphere* (krō′mə sfîr′), the layer just below the corona. Like the corona, the chromosphere can be seen only during a total eclipse. The chromosphere appears pinkish.

- Beneath the chromosphere is the *photosphere* (fō′tə sfîr′). This is the part of the Sun that is visible. The photosphere is basically the "surface" of the Sun. The temperature of the photosphere is about 6,000°C. That makes the Sun a yellow star. It is placed about in the middle of the H-R diagram, a middle-aged star. Of course, never look at the Sun directly. Its brightness can harm your eyes.

- Once past the photosphere, you're in the interior of the Sun. Here you see gases and light, moving toward the surface. Energy travels outward toward the Sun's surface by means of radiation and convection.

- The core, or center, of the Sun is the source of all the Sun's energy. The core is about the size of Jupiter.

The Sun is 92 percent hydrogen. It is slowly being changed into helium in a nuclear reaction. Hydrogen atoms are fused together, producing helium atoms and light energy. Scientists think the Sun has enough hydrogen to last another five billion years!

Sun Facts

- **Diameter:** 1,392,000 kilometers (865,000 miles)
- **Distance from Earth:** 149,600,000 kilometers (92,960,000 miles)
- **Rotation:** 27 Earth days
- **Gravity:** If you weigh 85 pounds on Earth, your weight on the Sun would be 2,363 pounds.

Diagram labels: Solar wind (particles streaming off the Sun), Corona, Solar flare, Photosphere, Sunspots, Chromosphere, Core (zone of nuclear reaction), Prominence

READING DIAGRAMS

1. **REPRESENT** Draw a diagram made of circles, one inside another. How many would it take to represent the parts of the Sun?
2. **REPRESENT** Label each circle in your diagram.

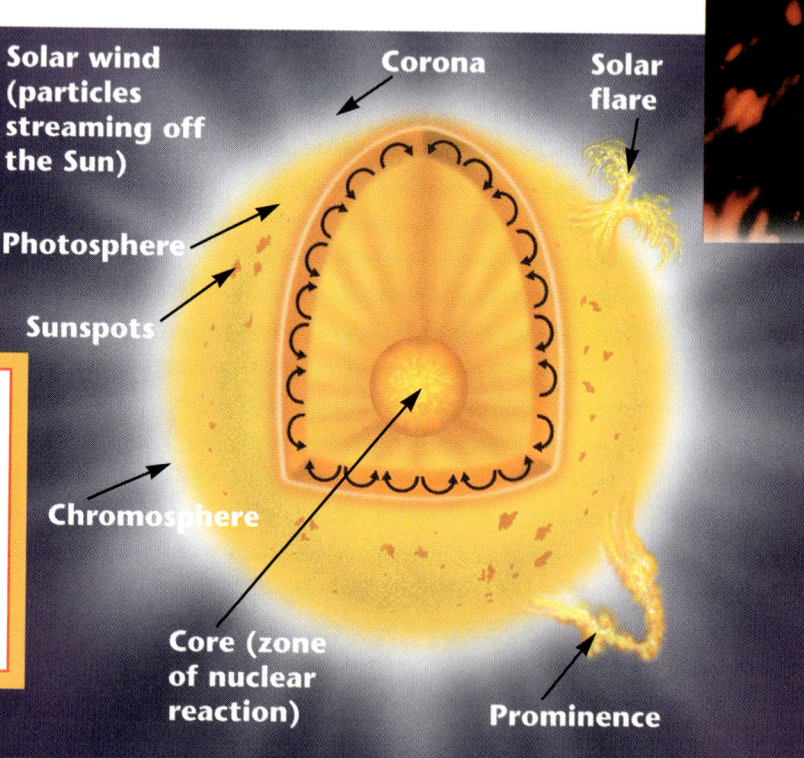

What Are Sunspots?

As you leave the Sun, you once again see the churning motion of gases in the photosphere. Some areas are dark. These dark areas are sunspots. Sunspots are caused by the Sun's rotation and its powerful magnetic field.

Sunspots tend to appear in groups and seem to follow an 11-year cycle of activity from peak to peak.

WHY IT MATTERS

The Sun is a main sequence star. Its life cycle will end in several billion years. In the meantime the Sun is an inexhaustible source of energy for Earth. Plants and other producers trap its energy by making food. Thus it makes possible the life cycles of all living things on Earth, including your own.

Plant matter decaying underground over millions of years produced today's limited fuel supplies of oil, natural gas, and coal. This fuel that is used today can be traced back to the Sun.

A sunspot "up close"

REVIEW

1. How is the distance to a star determined?
2. How is the temperature of a star related to its brightness?
3. **SEQUENCE** How would you put in order from youngest to oldest: neutron star, supergiant, protostar, main-sequence star, nebula, supernova?
4. How are the parts of the Sun arranged from innermost to outermost?
5. **CRITICAL THINKING** *Analyze* Why do you think the life cycle of a star depends on its mass?

WHY IT MATTERS THINK ABOUT IT
How are you changing as you get older?

WHY IT MATTERS WRITE ABOUT IT
Change can go in one direction without repeating. Some changes, however, happen over and over again in patterns, or cycles. What are some changes in the night sky that happen in cycles?

SCIENCE MAGAZINE

The Stuff Stars Are Made Of

How do scientists know what a star is made of and how old it is? The light from the star tells them!

At high temperatures elements become gases. Each gives off a unique pattern of light wavelengths, or spectrum. Astronomers use special equipment to separate a star's light into its wavelengths. From that they know which elements make up each star.

In 1885 American astronomer Edward Charles Pickering began studying the composition of stars. He hired Annie Jump Cannon to help. She analyzed hundreds of thousands of stars and was the first to classify them by brightness and temperature. Her observations are still used today.

By analyzing the amount of hydrogen and other elements in a star, scientists can estimate the star's age. Once the age is determined, scientists know the star's stage of development!

M stars, called red dwarfs, are the smallest and coolest. They reach 3,000°C (5,400°F) and are noted for their metallic-oxide molecules, such as titanium oxide.

K stars are orange. They have a temperature of about 4,700°C (8,400°F) and are smaller than the Sun. They have calcium and many metals.

Math Activity Make a graph of the temperatures of the kinds of stars mentioned on pages 368 and 369. Discuss the temperature differences.

Math Link

G stars have calcium, hydrogen, and many metals, particularly iron. These yellow stars are called solar stars because the Sun is one. They have a temperature of about 6,000°C (10,800°F).

F stars are yellow-white stars and have a temperature of about 7,500°C (13,500°F). They have a lot of calcium and hydrogen.

A stars, called white stars, have a lot of hydrogen and a temperature of about 10,000°C (18,000°F). Sirius, an A star, is the brightest star.

DISCUSSION STARTER

1. What did Annie Jump Cannon do to further astronomy?
2. What can scientists tell about stars from analyzing their elements?

B stars have the most helium. These blue-white stars have a temperature of about 20,000°C (36,000°F).

O stars are the hottest, brightest, and largest stars. Called blue giants, these stars are made of helium, oxygen, and nitrogen and have a temperature of about 35,000°C (63,000°F).

To learn more about stars, visit *www.mhschool.com/science* and select the keyword STARCLASS.

*inter*NET CONNECTION

Topic 7
EARTH SCIENCE

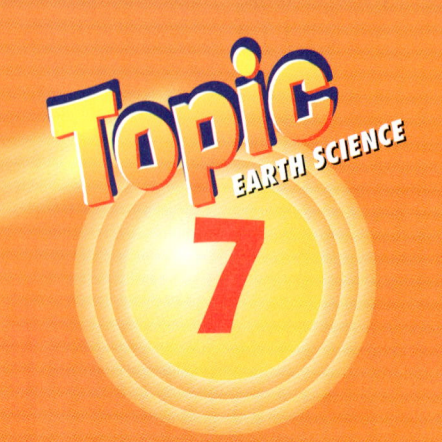

WHY IT MATTERS

With tools and ideas, people are learning more about the universe every day.

SCIENCE WORDS

galaxy a large group of stars held together by gravity

Milky Way our home galaxy

spectrum a band of colors made when white light is broken up

expansion redshift the shift of a spectrum of a galaxy toward longer (redder) wavelengths due to the expansion of space

big bang the beginning of the universe, when the density of the universe was very high

background radiation electromagnetic radiation left over from the big bang

quasar an extremely bright, extremely distant, high-energy source

Galaxies and Beyond

How do you think stars are arranged? Stars are in vast groups in the universe. These groups have immense spaces in between them. The pictures here show the star group that the Sun is in.

Is the Sun at the center of the star group? At the edge? Somewhere in between? If so, how far from the center is the Sun?

EXPLORE

HYPOTHESIZE How can we tell where the Sun is located in this star group? How do we know it is not in any of the other locations? Write a hypothesis in your *Science Journal*. Test your ideas.

EXPLORE ACTIVITY

Design Your Own Experiment

HOW CAN WE TELL WHERE THE SUN IS?

PROCEDURES

1. **MAKE A MODEL** Design a model of this star group. Make it large enough to walk through to positions A, B, C, and D. Choose ways of representing stars—students, desks, books, or another way. Arrange them to resemble an outline of this star group.

2. **OBSERVE** You will represent a person on Earth. Earth is so close to the Sun that you also represent the Sun. Move to positions A, B, and C in your model of the star group, and observe the stars around you.

3. **OBSERVE** Decide on a way to make observations at each location. Look forward, backward, left, and right—or any way you choose. Record your observations in your *Science Journal*.

MATERIALS
- art materials (optional)
- students, desks, or other ways to represent stars
- *Science Journal*

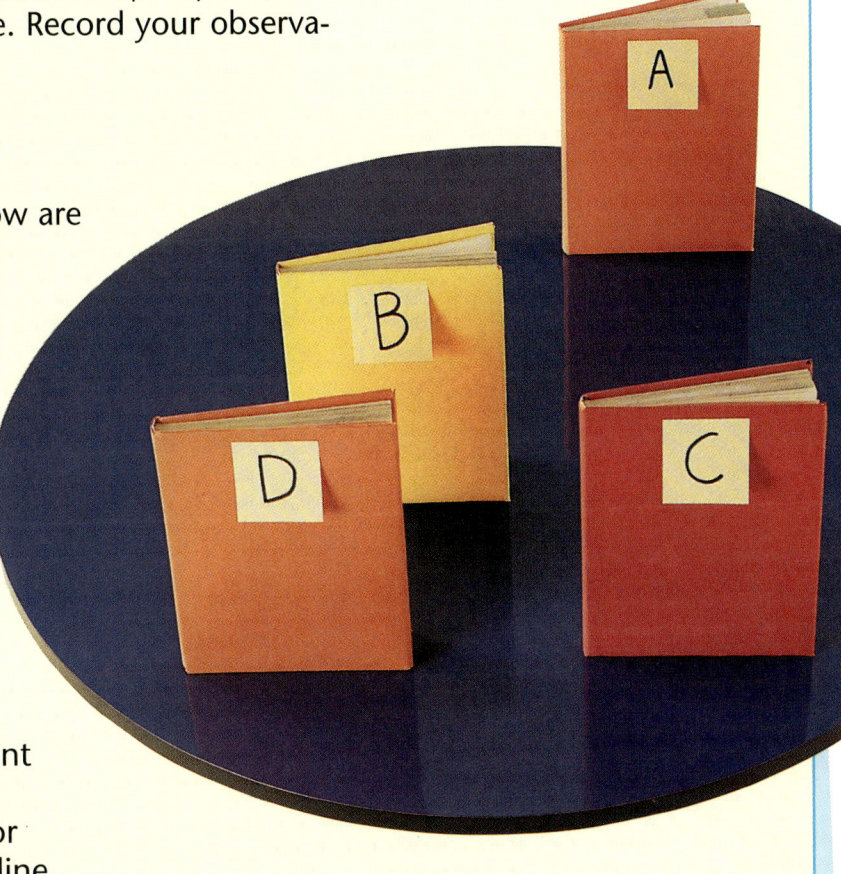

CONCLUDE AND APPLY

1. **COMPARE AND CONTRAST** How are your observations different at each location, looking in each direction?

2. **INFER** How do you think these differences can be used to tell where we are located when scientists make actual observations of the stars?

GOING FURTHER:
Problem Solving

3. **EXPERIMENT** Design a different kind of star group, with stars clustered in different places or with an entirely different outline. How will your observations differ?

371

How Are Stars Grouped?

How far apart are stars? Tremendously far! However, stars are grouped together throughout the universe. They are in groups called **galaxies**. Galaxies are large groups of stars held together by gravity. These stars are also moving. They orbit the center of their galaxy.

A galaxy may contain around 200 billion stars. There are around 100 billion galaxies in the universe. Just as stars belong to a galaxy, galaxies are usually part of a large group, or cluster.

You know that stars are different in size and structure. Galaxies also differ in size and structure. Astronomers classify galaxies into three groups, based on the shapes that galaxies can have.

- A *spiral galaxy* is a whirlpool-like galaxy. Spiral galaxies can be tightly or loosely wound. They often have lots of dust in their spirals. Some spirals even have a bar that goes through the center, the spirals going out from the bar.
- An *elliptical galaxy* is football- or basketball-shaped. It has no spirals and very little or no dust.
- An *irregular galaxy* does not have any recognizable shape. Many irregular galaxies have been involved in collisions with other galaxies.

Brain Power

An organism has levels of organization—cells, tissues, organs, and so on. What levels of organization might you say the universe has?

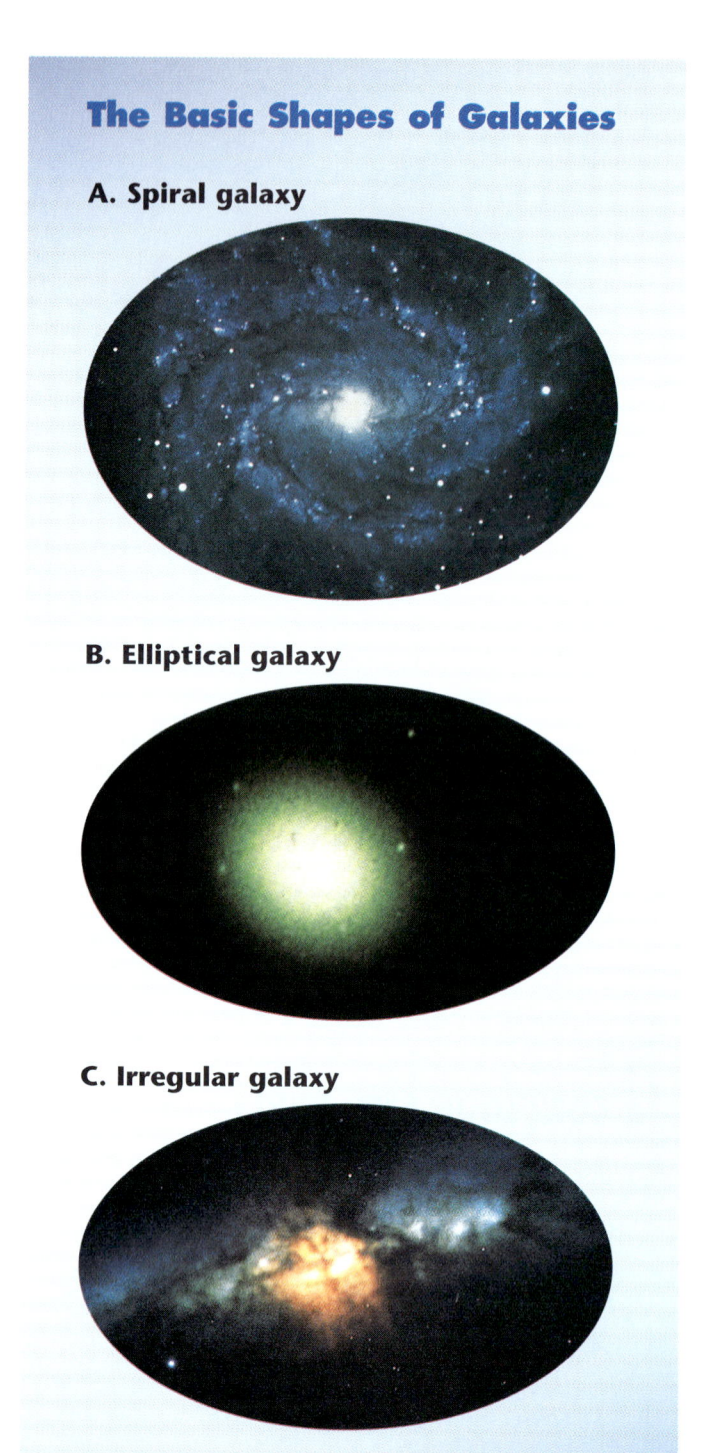

The Basic Shapes of Galaxies

A. Spiral galaxy

B. Elliptical galaxy

C. Irregular galaxy

Without a telescope galaxies look to us like points of light in the night sky, much like stars. Only with powerful telescopes can we look closer to see that the point of light is made up of many stars. The shape we observe also depends on the position from which they are viewed. Galaxies are three-dimensional, not flat. They look different if we see them head-on, at an angle, or edge-on.

How Can We Tell Where the Sun Is?

You're out in the countryside, away from city lights. The Moon has set, and it is dark and cloudless. It's a beautiful summer night. You look at the sky overhead. What do you see? You might see a broad, patchy band of light stretching across the sky. You are looking at part of our home galaxy, the **Milky Way**.

As you can see from the pictures below, the Milky Way is a spiral galaxy. It has some characteristic features.

- Stars are grouped in a kind of bulge in and around the center. All the stars in the Milky Way orbit its center. In general the closer a star is to the center, the faster it moves in its orbit.

- Several spiral arms, or narrow "lanes" of stars, extend out from the center. Getting farther and farther away from the center of the galaxy, stars become fewer in number.

- Surrounding the outer region of the Milky Way is a "halo." This halo is ball shaped and is made up of mostly faint stars.

Our solar system is located on one of the spiral arms. The Explore Activity on page 371 shows that from our vantage point on an arm, we see a large grouping of stars when we look toward the center of our galaxy. As we look in other directions, stars appear less crowded.

To find the Milky Way's center, we look in the direction of the constellation Sagittarius. However, we cannot actually see the center because we are looking through the Sagittarius arm. The spiral arm contains lots of gas and dust. The spiral arm's dust hides the Milky Way's center from us.

An artist's picture of what the Milky Way looks like from the "top" (left) and the "side" (right)

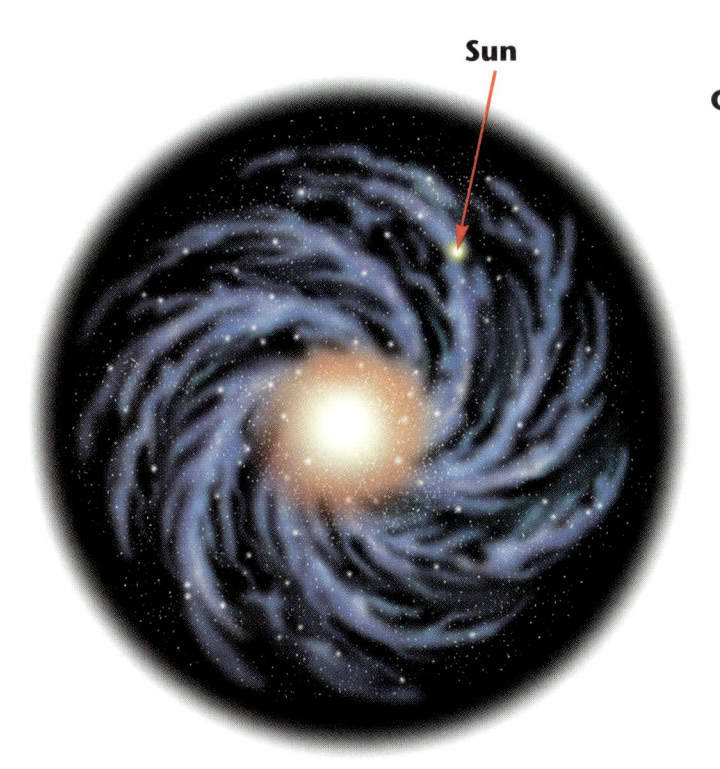

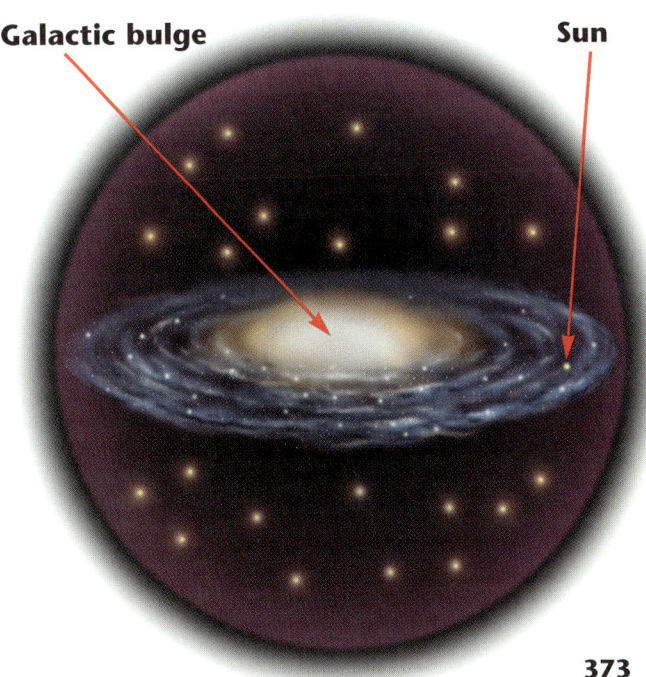

Sun

Galactic bulge   Sun

Are Galaxies Moving Away from Each Other?

Do galaxies change their distance from each other? Let's see how astronomers answer this question.

Think of a rainbow. It is formed by drops of water. When a beam of light goes through a drop of water, the wavelengths become separated. We see a band of colors, from violet to red. This band is part of the electromagnetic spectrum, discussed in Topic 1. A similar thing happens if you heat up a gas. The heated gases of stars produce waves of light. The light produces a **spectrum**. Only, instead of just a band of colors, you also see a pattern of dark lines. When light from a star passes through the star's outer gases, some of the wavelengths of light are absorbed by these gases. The absorbed wavelengths "drop out" from the spectrum in the form of dark lines.

The dark lines help us identify a star or a galaxy. Each star or galaxy has its own pattern of lines.

When we look at spectra from the light from galaxies, the dark lines shift. Some shift to the blue end of the spectrum. On the average, however, the lines shift to the red end. What can this mean?

Galaxies move away from each other because the space between the galaxies is expanding. It is something like a piece of rubber expanding. As space expands, the wavelength of light traveling through space also expands. This increase in wavelength of light due to space expanding is called an **expansion redshift**. It is called a redshift because the light's spectrum has been shifted to longer (redder) wavelengths.

Scientists can use this information. If the light from a galaxy is shifted to the red end, then the distance between us and the galaxy is increasing.

WAVELENGTH SHIFT

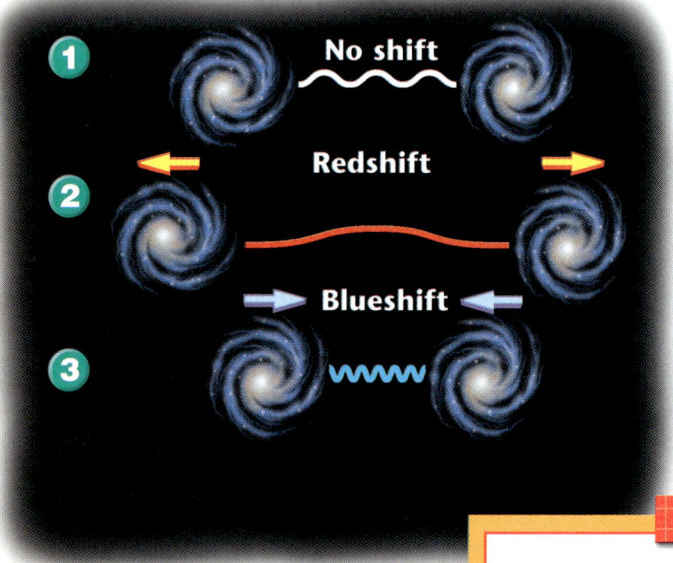

① This is a wave of light between our galaxy and another galaxy if they were not moving.

② If they are moving away from each other, the wavelength stretches out. It becomes longer.

③ If they are moving closer together, the wavelength is compressed. It gets shorter.

READING DIAGRAMS

1. **WRITE** What causes a shift to the red end, a redshift?
2. **WRITE** What causes a shift to the blue end, a blueshift?

How Does the Universe Expand?

The model in the Quick Lab helps describe how galaxies are moving away from each other. There is no "center" to the expansion. Observers on each galaxy could consider themselves to be at the center. This is because each observer would see the other galaxies moving away. It is useful to think of this as an expansion of space, not an explosion in space.

Looking "backward in time," astronomers say that in the past the galaxies must have been closer to each other. If you continue to let air out of the balloon, all the galaxies will be compressed into a very small volume. The early universe was very compressed. Because it was at a high pressure, its temperature was very high.

This beginning moment when the universe was very dense is called the **big bang.** The universe has expanded ever since the big bang. As the universe expands, its density decreases.

Astronomers do not know if the universe will continue to expand forever. It may, instead, stop expanding and then start contracting.

QUICK LAB

Expanding Dots

HYPOTHESIZE What happens to galaxies if the universe is changing size? Write a hypothesis in your *Science Journal*.

MATERIALS
- 9-in. round balloon, any light color
- permanent black marker
- *Science Journal*

PROCEDURES

1. Blow up the balloon just until it has a round shape (about 5 cm in diameter). Draw several dots over the surface of the balloon.

2. **OBSERVE** Now blow up the balloon until it is about 20 cm in diameter. While you blow up the balloon, your partner should observe what is happening to the dots.

3. **OBSERVE** Slowly release the air from the balloon. Observe what happens to the dots.

CONCLUDE AND APPLY

1. **OBSERVE** As the balloon was blown up, what happened to the dots on its surface?

2. **OBSERVE** What happened to the dots as you let the air out of the balloon?

3. **INFER** If the balloon represents the universe, what do the black dots represent?

375

What's the Matter?

What else does the big bang theory tell us? We can use it to explain the formation of matter in the universe.

According to the big bang theory, at some point in the past, all matter was in the form of a huge, compact ball. This ball was at a very high temperature. The high temperature and pressure resulted in a tremendous explosion. This big bang sent matter in all directions. As the matter expanded outward, gravity made the matter eventually collect into clumps. These clumps eventually became the stars and galaxies. These galaxies continue to move outward.

The big bang helps explain why there is a different amount of each element in the universe. For example, it tells us that originally the universe was made of electrons and other particles. As the temperature of the universe cooled down after the big bang, the small particles began to combine into hydrogen atoms. Most other elements were made inside the newly formed stars as hydrogen atoms were burned as fuel. The universe presently contains about 90 percent hydrogen.

Astronomers have discovered a form of electromagnetic waves coming from all directions in space. This radiation is left over from the beginning of the universe. It's called **background radiation**. Most of this energy is in the microwave part of the electromagnetic spectrum. The big bang theory predicted the existence of the background radiation in the 1940s. The background radiation was discovered in the 1960s. This was strong evidence for the big bang theory.

EXPANDING UNIVERSE

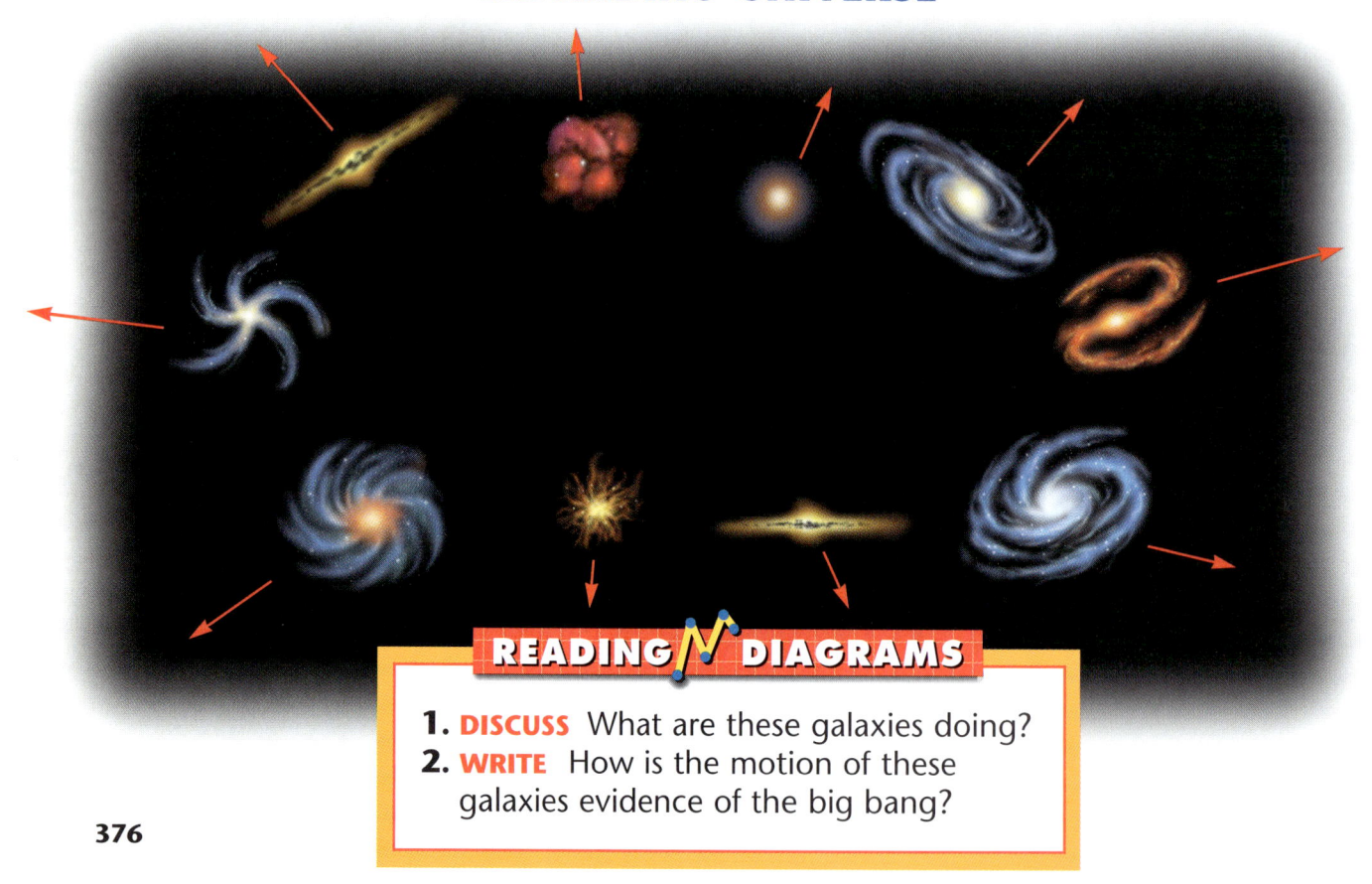

READING DIAGRAMS

1. **DISCUSS** What are these galaxies doing?
2. **WRITE** How is the motion of these galaxies evidence of the big bang?

How Did the Solar System Form?

One of the big questions astronomers ask is "Where did the solar system come from?" Let's look at this question from the point of view of the big bang.

- Several billion years after the big bang, many galaxies have formed. Much dust and hydrogen gas remains. Some of it has gathered into clouds, or nebulae. A few nebulae are massive enough to rotate slightly.

- Then something happens to one of the nebulae. Perhaps a star passes nearby. More likely the shock wave from a supernova hits the nebula. The wave makes small clumps of gas and dust form. Under the force of gravity, these clumps begin to contract. The supernova explosion, by the way, also carries with it heavier elements such as oxygen, carbon, and iron. These elements make up most of the inner planets.

- As the cloud contracts, it begins to rotate faster. The gravity at the center of the cloud gets stronger. Most of the clumps drift into the center of the spinning cloud. Not all the clumps move to the center, though. The clumps that move to the center will gradually become the proto-Sun. The other clumps will eventually become the protoplanets. These protoplanets move in approximately circular orbits around the proto-Sun. As they move in their orbits, the protoplanets sweep up some of the gas and dust. They add it to their growing mass.

- The center of the cloud gets more massive. The temperature at the core of the proto-Sun climbs. Eventually, the temperature becomes high enough to start nuclear reactions. The star—the Sun—is now a full-fledged main-sequence star.

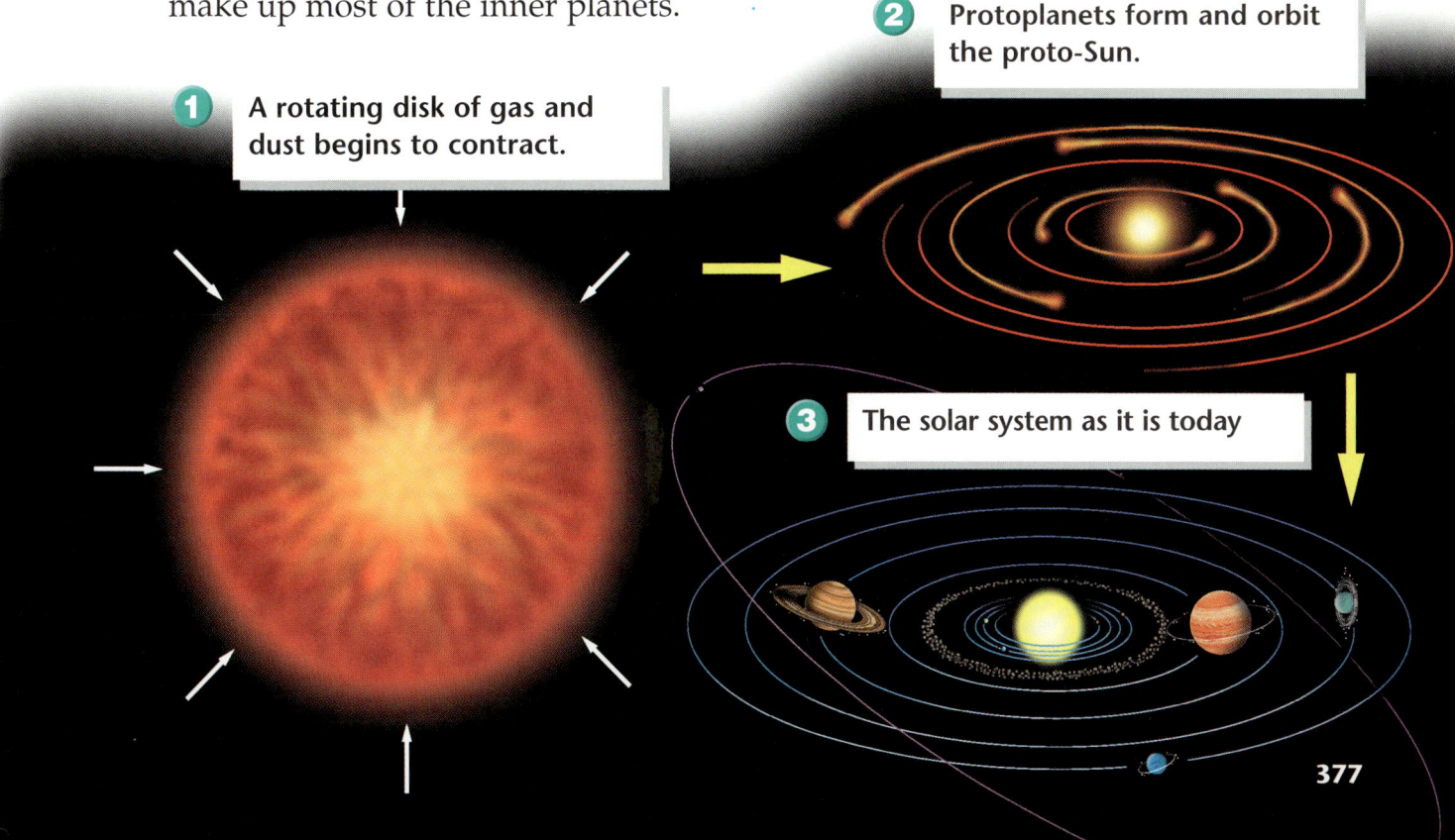

1 A rotating disk of gas and dust begins to contract.

2 Protoplanets form and orbit the proto-Sun.

3 The solar system as it is today

What Is a Quasar?

Why do some objects in the universe shine brighter than trillions of Suns? They have a size about that of the solar system. They are **quasars** (kwā′zärz). A quasar is an extremely bright, extremely distant, high-energy source.

Since quasars are at a great distance, the light coming from them reaches Earth after traveling billions of years. That means quasars must be very, very old. In the time the light has been traveling, the space between the quasars and Earth has grown, because the universe is getting larger. Thus, the wavelength of light coming from them has lengthened. It has been shifted to the red end of the spectrum.

One interesting idea about quasars is that they might be galaxies in an infant stage. It has taken so long for the light from them to reach Earth that in the meantime they have become galaxies. If so, we won't get light from these galaxies for billions of years to come!

Quasars might also be connected to black holes. In the past everything was closer together, and galaxies had a greater chance of colliding. Many astronomers hypothesize that when galaxies collide, they may feed material to supermassive black holes. These black holes would be able to gobble up entire stars. This feast would release tremendous amounts of energy, as the stars spiraled into the black hole. This energy is the energy we see as a quasar. Some Hubble photographs support this hypothesis. However, galaxies have been found around quasars that show no violent activity or collisions going on.

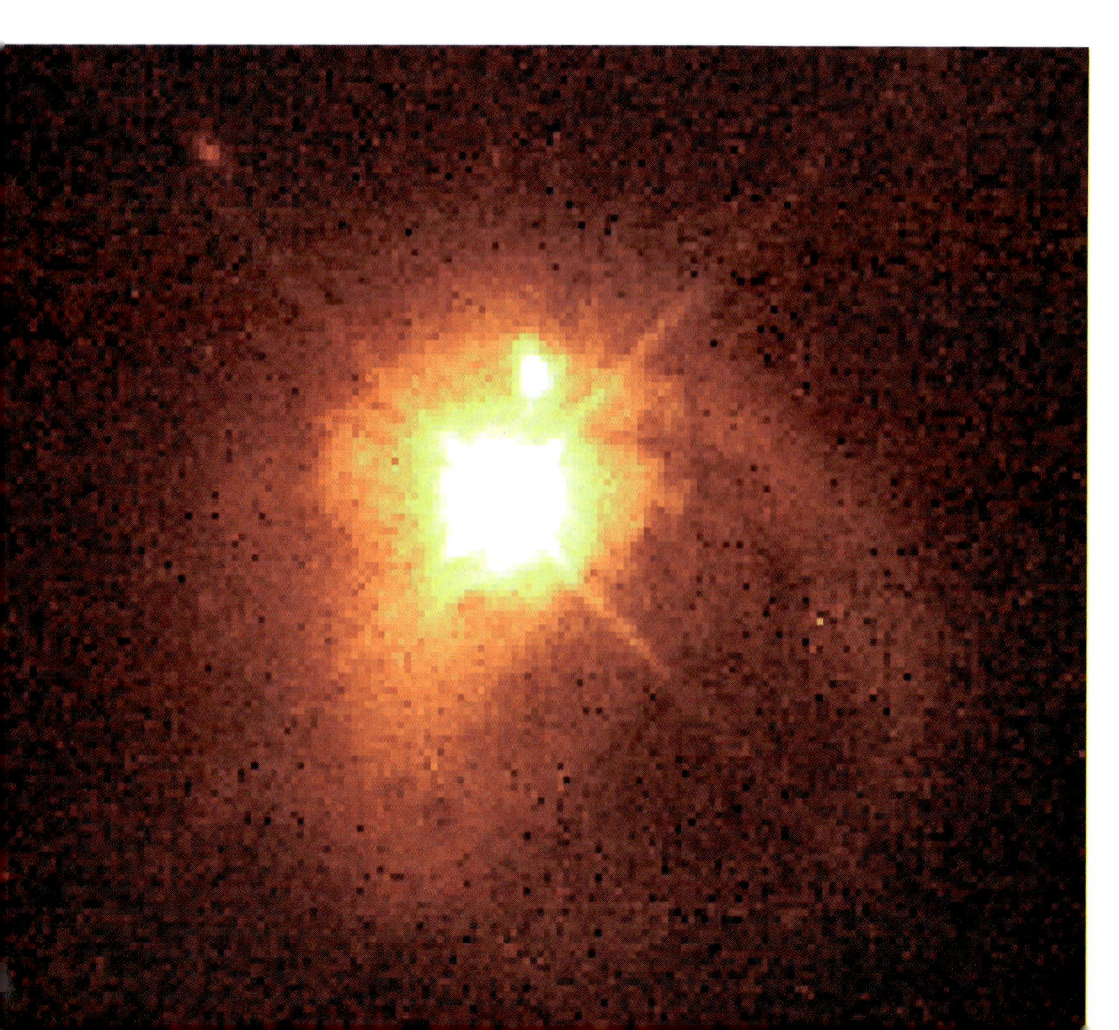

Astronomers believe this image shows a collision between a quasar and a galaxy.

What's Next

Where is astronomy headed? Astronomers are asking many questions. These are just some of them.

- How did galaxies form? Do galaxies form the same way now as they did in the past?
- How old is the universe? Will the universe expand forever or will it once again contract?
- Do planets revolve around other stars? Could they support life?

WHY IT MATTERS

When you look into the night sky, you look into the past. Light from stars and galaxies has been traveling for a long, long time. It left its source ages ago. Historians study what has happened in the past. They do this to explore the present and the future.

Astronomers also study the past. They look into space to understand what is happening now and to help prepare for the future.

We have tools to help us, such as the Hubble Space Telescope, the *Mars Pathfinder*, the *Cassini* probe, and the *Pluto Express*. What new things will you discover? It's all up to you.

Saturn as photographed by the Hubble Space Telescope

REVIEW

1. **COMPARE AND CONTRAST** What is a galaxy? List the characteristics of each of the three types of galaxies.

2. What kind of galaxy is the Milky Way? What is the approximate location of the solar system in the Milky Way?

3. Why are the spectra of galaxies shifted toward the red end?

4. What does the big bang mean? How does it explain the formation of galaxies?

5. **CRITICAL THINKING** *Analyze* What might we learn by studying quasars?

WHY IT MATTERS THINK ABOUT IT
Do you think the universe will continue to expand or will it stop? What would you use to support your idea?

WHY IT MATTERS WRITE ABOUT IT
Why is studying astronomy like studying the past? Why is studying the past important?

SCIENCE MAGAZINE

A Closer Look

When Galaxies Collide

Sixty-three million light years away, a dramatic event occurred. It happened 65 million years ago. What's strange is that the Hubble Space Telescope caught the action on film in late 1997!

Hubble photographed two galaxies colliding in the Antennae galaxy. The result of the crash? A gigantic new galaxy! It won't happen immediately, however. Astronomers estimate the process can take a half billion years.

Astronomers have wondered what would happen if two spiral galaxies collided. (Spiral galaxies, like our Milky Way, have curved arms that whirl around a center. Elliptical galaxies are compact.) The result, based on the pictures of Antennae, is an elliptical galaxy.

The collision also suggests what's ahead for our galaxy. The Andromeda galaxy is headed straight for the Milky Way! Don't put on your crash helmet yet. It probably won't happen for five billion years, long after the Sun is a burnt-out star!

More than a thousand clusters of stars showered the sky when the two galaxies collided. Each cluster may have up to a million stars!

DISCUSSION STARTER

1. What happened when the Antennae galaxies collided?
2. Why is this collision of interest to inhabitants of the Milky Way?

To learn more about the collision, visit *www.mhschool.com/science* and select the keyword GALAXY.

interNET CONNECTION

CHAPTER 8 REVIEW

SCIENCE WORDS

black hole p.363
comet p.350
galaxy p.372
light-year p.358
meteoroid p.351
nebula p.362
parallax p.358
planet p.334
quasar p.378
solar system p.334
star p.358
supernova p.363

USING SCIENCE WORDS

Number a paper from 1 to 10. Fill in 1 to 5 with words from the list above.

1. The distance to close stars can be measured using ___?___.
2. A distant bright source of high energy is called a(n) ___?___.
3. One type of exploding star is called a(n) ___?___.
4. A group of stars held together by gravity is a(n) ___?___.
5. The Sun and all the objects in orbit around it is the ___?___.
6–10. **Pick five words from the list above that were not used in 1 to 5, and use each in a sentence.**

UNDERSTANDING SCIENCE IDEAS

11. What object's gravity is so strong that even light cannot escape it?
12. What can we use to predict the motion of planets?
13. What do astronomers call the patterns that we see in the stars?
14. What do astronomers call a meteor that has landed on Earth?
15. What objects in the universe are moving away from each other?

USING IDEAS AND SKILLS

16. The universe is expanding. What evidence supports this theory?
17. **READING SKILL: COMPARE AND CONTRAST** How is the speed of a planet related to its distance from the Sun?
18. What are the possible final states of a star?
19. **EXPERIMENT** What determines whether an object falls to Earth's surface or orbits Earth?
20. **THINKING LIKE A SCIENTIST** The galaxies are moving away from each other. What force acts to oppose this expansion? Is this the same force that causes a ball to return to Earth after it is thrown upward?

PROBLEMS and PUZZLES

Sky View Borrow some binoculars, go as far from city lights as you can, and observe the night sky. What stars can you identify? Use a star map as a guide, if you can.

381

UNIT 4 REVIEW

SCIENCE WORDS

asteroid p.340
comet p.350
galaxy p.372
meteorite p.351
refraction p.294
revolution p.312
rotation p.308
solar eclipse p.323
supernova p.363
tide p.324

USING SCIENCE WORDS

Number a paper from 1 to 10. Beside each number write the word or words that best complete the sentence.

1. The bending of waves as they go from one substance to another is called __?__.

2. A complete spin of a planet on its axis is called a(n) __?__.

3. A complete trip around the Sun is called __?__.

4. A blocking out of a view of the Sun when Earth passes through the Moon's shadow is a(n) __?__.

5. The Moon's gravity (pull) causes ocean __?__.

6. A rocky, metallic object that orbits the Sun is a(n) __?__.

7. After a meteor hits Earth, whatever is left is called a(n) __?__.

8. The tail or tails of a __?__ always point away from the Sun.

9. A star that explodes is a(n) __?__.

10. The Milky Way is our __?__.

UNDERSTANDING SCIENCE IDEAS

Write 11 to 15. For each number write the letter for the best answer. You may wish to use the hints provided.

11. Kepler's model of the solar system is not correct because
    a. it is too small
    b. it is too old
    c. it uses geometric shapes
    d. it contradicts observations
    (Hint: Read page 293.)

12. Planets were noticeably different from stars to ancient peoples because
    a. planets "wandered" among stars
    b. planets appeared to be smaller than stars
    c. stars were farther away
    d. the skies were much clearer
    (Hint: Read page 334.)

13. Galileo discovered that Jupiter
    a. had moons
    b. was made of asteroids
    c. was covered with ice
    d. had rings
    (Hint: Read page 352.)

14. The brightness of a star is its
    a. parallax
    b. magnitude
    c. phase
    d. wavelength
    (Hint: Read page 359.)

15. The universe is
    a. a galaxy
    b. getting larger all the time
    c. the result of a red shift
    d. getting denser as it gets older
    (Hint: Read page 375.)

UNIT 4 REVIEW

USING IDEAS AND SKILLS

16. **MAKE A MODEL** What is a common model of Earth? What is the difference between a model and the real thing?

17. Why are standard time zones 15° wide in longitude?

18. How is a sundial used to tell time?

19. How does a solar eclipse happen?

20. How are comets and asteroids alike? How are they different?

21. List the planets Saturn, Jupiter, and Uranus in order of their distance from the Sun. Label one biggest, another smallest.

22. How is Pluto different from the other outer planets?

23. What theory did the discovery of the background radiation help support? Explain.

THINKING LIKE A SCIENTIST

24. **EXPERIMENT** The stars in a constellation seem to be close together. How could you demonstrate that they are not close but can appear to be.

25. What happens to a spectrum of light from a galaxy that is moving away from our viewpoint?

interNET CONNECTION

For help in reviewing this unit, visit www.mhschool.com/science

WRITING IN YOUR JOURNAL

SCIENCE IN YOUR LIFE
Describe one way that space exploration has changed the way people communicate with each other around the world.

SCIENCE TODAY/TOMORROW
Why do you think people are interested in learning more about other planets? Why might you want to explore a planet one day? What might you wonder that you'd find?

HOW SCIENTISTS WORK
Why do you think people were able to describe stars and planets long before telescopes were invented?

Design your own Experiment

A sundial allows you to tell time when the Sun is up. Can you think of a way to tell time from the sky at night? Check with your teacher before carrying out the experiment.

383

UNIT 4 REVIEW

PROBLEMS and PUZZLES

Life on Earth-2

The planet Earth-2 is just like Earth in almost every way. It has the same size, shape, atmosphere, and distance to its sun as Earth. There is one characteristic that Earth-2 does not share with Earth: Earth-2 has no seasons. There is no winter or summer on Earth-2. The temperatures at any place tend to be the same all year round. Can you think of a reason why Earth-2 might not have seasons? Include a diagram in your explanation.

Earth-2, similar to Earth in almost every way

Star Puzzle

Three stars—star A, star B, and star C—are all visible in the night sky. In apparent magnitude—how bright the stars appear to be—A seems brighter than B and less bright than C. In absolute magnitude—how much light energy the stars actually give off—A is brighter than C but less bright than B.

Which star is closest to Earth? Farthest from Earth? Use the information above and the table to determine the relative distance of each star from Earth. Rank each star from 1 to 3 in each category.

Star	Apparent Magnitude (how bright it appears)	Absolute Magnitude (how bright it really is)	Closeness
A			
B			
C			

Marble Drop

SAFETY Wear goggles.

Pour about 3 cm of aquarium gravel into a deep 6- to 9-in. pie tin. On top of the gravel place about 3 cm of flour. Over the flour sprinkle a very thin layer of fine soil or powdered cocoa. Place the pie tin in the center of a large sheet of newspaper. Drop a marble from a height of 50 cm into the center of your pie tin. Carefully remove the marble. Do this several times. You can also vary the height or angle at which your marble hits the pie tin. Describe how this model suggests how craters on the Moon, Mercury, and the moons of the outer planets may have formed.

REFERENCE SECTION

HANDBOOK
MEASUREMENTS R2
SAFETY R4
COLLECT DATA
- HAND LENS R6
- MICROSCOPE R7
- COLLECTING NET AND COMPASS R8
- TELESCOPE R9
- CAMERA, TAPE RECORDER, MAP, AND COMPASS . . . R10

MAKE MEASUREMENTS
- LENGTH R11
- TIME R12
- VOLUME R13
- MASS R14
- WEIGHT/FORCE R16
- TEMPERATURE R17

MAKE OBSERVATIONS
- WEATHER R18

USE TECHNOLOGY
- COMPUTER R20
- CALCULATOR R22

REPRESENT DATA
- GRAPHS R24
- MAPS R25
- TABLES AND CHARTS R26

GLOSSARY R27

INDEX R39

MEASUREMENTS

"The temperature is 77 degrees Fahrenheit."

"That is the same as 25 degrees Celsius."

"Water boils at 212 degrees Fahrenheit."

"Water freezes at 0 degrees Celsius."

"I weigh 85 pounds."

"That baseball bat weighs 32 ounces."

"32 ounces is the same as 2 pounds."

"The mass of the bat is 907 grams."

"This classroom is 10 meters wide and 20 meters long."

"That means the area is 200 square meters."

This bottle of juice has a volume of 1 liter.

That is a little more than 1 quart.

She can walk 20 meters in 5 seconds.

That means her speed is 4 meters per second.

Table of Measurements

SI (INTERNATIONAL SYSTEM) OF UNITS

Temperature

Water freezes at 0°C and boils at 100°C.

Length and Distance

1,000 meters = 1 kilometer
100 centimeters = 1 meter
10 millimeters = 1 centimeter

Volume

1,000 milliliters = 1 liter
1 cubic centimeter = 1 milliliter

Mass

1,000 grams = 1 kilogram

ENGLISH SYSTEM OF UNITS

Temperature

Water freezes at 32°F and boils at 212°F.

Length and Distance

5,280 feet = 1 mile
3 feet = 1 yard
12 inches = 1 foot

Volume of Fluids

4 quarts = 1 gallon
2 pints = 1 quart
2 cups = 1 pint
8 fluid ounces = 1 cup

Weight

2,000 pounds = 1 ton
16 ounces = 1 pound

SAFETY

In the Classroom

The most important part of doing any experiment is doing it safely. You can be safe by paying attention to your teacher and doing your work carefully. Here are some other ways to stay safe while you do experiments.

Before the Experiment

- Read all of the directions. Make sure you understand them. When you see 🚧 be sure to follow the safety rule.
- Listen to your teacher for special safety directions. If you don't understand something, ask for help.
- Wash your hands with soap and water before an activity.

During the Experiment

- Wear safety goggles when your teacher tells you to wear them and whenever you see 🥽.
- Wear splash-proof goggles when working with liquids.
- Wear goggles when working with anything that can fly into your eyes.
- Wear a safety apron if you work with anything messy or anything that might spill.
- If you spill something, wipe it up right away or ask your teacher for help.
- Tell your teacher if something breaks. If glass breaks do not clean it up yourself.
- Keep your hair and clothes away from open flames. Tie back long hair and roll up long sleeves.
- Be careful around a hot plate. Know when it is on and when it is off. Remember that the plate stays hot for a few minutes after you turn it off.
- Keep your hands dry around electrical equipment.
- Don't eat or drink anything during the experiment.

After the Experiment

- Put equipment back the way your teacher tells you.
- Dispose of things the way your teacher tells you.
- Clean up your work area and wash your hands with soap and water.

In the Field

- Always be accompanied by a trusted adult—like your teacher or a parent or guardian.
- Never touch animals or plants without the adult's approval. The animal might bite. The plant might be poison ivy or another dangerous plant.

Responsibility

Acting safely is one way to be responsible. You can also be responsible by treating animals, the environment, and each other with respect in the class and in the field.

Treat Living Things with Respect

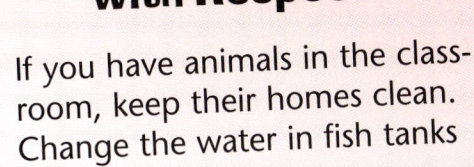

- If you have animals in the classroom, keep their homes clean. Change the water in fish tanks and clean out cages.
- Feed classroom animals the right amount of food.
- Give your classroom animals enough space.
- When you observe animals, don't hurt them or disturb their homes.
- Find a way to care for animals while school is on vacation.

Treat the Environment with Respect

- Do not pick flowers.
- Do not litter, including gum and food.
- If you see litter, ask your teacher if you can pick it up.
- Recycle materials used in experiments. Ask your teacher what materials can be recycled instead of thrown away. These might include plastics, aluminum, and newspapers.

Treat Each Other with Respect

- Use materials carefully around others so that people don't get hurt or get stains on their clothes.
- Be careful not to bump people when they are doing experiments. Do not disturb or damage their experiments.
- If you see that people are having trouble with an experiment, help them.

HANDBOOK

COLLECT DATA

Use a Hand Lens

One of the most important things you do in science is something that you do every day—make observations. You make an observation every time you use your senses to learn about the world around you. Whether you are watching a bird build a nest, listening to the rumble of distant thunder, or feeling the pull of a refrigerator magnet, you are using your senses to learn.

Sometimes your senses need a little help, especially during experiments. A hand lens, for example, magnifies an object, or makes the object look larger. With a hand lens, you can see details that would be hard to see otherwise.

Magnify a Piece of Cereal

1. Place a piece of your favorite cereal on a flat surface. Look at the cereal carefully. Draw a picture of it.
2. Look at the cereal through the large lens of a hand lens. Move the lens toward or away from the cereal until it looks larger and in focus. Draw a picture of the cereal as you see it through the hand lens. Fill in details that you did not see before.
3. Look at the cereal through the smaller lens, which will magnify the cereal even more. If you notice more details, add them to your drawing.
4. Repeat this activity using objects you are studying in science. It might be a rock, some soil, or a seed.

Observe Mold in a Petri Dish

A petri dish is a shallow, clear, round dish with a cover. It's useful for growing microscopic organisms such as mold.

1. Place a piece of bread about the size of your palm in a petri dish. It is best if the bread is a few days old and not made with preservatives.
2. Wet the bread by sprinkling water on it. Put the lid on the petri dish, and place the dish in a warm place.
3. After a few days, mold will start to grow on the bread. Use a hand lens to observe the mold through the clear petri dish. Draw what you see. Do not remove the cover from the dish.

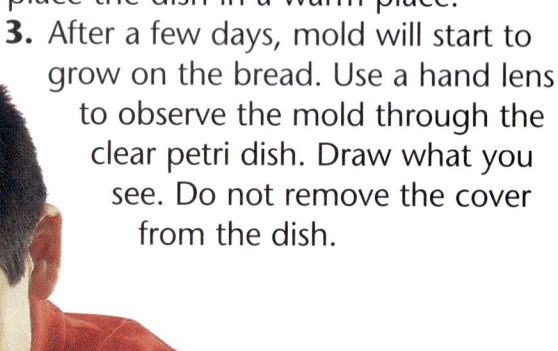

Use a Microscope

Hand lenses make objects look several times larger. A microscope, however, can magnify an object to look hundreds of times larger.

Examine Salt Grains

1. Look at the photograph to learn the different parts of your microscope.
2. Place the microscope on a flat surface. Always carry a microscope with both hands. Hold the arm with one hand, and put your other hand beneath the base.
3. Move the mirror so that it reflects light up toward the stage. Never point the mirror directly at the Sun or a bright light. Bright light can cause permanent eye damage.
4. Place a few grains of salt on the slide. Put the slide under the stage clips. Be sure that the salt grains you are going to examine are over the hole in the stage.
5. Look through the eyepiece. Turn the focusing knob slowly until the salt grains come into focus.
6. Draw what the grains look like through the microscope.
7. Look at other objects through the microscope. Try a piece of leaf, a human hair, or a pencil mark.

COLLECT DATA

Use a Collecting Net

You can use a collecting net to catch insects and observe them. You can try catching an insect in midair, but you might have better luck waiting for it to land on a plant. Put the net over the whole plant. Then you can place the insect in a jar with holes in the lid. With the help of your teacher, plan a research project about insects that includes using a collecting net.

Use a Compass

You use a compass to find directions. A compass is a small, thin magnet that swings freely, like a spinner in a board game. One end of the magnet always points north. This end is the magnet's north pole. How does a compass work?

1. Place the compass on a surface that is not made of magnetic material, such as a wooden table or a sidewalk.

2. Find the magnet's north pole. The north pole is marked in some way, usually with a color or an arrowhead.
3. Notice the letters *N*, *E*, *S*, and *W* on the compass. These letters stand for the directions north, east, south, and west. When the magnet stops swinging, turn the compass so that the *N* lines up with the north pole of the magnet.
4. Face to the north. Then face to the east, to the south, and to the west.
5. Repeat this activity by holding the compass in your hand and then at different places indoors and outdoors.

R8

Use a Telescope

You make most observations for science class during the day. Some things are observed best at night—like the Moon and the stars.

You can observe the Moon and the stars simply by looking up into a clear night sky. However, it's hard to see much detail on the Moon, such as craters and mountains. Also you can see only a tiny fraction of the stars and other objects that are actually in the sky. A telescope improves those observations.

A telescope uses lenses or mirrors to gather light and magnify objects. You can see much greater detail of the Moon's surface with a telescope than with just your eyes. A telescope gathers light better than your eyes can. With a telescope you can see stars that are too faint to see with just your eyes. See for yourself how a telescope can improve your observations.

1. Look at the Moon in the night sky, and draw a picture of what you see. Draw as many details as you can.
2. Point a telescope toward the Moon. Look through the eyepiece of the telescope. Move the telescope until you see the Moon. Turn the knob until the Moon comes into focus.

Objective lens
Eyepiece lens
Focusing knob

3. Draw a picture of what you see, including as many details as you can. Compare your two pictures.
4. Find the brightest star in the sky. Notice if there are any other stars near it.
5. Point a telescope toward the bright star. Look through the eyepiece and turn the knob until the stars come into focus. Move the telescope until you find the bright star.
6. Can you see stars through the telescope that you cannot see with just your eyes?

COLLECT DATA

Use a Camera, Tape Recorder, Map, and Compass

Camera

You can use a camera to record what you observe in nature. When taking photographs keep these tips in mind.

1. Hold the camera steady. Gently press the shutter button so that you do not jerk the camera.
2. Try to take pictures with the Sun at your back. Then your pictures will be bright and clear.
3. Don't get too close to the subject. Without a special lens, the picture could turn out blurry.
4. Be patient. If you are taking a picture of an animal, you may have to wait for the animal to appear.

Tape Recorder

You can record observations on a tape recorder. This is sometimes better than writing notes because, with a tape recorder, you can record your observations at the exact time you are making them. Later you can listen to the tape and write down your observations.

Use a Map and a Compass

When you are busy observing nature, it might be easy to get lost. You can use a map of the area and a compass to find your way. Here are some tips.

1. Lightly mark on the map your starting place. It might be the place where the bus parked.
2. Always know where you are on the map compared to your starting place. Watch for landmarks on the map, such as a river, a pond, trails, or buildings.
3. Use the map and compass to find special places to observe, such as a pond. Look at the map to see what direction the place is from you. Hold the compass to see where that direction is.
4. Use your map and compass with a friend.

MAKE MEASUREMENTS

Length

Find Length with a Ruler

1. Look at this section of a ruler. Each centimeter is divided into 10 millimeters. How long is the paper clip?
2. The length of the paper clip is 3 centimeters plus 2 millimeters. You can write this length as 3.2 centimeters.
3. Place the ruler on your desk. Lay a pencil against the ruler so that one end of the pencil lines up with the left edge of the ruler. Record the length of the pencil.
4. Trade your pencil with a classmate. Measure and record the length of each other's pencil. Compare your answers.

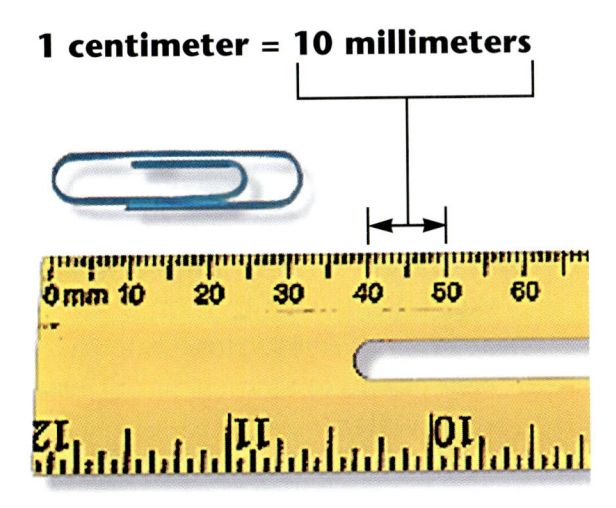

1 centimeter = 10 millimeters

Find Length with a Meterstick

1. Line up the meterstick with the left edge of the chalkboard. Make a chalk mark on the board at the right end of the meterstick.
2. Move the meterstick so that the left edge lines up with the chalk mark. Keep the stick level. Make another mark on the board at the right end of the meterstick.
3. Continue to move the meterstick and make chalk marks until the meterstick meets or overlaps the right edge of the board.
4. Record the length of the chalkboard in centimeters by adding all the measurements you've made. Remember, a meterstick has 100 centimeters.

Measuring Area

Area is the amount of surface something covers. To find the area of a rectangle, multiply the rectangle's length by its width. For example, the rectangle here is 3 centimeters long and 2 centimeters wide. Its area is 3 cm x 2 cm = 6 square centimeters. You write the area as 6 cm^2.

1. Find the area of your science book. Measure the book's length to the nearest centimeter. Measure its width.
2. Multiply the book's length by its width. Remember to put the answer in cm^2.

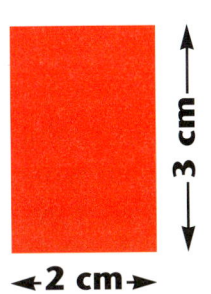

R11

MAKE MEASUREMENTS

Time

You use timing devices to measure how long something takes to happen. Some timing devices you use in science are a clock with a second hand and a stopwatch. Which one is more accurate?

Comparing a Clock and Stopwatch

1. Look at a clock with a second hand. The second hand is the hand that you can see moving. It measures seconds.
2. Get an egg timer with falling sand or some device like a wind-up toy that runs down after a certain length of time. When the second hand of the clock points to 12, tell your partner to start the egg timer. Watch the clock while the sand in the egg timer is falling.
3. When the sand stops falling, count how many seconds it took. Record this measurement. Repeat the activity, and compare the two measurements.
4. Switch roles with your partner.
5. Look at a stopwatch. Click the button on the top right. This starts the time. Click the button again. This stops the time. Click the button on the top left. This sets the stopwatch back to zero. Notice that the stopwatch tells time in minutes, seconds, and hundredths of a second.
6. Repeat the activity in steps 1–3, using the stopwatch instead of a clock. Make sure the stopwatch is set to zero. Click the top right button to start timing the reading. Click it again when the sand stops falling. Make sure you and your partner time each other twice.

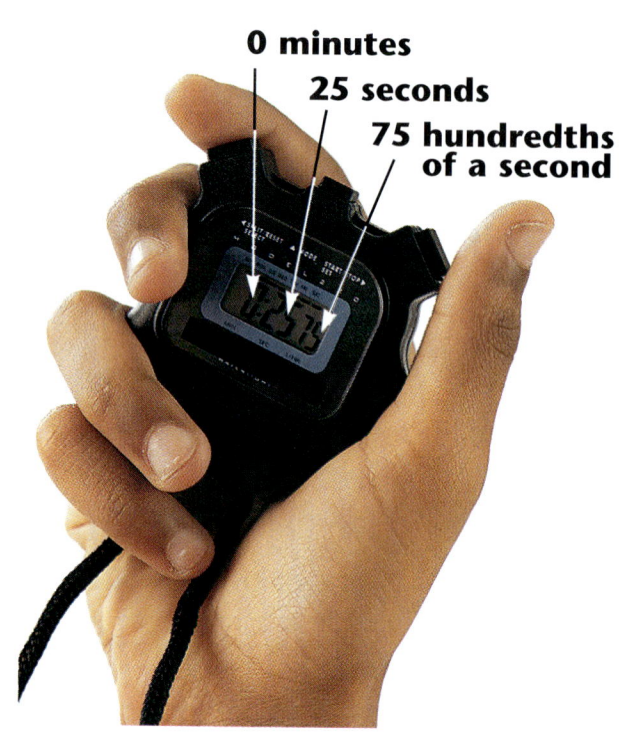

0 minutes
25 seconds
75 hundredths of a second

More About Time

1. Use the stopwatch to time how long it takes an ice cube to melt under cold running water. How long does an ice cube take to melt under warm running water?
2. Match each of these times with the action you think took that amount of time.

a. 0:00:14:55
b. 0:24:39:45
c. 2:10:23:00

1. A Little League baseball game
2. Saying the Pledge of Allegiance
3. Recess

Volume

Volume is the amount of space something takes up. If you've ever helped bake a cake or do other cooking, you might have measured the volume of water, vegetable oil, or melted butter. In science you usually measure the volume of liquids by using beakers and graduated cylinders. These containers are marked in milliliters (mL).

Measure the Volume of a Liquid

1. Look at the beaker and at the graduated cylinder. The beaker has marks for each 25 mL up to 200 mL. The graduated cylinder has marks for each 1 mL up to 100 mL.
2. The surface of the water in the graduated cylinder curves up at the sides. You measure the volume by reading the height of the water at the flat part. What is the volume of water in the graduated cylinder? How much water is in the beaker? They both contain 75 mL of water.
3. Pour 50 mL of water from a pitcher into a graduated cylinder. The water should be at the 50-mL mark on the graduated cylinder. If you go over the mark, pour a little water back into the pitcher.
4. Pour the 50 mL of water into a beaker.
5. Repeat steps 3 and 4 using 30 mL, 45 mL, and 25 mL of water.
6. Measure the volume of water you have in the beaker. Do you have about the same amount of water as your classmates?

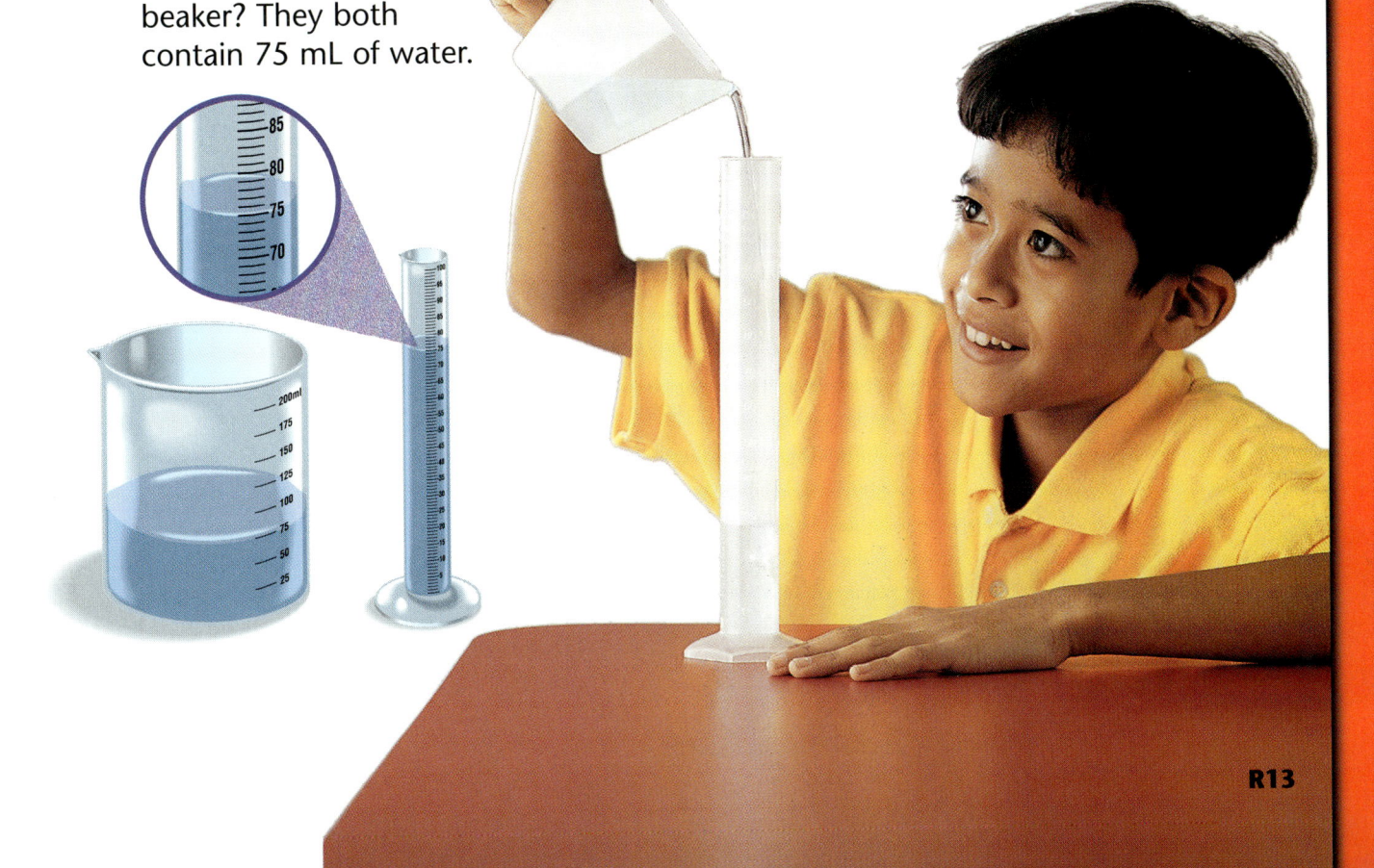

MAKE MEASUREMENTS

Mass

Mass is the amount of matter an object has. You use a balance to measure mass. To find the mass of an object, you balance it with objects whose masses you know. Let's find the mass of a box of crayons.

Measure the Mass of a Box of Crayons

1. Place the balance on a flat, level surface. Check that the two pans are empty and clean.
2. Make sure the empty pans are balanced with each other. The pointer should point to the middle mark. If it does not, move the slider a little to the right or left to balance the pans.
3. Gently place a box of crayons on the left pan. This pan will drop lower.
4. Add masses to the right pan until the pans are balanced.
5. Add the numbers on the masses that are in the right pan. The total is the mass of the box of crayons, in grams. Record this number. After the number write a *g* for "grams."

R14

Predict the Mass of More Crayons

1. Leave the box of crayons and the masses on the balance.
2. Get two more crayons. If you put them in the pan with the box of crayons, what do you think the mass of all the crayons will be? Record what you predict the total mass will be.
3. Check your prediction. Gently place the two crayons in the left pan. Add masses to the right pan until the pans are balanced.
4. Add the numbers on the masses as you did before. Record this number. How close is it to your prediction?

More About Mass

What was the mass of all your crayons? It was probably less than 100 grams. What would happen if you replaced the crayons with a pineapple? You may not have enough masses to balance the pineapple. It has a mass of about 1,000 grams. That's the same as 1 kilogram because *kilo* means "1,000."

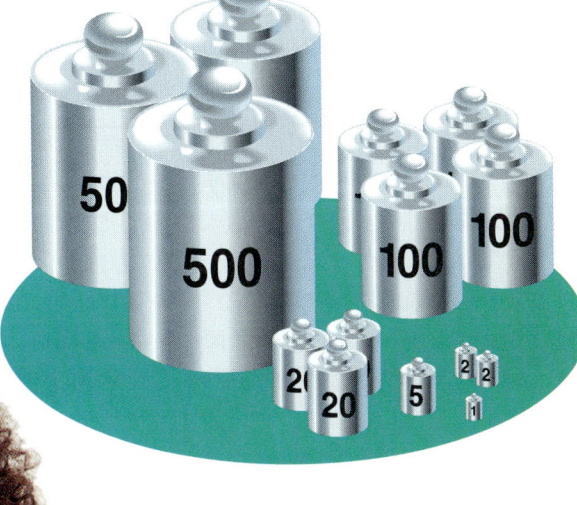

1. How many kilograms do all these masses add up to?
2. Which of these objects have a mass greater than 1 kilogram?
    a. large dog
    b. robin
    c. desktop computer
    d. calculator
    e. whole watermelon

R15

MAKE MEASUREMENTS

Weight/Force

You use a spring scale to measure weight. An object has weight because the force of gravity pulls down on the object. Therefore, weight is a force. Weight is measured in newtons (N) like all forces.

Measure the Weight of an Object

1. Look at your spring scale to see how many newtons it measures. See how the measurements are divided. The spring scale shown here measures up to 5 N. It has a mark for every 0.1 N.
2. Hold the spring scale by the top loop. Put the object to be measured on the bottom hook. If the object will not stay on the hook, place it in a net bag. Then hang the bag from the hook.
3. Let go of the object slowly. It will pull down on a spring inside the scale. The spring is connected to a pointer. The pointer on the spring scale shown here is a small bar.
4. Wait for the pointer to stop moving. Read the number of newtons next to the pointer. This is the object's weight. The mug in the picture weighs 4 N.

More About Spring Scales

You probably weigh yourself by standing on a bathroom scale. This is a spring scale. The force of your body stretches a spring inside the scale. The dial on the scale is probably marked in pounds—the English unit of weight. One pound is equal to about 4.5 newtons.

Here are some other spring scales you may have seen.

Temperature *MATH LINK*

You use a thermometer to measure temperature—how hot or cold something is. A thermometer is made of a thin tube with colored liquid inside. When the liquid gets warmer, it expands and moves up the tube. When the liquid gets cooler, it contracts and moves down the tube. You may have seen most temperatures measured in degrees Fahrenheit (°F). Scientists measure temperature in degrees Celsius (°C).

Water boils
Room temperature
Water freezes

Read a Thermometer

1. Look at the thermometer shown here. It has two scales—a Fahrenheit scale and a Celsius scale. Every 20 degrees on the Fahrenheit scale has a number. Every 10 degrees on the Celsius scale has a number.
2. What is the temperature shown on the thermometer? At what temperature does water freeze? Give your answers in °F and in °C.

What Is Convection?

1. Fill a large beaker about two-thirds full of cool water. Find the temperature of the water by holding a thermometer in the water. Do not let the bulb at the bottom of the thermometer touch the sides or bottom of the beaker.
2. Keep the thermometer in the water until the liquid in the tube stops moving—about a minute. Read and record the temperature in °C.
3. Sprinkle a little fish food on the surface of the water in the beaker. Do not knock the beaker, and most of the food will stay on top.
4. Carefully place the beaker on a hot plate. A hot plate is a small electric stove. Plug in the hot plate, and turn the control knob to a middle setting.
5. After a minute measure the temperature of water near the bottom of the beaker. At the same time, a classmate should measure the temperature of water near the top of the beaker. Record these temperatures. Is water near the bottom of the beaker heating up faster than near the top?
6. As the water heats up, notice what happens to the fish food. How do you know that warmer water at the bottom of the beaker rises and cooler water at the top sinks?

HANDBOOK

R17

MAKE OBSERVATIONS

Weather

What information is included in a weather report? You might think of temperature, cloud cover, wind speed, amount of rainfall, and so on. Various instruments are used to measure these parts of the weather. Some of them are shown here.

Barometer

A barometer measures air pressure. Most barometers are like the one shown here. It contains a flat metal can with most of the air removed. When air pressure increases (rises), the air pushes more on the can. A pointer that is attached to the can moves toward a higher number on the scale. When air pressure decreases (falls), the air pushes less on the can. The pointer moves toward a lower number on the scale.

29.73 inches →

Notice that the barometer above measures air pressure in inches and in centimeters. The long arrow points to the current air pressure, which is 29.73 inches of mercury. That means the air pushing down on liquid mercury in a dish would force the mercury 29.73 inches up a tube, as the drawing shows. What is the air pressure in centimeters?

Follow these steps when you use a barometer.

1. Look at the current air pressure reading marked by the long arrow.
2. Turn the knob on the front of the barometer so the short arrow points to the current pressure reading.
3. Check the barometer several times a day to see if the pressure is rising, falling, or staying the same.

Rain Gauge

A rain gauge measures how much rain falls. This instrument is simply a container that collects water. It has one or more scales for measuring the amount of rain.

The rain gauge shown here has been collecting rain throughout the day. How much rain fell in inches? In centimeters?

R18

Weather Vane

A weather vane measures wind direction. A weather vane is basically an arrow that is free to spin on a pole. Wind pushes on the widest part of the arrow—the tail—so that the arrow points to the direction that the wind is coming from. Letters on the weather vane show directions. If the vane doesn't have letters, you can tell direction with a compass. What direction is the wind coming from in the picture?

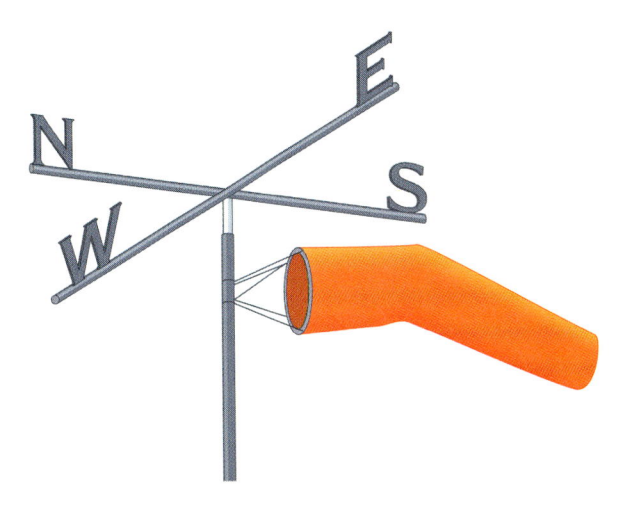

Windsock

A windsock also measures wind direction. You may have seen windsocks at airports. Windsocks are usually large and bright orange so that pilots can easily see which way the wind is blowing. The large opening of the windsock faces the wind. The narrow part of the windsock points in the direction that the wind is blowing. Which way is the wind blowing in the picture?

Anemometer

An anemometer measures wind speed. It is usually made of three shallow cones, or cups, that spin on an axle. The wind makes the cups and axle spin. The axle is attached to a dial that indicates wind speed. The faster the wind blows, the faster the cups turn.

R19

USE TECHNOLOGY

Computer

A computer has many uses. The Internet connects your computer to many other computers around the world, so you can collect all kinds of information. You can use a computer to show this information and write reports. Best of all you can use a computer to explore, discover, and learn.

You can also get information from CD-ROMs. They are computer disks that can hold large amounts of information. You can fit a whole encyclopedia on one CD-ROM.

Use Computers for a Project

Here is how one group of students uses computers as they work on a weather project.

1. The students use instruments to measure temperature, wind speed, wind direction, and other parts of the weather. They input this information, or data, into the computer. The students keep the data in a table. This helps them compare the data from one day to the next.

2. The teacher finds out that another group of students in a town 200 kilometers to the west is also doing a weather project. The two groups use the Internet to talk to each other and share data. When a storm happens in the town to the west, that group tells the other group that it's coming its way.

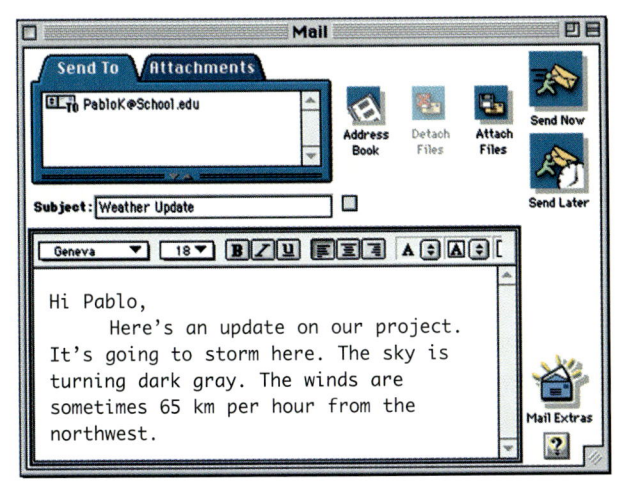

3. The students want to find out more. They decide to stay on the Internet and send questions to a local TV weather forecaster. She has a Web site and answers questions from students every day.

4. Meanwhile some students go to the library to gather more information from a CD-ROM disk. The CD-ROM has an encyclopedia that includes movie clips with sound. The clips give examples of different kinds of storms.

5. The students have kept all their information in a folder called Weather Project. Now they use that information to write a report about the weather. On the computer they can move around paragraphs, add words, take out words, put in diagrams, and draw their own weather maps. Then they print the report in color.

HANDBOOK

USE TECHNOLOGY

Calculator

Sometimes after you make measurements, you have to analyze your data to see what it means. This might involve doing calculations with your data. A calculator helps you do time-consuming calculations.

Find an Average

After you collect a set of measurements, you may want to get an idea of a typical measurement in that set. What if, for example, you are doing a weather project? As part of the project, you are studying rainfall data of a nearby town. The table shows how much rain fell in that town each week during the summer.

Week	Rain (cm)
1	2.0
2	1.4
3	0.0
4	0.5
5	1.2
6	2.5
7	1.8
8	1.4
9	2.4
10	8.6
11	7.5

What if you want to get an idea of how much rain fell during a typical week in the summer? In other words you want to find the average for the set of data. There are three kinds of averages—mean, median, and mode. Does it matter which one you use?

Find the Mean

The mean is what most people think of when they hear the word *average*. You can use a calculator to find the mean.

1. Make sure the calculator is on.
2. Add the numbers. To add a series of numbers, enter the first number and press [+]. Repeat until you enter the last number. See the hints below. After your last number, press [=]. Your total should be 29.3.
3. While entering so many numbers, it's easy to make a mistake and hit the wrong key. If you make a mistake, correct it by pressing the clear entry key, [CE]. Then continue entering the rest of the numbers.
4. Find the mean by dividing your total by the number of weeks. If 29.3 is displayed, press [÷] [1] [1] [=]. Rounded up to one decimal point, your mean should be 2.7.

Hints:
- If the only number to the right of the decimal point is 0, you don't have to enter it into the calculator. To enter 2.0, just press [2].
- If the only number to the left of the decimal point is 0, you don't have to enter it into the calculator. To enter 0.5, just press [.] [5].

R22

Find the Median

The median is the middle number when the numbers are arranged in order of size. When the rainfall measurements are arranged in order of size, they look like this.

0.0
0.5
1.2
1.4
1.4
1.8 ← there are five numbers above it and five numbers below it.
2.0
2.4
2.5
7.5
8.6

The median is 1.8. This number is in the middle;

Find the Mode

The mode is the number that occurs most frequently. From the ranked set of data above, you can see that the most frequent number is 1.4. It occurs twice. Here are your three different averages from the same set of data.

Average Weekly Rainfall (cm)
Mean	**2.7**
Median	**1.8**
Mode	**1.4**

Why is the mean so much higher than the median or mode? The mean is affected greatly by the last two weeks when it rained a lot. A typical week for that summer was much drier than either of those last two weeks. The median or mode gives a better idea of rainfall for a typical week.

Find the Mean, Median, and Mode

The table shows the length of 15 peanuts. Find the mean, median, and mode for this set of data. Which do you think best represents a typical peanut?

Peanut	Length (mm)
1	32
2	29
3	30
4	31
5	33
6	26
7	28
8	27
9	29
10	29
11	32
12	31
13	23
14	36
15	31

Find the Percent

Sometimes numbers are given as percents (%). *Percent* literally means "per hundred." For example, 28% means 28 out of 100. What if there are about 14,000 trees in the forest and 28% are over 50 years old? How many of them are over 50 years old? Use your calculator. You want to find 28% of 14,000. Press ① ④ ⓪ ⓪ ⓪ ⊗ ② ⑧ %. The answer should be 3,920.

R23

REPRESENT DATA

Make Graphs to Organize Data

When you do an experiment in science, you collect information. To find out what your information means, you can organize it into graphs. There are many kinds of graphs.

Circle Graphs

A circle graph is helpful to show how a complete set of data is divided into parts. The circle graph here shows how water is used in the United States. What is the single largest use of water?

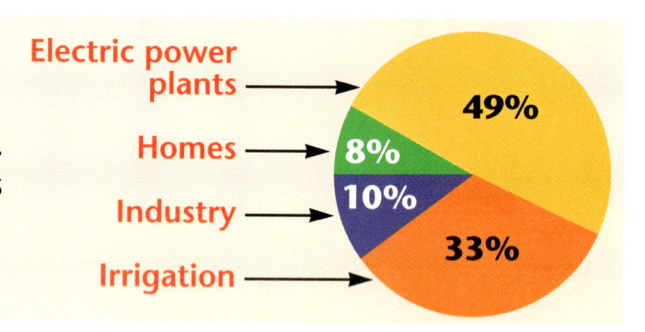

Electric power plants → 49%
Homes → 8%
Industry → 10%
Irrigation → 33%

Bar Graphs

A bar graph uses bars to show information. For example, what if you wrap wire around a nail and connect the ends to a battery? The nail becomes a magnet that can pick up paper clips. The graph shows that the more you wrap the wire around the nail, the more paper clips it picks up.

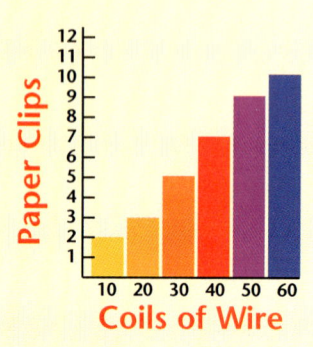

How many paper clips did the nail with 20 coils pick up? With 50 coils?

Line Graphs

A line graph shows information by connecting dots plotted on the graph. For example, what if you are growing a plant? Every week you measure how high the plant has grown. The line graph below organizes the measurements.

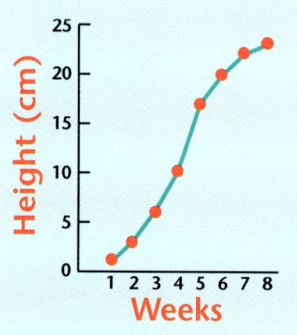

1. Between which two weeks did the plant grow most?
2. When did plant growth begin to level off?

Make a Graph

What if you collect information about how much water your family uses each day?

Activity	Water Used (L)
Drinking	10
Showering	180
Bathing	240
Brushing teeth	80
Washing dishes	140
Washing hands	30
Washing clothes	280
Flushing toilet	90

Decide what type of graph would best organize such data. Collect the information, and make your graph. Compare it with those of classmates.

R24

Make Maps to Show Information

Locate Places

A map is a drawing that shows an area from above. Most maps have coordinates—numbers and letters along the top and side. Coordinates help you find places easily. For example, what if you wanted to find the library on the map? It is located at B4. Place a finger on the letter B at the top of the map and another finger on the number 4 along the side. Then move your fingers straight across and down the map until they meet. The library is located where the coordinates B and 4 meet, or very nearby.

1. What color building is located at F6?
2. The hospital is located three blocks north and two blocks east of the library. What are its coordinates?
3. Make a map of an area in your community. It might be a park or the area between your home and school. Include coordinates. Use a compass to find north, and mark north on your map. Exchange maps with classmates, and answer each other's questions.

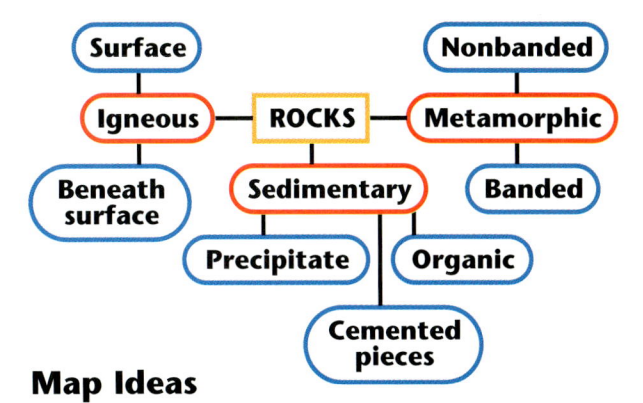

Map Ideas

The map shows how places are connected to each other. Idea maps, on the other hand, show how ideas are connected to each other. Idea maps help you organize information about a topic.

The idea map above connects ideas about rocks. This map shows that there are three major types of rock—igneous, sedimentary, and metamorphic. Connections to each rock type provide further information. For example, this map reminds you that igneous rocks are classified into those that form at Earth's surface and far beneath it.

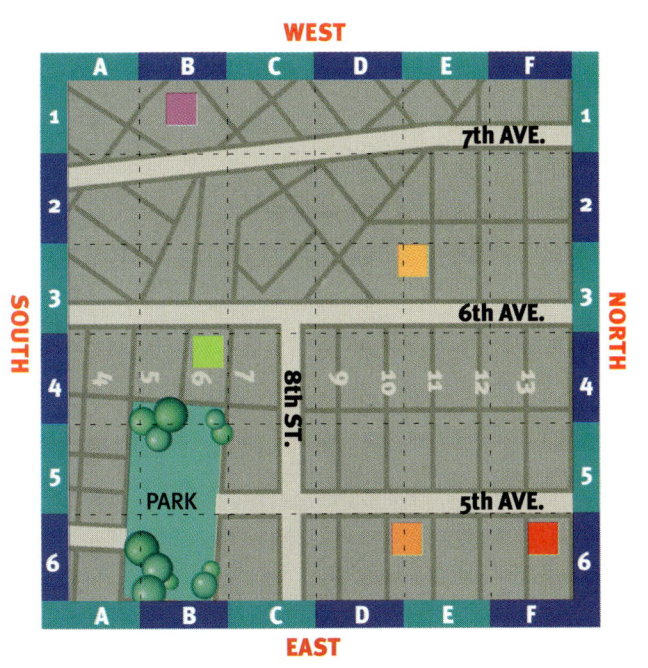

Make an idea map about a topic you are learning in science. Your map can include words, phrases, or even sentences. Arrange your map in a way that makes sense to you and helps you understand the ideas.

R25

REPRESENT DATA

Make Tables and Charts to Organize Information

MATH LINK

Tables help you organize data during experiments. Most tables have columns that run up and down, and rows that run across. The columns and rows have headings that tell you what kind of data goes in each part of the table.

A Sample Table

What if you are going to do an experiment to find out how long different kinds of seeds take to sprout? Before you begin the experiment, you should set up your table. Follow these steps.

1. In this experiment you will plant 20 radish seeds, 20 bean seeds, and 20 corn seeds. Your table must show how many radish seeds, bean seeds, and corn seeds sprouted on days 1, 2, 3, 4, and 5.

2. Make your table with columns, rows, and headings. You might use a computer to make a table. Some computer programs let you build a table with just the click of a mouse. You can delete or add columns and rows if you need to.

3. Give your table a title. Your table could look like the one here.

Make a Table

Now what if you are going to do an experiment to find out how temperature affects the sprouting of seeds? You will plant 20 bean seeds in each of two trays. You will keep each tray at a different temperature, as shown below, and observe the trays for seven days. Make a table you can use for this experiment.

Make a Chart

A chart is simply a table with pictures as well as words to label the rows or columns.

R26

GLOSSARY

This Glossary will help you to pronounce and understand the meanings of the Science Words introduced in this book. The page number at the end of the definition tells where the word appears.

A

absolute age (ab′sə lüt′ āj) The age of a rock in years, as determined by measuring the decay rate of its radioactive elements. (p. 470)

absolute magnitude (ab′sə lüt′ mag′ni tüd′) The actual brightness of a star. (p. 359)

acceleration (ak sel′ə rā′shən) The change in velocity of a moving object with time. (p. 206)

action-reaction pair (ak′shən rē ak′shən pâr) Two forces acting on different objects, having equal strength but opposite direction. (p. 230)

active transport (ak′tiv trans′pôrt′) The movement of molecules through a cell membrane, requiring energy. (p. 131)

adaptation (ad′ap tā′shən) A variation that increases an organism's chances for survival. (p. 564)

adolescence (ad′ə les′əns) The period of time between childhood and adulthood. (p. 617)

aftershock (af′tər shok′) Shaking of the crust after the initial shaking of an earthquake. (p. 404)

amnion (am′nē ən) A fluid-filled sac that surrounds the fetus for protection during pregnancy. (p. 608)

annual (an′ū əl) A plant that grows, reproduces, and dies all in one year. (p. 183)

apparent magnitude (ə par′ənt mag′ni tüd′) The brightness of a star as seen in the night sky on Earth. (p. 359)

artificial satellite (är′tə fish′əl sat′ə līt′) A device sent into orbit around Earth. (p. 299)

asexual reproduction (ā sek′shü əl rē′prə duk′shən) The production of a new organism from one parent. (p. 143)

associative neuron (ə sō′shē ā′tiv nûr′on) A nerve cell that passes impulses from sensory to motor neurons. (p. 581)

asteroid (as′tə roid′) A rocky, metallic object that orbits the Sun. (p. 340)

atom (at′əm) The smallest particle of an element that has the same chemical properties of the element. *See* **molecule**. (pp. 20, 118)

atomic number (ə tom′ik num′bər) The number of protons in an atom. (p. 23)

average speed (av′rij spēd) The total distance traveled by the amount of time. (p. 203)

axon (ak′son) A nerve fiber that carries messages away from the cell body. (p. 580)

B

background radiation (bak′ground′ rā′dē ā′shən) Electromagnetic radiation left over from the big-bang beginning of the universe. (p. 376)

balanced forces (bal′ənst fôrs′əz) Forces that cancel each other out when acting together on a single object. (p. 216)

PRONUNCIATION KEY

The following symbols are used throughout the McGraw-Hill Science 2000 Glossaries.

a	at	e	end	o	hot	u	up	hw	white	ə	about
ā	ape	ē	me	ō	old	ū	use	ng	song		taken
ä	far	i	it	ô	fork	ü	rule	th	thin		pencil
âr	care	ī	ice	oi	oil	u̇	pull	<u>th</u>	this		lemon
		îr	pierce	ou	out	ûr	turn	zh	measure		circus

′ = *primary accent; shows which syllable takes the main stress, such as* **kil** *in* **kilogram** (kil′ə gram′)

′ = *secondary accent; shows which syllables take the lighter stresses, such as* **gram** *in* **kilogram**

R27

batholith • community

batholith (bath′ə lith) An irregularly shaped structure that is the largest and deepest of underground magma formations. (p. 419)

biennial (bī en′ē əl) A plant that produces leaves and food one year and reproduces and dies the next year. (p. 183)

big bang (big bang) The beginning moment of the universe when the density and temperature of the universe were very high. (p. 375)

biodiversity (bī′ō di vûr′si tē) The wide variety of life on Earth. (p. 161)

biological feedback (bī′ə loj′i kəl fēd′bak′) The process the body uses to determine when to release a hormone and when to stop. (p. 594)

biomass conversion (bī′ō mas′ kən vûr′zhən) Getting energy from plant and animal materials by changing them into high-quality fuels. (p. 83)

black hole (blak hōl) An object whose gravity is so strong that light cannot escape it. (p. 363)

boiling (boil′ing) The formation of bubbles of vapor that escape from a liquid that is being heated. (p. 71)

boiling point (boil′ing point) The temperature at which a substance turns from a liquid to a gas. (p. 7)

budding (bə′ding) A kind of asexual reproduction in which a new organism develops from a bump (bud) on the side of the parent. (p. 180)

C

caldera (kal dâr′ə) A very wide crater formed by the collapse of a volcano. (p. 415)

calorie (kal′ə rē) How much energy is in food. (p. 123)

carbohydrate (kär′bō hī′drāt) One of the carbon compounds, such as sugars and starches, that supply energy for cell activities. (p. 122)

carrier (kar′ē ər) An individual who has inherited a factor for a trait but does not show the trait. (p. 504)

cast (kast) The seeping of minerals into a mold to form a stone fossil. (p. 547)

cell (sel) The basic unit of life. (p. 101)

cell membrane (sel mem′brān) A cell's outer covering. (p. 114)

cell wall (sel wôl) A stiff covering outside the cell membrane of a plant cell. (p. 117)

chain reaction (chān rē ak′shən) A reaction that is kept going by products of the reaction. (p. 84)

chemical bond (kem′i kəl bond) A link that atoms or electrically charged particles can form with each other. (p. 35)

chemical change (kem′i kəl chānj) A change in matter that produces a new substance with different properties from the original. (p. 12)

chemical formula (kem′i kəl fôr′myə lə) A way of using letters and numbers to show how much of each element is in a substance. (p. 35)

chemical property (kem′i kəl prop′ər tē) A way of describing how a substance changes chemically with other substances. (p. 41)

chemical weathering (kem′i kəl weth′ər ing) The breaking down of rocks by oxidation or the dissolving action of acids. (p. 431)

chloroplast (klôr′ə plast′) A green structure in a plant cell where food is produced. Chloroplasts contain the green pigment chlorophyll and are also found in some protist cells. (p. 117)

chromosome (krō′mə sōm′) A strand in the nucleus that stores directions for cell activities. Chromosomes act like blueprints for transferring information to the next generation of cells. (p. 114)

chromosphere (krō′mə sfîr′) The pinkish layer of the Sun just below the corona that can be seen only during a total eclipse. (p. 366)

cinder-cone volcano (sin′dər kōn vol kā′nō) A steep-sided cone that forms from explosive eruptions of hot rocks, ranging from particles to boulders. (p. 416)

class (klas) One of the groupings of similar members within a phylum. (p. 157)

comet (kom′it) A ball of ice and rock that orbits the Sun. Comets come from the outer fringes of the solar system and circle the Sun in long elliptical orbits. (p. 350)

community (kə mū′ni tē) All the populations living together in the same place. (p. 106)

composite volcano • DNA

competition (kom′pi tish′ən) The struggle among living things to obtain the resources they need to survive. (p. 567)

composite volcano (kəm poz′it vol kā′nō) A cone formed from explosive eruptions of hot rocks followed by a flow of lava, over and over. (p. 416)

compound (*n.*, kom′pound) A chemical combination of two or more elements. (pp. 34, 121)

compound machine (kom′pound mə shēn′) A combination of two or more machines. (p. 281)

condensation (kon′den sā′shən) The change of a gas into a liquid as molecules attract each other. (p. 71)

conduction (kən duk′shən) The transfer of energy by direct contact of molecules. (p. 57)

conjugation (kon′jə gā′shən) A kind of sexual reproduction in which two parent cells join and exchange material from their nuclei before they divide. The result is offspring that are not identical to either parent. (p. 180)

conservation of momentum (kon′sər vā′shən uv mō men′təm) The total momentum of a group that does not change unless the group is acted upon by outside forces. (p. 233)

constellation (kon′stə lā′shən) A number of stars that appears to form a pattern. (p. 359)

continental drift (kon′tə nen′təl drift) The idea that a supercontinent split apart into pieces, the continents, which drifted in time to their present locations. (p. 389)

convection (kən vek′shən) The transfer of energy by the flow of a liquid or gas. (p. 57)

convection current (kən vek′shən kûr′ənt) The rising of warm matter and sinking of cooled matter. (p. 396)

convergent boundary (kən vûr′jənt boun′də rē) Places where tectonic plates are colliding. (p. 394)

corona (kə rō′nə) The outermost part of the Sun that can be seen only in a total eclipse. (p. 366)

crater (krā′tər) **1.** A depression in the Moon's surface formed by the impact of objects from space. (p. 326) **2.** A cuplike hollow that forms at the top of a volcano around the vent. (p. 415)

cross-breeding (krôs′brēd′ing) Producing offspring by mating parent plants or animals with different forms of a trait. (p. 492)

cross-pollination (krôs′po′lə nā′shən) When pollen from one flower is transported to a different flower. (p. 487)

crust (krust) Earth's solid, rocky surface containing the continents and ocean floor. (p. 388)

cytoplasm (sī′tə plaz′əm) A gel-like substance inside the cell membrane, where most cell activities occur. Cytoplasm surrounds the nucleus and contains a large amount of water. (p. 115)

D

dendrite (den′drīt) A nerve fiber that carries messages toward the cell body. (p. 580)

density (den′si tē) The amount of mass in a certain volume of material; found by dividing the mass of an object by its volume. (p. 5)

deposition (dep′ə zish′ən) The dropping off of sediment. (p. 440)

diffusion (di fū′zhən) The movement of molecules from areas of higher to lower concentration. (p. 128)

dike (dīk) An underground structure that forms when magma hardens in vertical cracks. (p. 419)

distance (dis′təns) The length between any two points on the path of an object. (p. 201)

divergent boundary (di vûr′jənt boun′də rē) Places where tectonic plates are moving apart. (p. 394)

DNA (dē en ā) A long, complex molecule that contains the codes that control your cells' activities, your chemical makeup, and heredity. (p. 517)

PRONUNCIATION KEY

a **a**t; ā **a**pe; ä f**a**r; âr c**a**re; e **e**nd; ē m**e**; i **i**t; ī **i**ce; îr p**ie**rce; o h**o**t; ō **o**ld; ô f**o**rk; oi **oi**l; ou **ou**t; u **u**p; ū **u**se; ü r**u**le; u̇ p**u**ll; ûr t**ur**n; hw **wh**ite; ng so**ng**; th **th**in; <u>th</u> **th**is; zh mea**s**ure; ə **a**bout, tak**e**n, p**e**ncil, lem**o**n, circ**u**s

dome mountain • fetus

dome mountain (dōm moun′tən) A broad, circular mountain formed from uplifted rock layers. (p. 419)

dominant factor (dom′ə nənt fak′tər) The trait expressed in offspring when the factors in a pair are different. (p. 491)

dominant trait (dom′ə nənt trāt) A form of a trait that appears in the hybrid generation. (p. 489)

dormant volcano (dôr′mənt vol kā′nō) A volcano that has not been active for a long time but has erupted before. (p. 418)

drag force (drag fôrs) A force that opposes motion of an object through a liquid or gas. (p. 213)

E

ecosystem (ek′ō sis′təm) The living and nonliving things in an area interacting with each other. (p. 108)

efficiency (i fish′ən sē) A ratio of the work done by a machine compared with the work put into the machine. (p. 282)

effort force (ef′ərt fôrs) The force applied to a machine. (p. 258)

egg (eg) A female sex cell. (p. 144)

electromagnetic spectrum (i lek′trō mag net′ik spek′trəm) Waves of light in order by wavelength. (p. 295)

electromagnetic wave (i lek′trō mag net′ik wāv) A type of wave that can travel through empty space. (p. 56)

electron (i lek′tron) A negatively charged particle that moves around an atom's nucleus. (p. 22)

element (el′ə mənt) A substance that cannot be broken down any further into anything simpler. (p. 20)

elliptical galaxy (i lip′ti kəl gal′ək sē) A galaxy shaped like a football or basketball with no spiral arms and very little or no galactic dust. (p. 372)

embryo (em′brē ō′) An organism in the early stages of development. (p. 607)

endocrine gland (en′də krin gland) A gland that produces hormones. (p. 594)

endothermic (en′dō thûr′mik) A reaction that absorbs heat. (p. 44)

epicenter (ep′i sen′tər) The point on Earth's surface directly above the focus of an earthquake. (p. 404)

equilibrium (ē′kwə lib′rē əm) Balance, such as an equal concentration of water molecules on both sides of a cell membrane. (p. 130)

era (îr′ə) One of the long stretches of time that Earth's history is divided into. (p. 470)

erosion (i rō′zhən) The picking up and removal of rock particles. (p. 429)

evaporation (i vap′ə rā′shən) The vaporization of molecules from the surface of a liquid. (p. 71)

evolution (ev′ə lü′shən) The theory that species change over time, resulting in new species. (p. 545)

exothermic (ek′sō thûr′mik) A reaction that gives off heat. (p. 44)

expansion redshift (ek span′shən red′shift′) The spectrum shift of a galaxy toward longer (redder) wavelengths because of the expansion of space. (p. 374)

extinct (ek stingkt′) Died out (referring to an entire species). (p. 545)

F

family (fam′ə lē) One of the groupings of similar members within an order. (p. 157)

fault (fôlt) A huge crack in Earth's crust at or below the surface, the sides of which may show evidence of motions. (p. 403)

fault-block mountain (fôlt blok moun′tən) A mountain made by huge tilted blocks of rocks separated from surrounding rocks by faults. (p. 428)

fermentation (fûr′men tā′shən) A form of respiration without oxygen. (p. 133)

fertilization (fûr′tə lə zā′shən) The joining of the male sex cell and female sex cell into one cell. (pp. 145, 486)

fetus (fē′təs) The embryo after all the organ systems are present. (p. 608)

First Law of Motion, Newton's • gravitational potential energy

First Law of Motion, Newton's (fûrst lô uv mō′shən, nü′tənz) An object's velocity can only be changed by applying an unbalanced force to it. (p. 220)

First Quarter (fûrst kwôr′tər) A phase of the waxing Moon in which the right half is visible and growing larger. (p. 320)

fission (fish′ən) A kind of asexual reproduction in which one parent cell divides into two offspring cells, each with chromosomes identical to the parent. (p. 180)

focus (fō′kəs) The point where an earthquake starts as rocks begin to slide past each other. (p. 404)

fold mountain (fōld moun′tən) A mountain made up mostly of rock layers folded by being squeezed together. (p. 428)

Food Guide Pyramid (füd gīd pir′ə mid′) A chart that organizes food into five groups that supply the body with nutrients. (p. 618)

force (fôrs) A push or pull exerted by one object on another, causing a change in motion. (p. 210)

fossil (fos′əl) Any trace, imprint, or remains of a living thing preserved in Earth's crust. (pp. 468, 544)

freezing (frēz′ing) The change of a liquid into a solid. (p. 71)

frequency (frē′kwən sē) The number of waves that pass through a point in a second. (p. 295)

friction (frik′shən) A force that opposes motion of an object in contact with a surface. (p. 211)

fulcrum (fůl′krəm) The pivot point of a lever. (p. 259)

Full Moon (fůl mün) or **Second Quarter** (sek′ənd kwôr′tər) The phase of the Moon in which all of its sunlit half is visible from Earth. (p. 320)

G

galaxy (gal′ək sē) A large group of stars that are held together by gravity. The main three types of galaxies are: spiral, elliptical, and irregular. (p. 372)

Galilean satellite (gal′ə lē′ən sat′ə līt′) The four largest moons of Jupiter, first seen by Galileo in 1610. (p. 347)

gene (jēn) A portion of a chromosome that controls a particular inherited trait. (p. 516)

generation (jen′ə rā′shən) Parents and offspring; parents are one *generation*, their offspring another. (p. 484)

gene-splicing (jēn splī′sing) Attaching the genes from one organism to the genes in another organism. (p. 534)

genetic engineering (jə net′ik en′jə nîr′ing) A way of changing the DNA sequence in a gene so that the gene will produce a particular trait. (p. 533)

geneticist (jə net′ə sist) A scientist who studies how heredity works. (p. 491)

genetics (jə net′iks) The study of how heredity works. (p. 485)

genus (jēn′əs) A grouping of the most similar family members. (p. 157)

geologic column (jē′ə loj′ik kol′əm) A listing of Earth's rock layers in order from oldest to youngest. (p. 466)

geothermal energy (jē′ō thûr′məl en′ər jē) Heat from below Earth's surface. (p. 421)

germination (jûr′mə nā′shən) The sprouting of new plant structures from a seed. (p. 182)

glacier (glā′shər) A huge sheet of ice and snow that moves slowly over the land. (p. 444)

glassy (glas′ē) How smooth a mineral feels to the touch. (p. 453)

gravitational potential energy (grav′i tā′shən əl pə ten′shəl en′ər jē) The gain in potential energy when an object is lifted up against gravity. (p. 244)

PRONUNCIATION KEY

a **a**t; ā **a**pe; ä f**a**r; âr c**a**re; e **e**nd; ē m**e**; i **i**t; ī **i**ce; îr p**ie**rce; o h**o**t; ō **o**ld; ô f**o**rk; oi **oi**l; ou **ou**t; u **u**p; ū **u**se; ü r**u**le; ů p**u**ll; ûr t**ur**n; hw **wh**ite; ng so**ng**; th **th**in; <u>th</u> **th**is; zh mea**s**ure; ə **a**bout, tak**e**n, penc**i**l, lem**o**n, circ**u**s

gravity (grav′i tē) A force of attraction that exists between any objects with mass. (p. 214)

groundwater (ground′wô′tər) Water that soaks into soil and rock by collecting in spaces between rock particles. (p. 434)

H

half-life (haf′līf′) The time it takes for half the mass of an original element to change into a new product. (p. 470)

hardness (härd′ness) How a mineral resists scratching. (p. 452)

heat (hēt) Energy that flows between objects that have different temperatures. (p. 55)

hemodialysis (hē′mō dī al′ə sis) The artificial filtering of blood by use of a kidney machine. (p. 134)

heredity (hə red′i tē) The passing of inherited traits from parents to offspring. (p. 484)

Hertzsprung-Russell (H-R) diagram (hert′sprŭng rus′əl dī′ə gram′) A table comparing the temperatures of stars to their absolute magnitudes. (p. 361)

highland (hī′lənd) Light-colored, heavily cratered regions on the Moon at higher elevations than maria. (p. 326)

hominid (hom′ə nid) A member of the family *Hominidae* of the order primates (p. 554)

hormone (hôr′mōn) A chemical that controls body functions by influencing how cells work. (p. 594)

hot spot (hot spot) A very hot part of the mantle, where magma can melt through a plate moving above it. (p. 414)

hot spring (hot spring) An opening in the ground where hot water and gases escape from magma heated deep underground. (p. 420)

humus (hū′məs) Material in soil formed by the breakdown of plant and animal material. (p. 433)

hybrid (hī′brid) An organism produced by the crossing of parents that have different forms of the same trait. (p. 488)

hydroelectricity (hī′drō i lek tris′i tē) The use of flowing water to generate electricity. (p. 89)

I

igneous rock (ig′nē əs rok) A rock that forms when hot, liquid lava cools and hardens into a solid. (p. 454)

inclined plane (in klīnd′ plān) A straight, slanted surface that is not moved when it is used. (p. 274)

incomplete dominance (in′kəm plēt′ dom′ə nəns) A genetic pattern in which neither of the two forms of a trait completely masks the other. (p. 506)

index fossil (in′deks fos′əl) The remains of a living thing that was widespread but lived for only a short part of Earth's history. (p. 469)

inertia (i nûr′shə) The tendency of an object to oppose a change in motion. (p. 218)

inherited trait (in her′i təd trāt) A characteristic that is passed from parent to offspring. (p. 484)

inner planet (in′ər plan′it) One of the four planets closer to the Sun—Mercury, Venus, Earth, or Mars. (p. 339)

insulation (in′sə lā′shən) Preventing heat from flowing in or out of a material. (p. 60)

International Date Line (in′tər nash′ə nəl dāt līn) The 180° line of longitude. Going west across this line adds one day to the date; going east subtracts a day. (p. 311)

ion (ī′ən) An electrically charged particle with unequal numbers of protons and electrons. (p. 37)

irregular galaxy (i reg′yə lər gal′ək sē) A galaxy that has no recognizable shape, possibly as the result of a galactic collision. (p. 372)

island arc (ī′lənd ark) A string of volcanic islands made when melted rock rises up from beneath the sea floor. (p. 396)

isolation (ī′sə lā′shən) The separation of one group from others of the same species. (p. 569)

K

Kepler's laws (kep′lərz lôz) Laws that summarize the movement of the planets. (p. 334)

kinetic energy (ki net′ik en′ər jē) The energy of a moving object. *See* **potential energy**. (pp. 53, 245)

kingdom • metamorphic rock

kingdom (king′dəm) One of the largest groups used to classify living things. (p. 156)

Kuiper Belt (kī′pər belt) A region of the solar system that stretches 45 billion kilometers beyond Pluto's orbit and contains tens of thousands of comets. (p. 350)

L

lava (lä′və) Magma that reaches Earth's surface and flows out of a vent. (p. 415)

lever (lev′ər) A simple machine made of a rigid bar on a pivot point. (p. 259)

life cycle (līf sī′kəl) The life stages of a living organism—infancy, childhood, adolescence, and maturity. (p. 617)

light-year (līt′yîr′) The distance light travels in a year. (p. 358)

lipid (lip′id) Fat; one of the carbon compounds that release even more energy than carbohydrates. (p. 122)

lunar eclipse (lü′nər i klips′) A blocking of a view of the Full Moon when the Moon passes into Earth's shadow. (p. 322)

luster (lus′tər) How a mineral reflects light. (p. 452)

M

magma (mag′mə) Hot, molten rock below Earth's surface. (p. 390)

magnitude (mag′ni tüd′) **1.** The brightness of a star. (p. 359) **2.** The amount of energy released by an earthquake. (p. 407)

main-sequence star (mān sē′kwəns stär) A star that fuses hydrogen into helium. (p. 362)

mantle (man′təl) The layer beneath Earth's crust. (p. 393)

mare (mär′ā), *pl.* **maria** (mär′ē ə) A large, flat, dark area on the Moon formed by huge lava flows billions of years ago. (p. 326)

mass (mas) A measure of how hard it is to push or pull an object. (p. 4)

mass wasting (mas wās′ting) The downhill movement of Earth material caused by gravity. (p. 440)

matter (mat′ər) Any solid, liquid, or gas. (p. 4)

mature (mə chúr′) The final or fully developed stage in a process. *Mature* sex cells are those that are capable of reproduction. (p. 144)

mechanical advantage (mə kan′i kəl ad van′tij) The number of times a machine multiplies the force applied. (p. 262)

mechanical weathering (mə kan′i kəl weth′ər ing) The breaking down of rock by physical changes. (p. 430)

meiosis (mī ō′sis) The division of the nucleus resulting in sex cells with half as many chromosomes as in body cells. (pp. 144, 514)

melting (melt′ing) The change of a solid into a liquid. (p. 70)

melting point (melt′ing point) The temperature at which a substance changes from a solid to a liquid. (p. 7)

menopause (men′ə pôz′) The time in a woman's life when menstruation ends. (p. 617)

menstruation (men′strü ā′shən) The time when the uterus lining leaves the body. (p. 607)

metabolism (mə tab′ə liz′əm) The sum of all the chemical reactions that occur in your body. (p. 596)

metal (met′əl) Any of a group of elements that conducts heat and electricity, and is shiny and bendable. (p. 27)

metamorphic (met′ə môr′fik) Changed, as when one kind of rock is turned into rock with different properties. (p. 458)

metamorphic rock (met′ə môr′fik rok) A rock that forms from another kind of rock that is changed by heat, pressure, or a chemical reaction. (p. 458)

PRONUNCIATION KEY

a **a**t; ā **a**pe; ä f**a**r; âr c**a**re; e **e**nd; ē m**e**; i **i**t; ī **i**ce; îr p**ie**rce; o h**o**t; ō **o**ld; ô f**o**rk; oi **oi**l; ou **ou**t; u **u**p; ū **u**se; ü r**u**le; ú p**u**ll; ûr t**ur**n; hw **wh**ite; ng so**ng**; th **th**in; <u>th</u> **th**is; zh mea**s**ure; ə **a**bout, tak**e**n, penc**i**l, lem**o**n, circ**u**s

R33

metamorphosis • nutrient

metamorphosis (met′ə môr′fə sis) The changes of body form that some animals go through in their life cycle. Complete metamorphosis includes four different stages—egg, larva, pupa, adult; incomplete metamorphosis includes three—egg, nymph, adult. (p. 184)

meteor (mē′tē ər) A meteoroid that enters Earth's atmosphere and burns with a streak of light. (p. 351)

meteorite (mē′tē ə rīt′) Any part of a meteoroid that reaches Earth's surface. (p. 351)

meteoroid (mē′tē ə roid′) Small, rocky objects that orbit the Sun in both the outer and inner regions of the solar system. (p. 351)

microbe (mī′krōb) A living thing so small that it can be seen only with a microscope. (p. 170)

Milky Way (mil′kē wā), The medium-sized spiral galaxy that is our home galaxy. (p. 373)

mineral (min′ər əl) A naturally occurring solid in Earth's crust with a definite structure and composition. (p. 452)

mitochondrion (mī′tə kon′drē ən), pl. **mitochondria** (-drē ə) A rod-shaped structure in the cytoplasm that supplies the cell with energy. (p. 115)

mitosis (mī tō′sis) The division of the nucleus while a cell is dividing into two identical cells. (pp. 141, 514)

mold (mōld) The rock surrounding an empty space that once contained a dead organism. The shape of the model is exactly the same as the organism. (p. 547)

molecule (mol′ə kūl′) A group of bonded atoms that acts like a single particle. (p. 38)

momentum (mō mən′təm) The mass of an object multiplied by its velocity. (p. 232)

moraine (mə rān′) A deposit of many sizes of sediment in front of or along the sides of a glacier. (p. 446)

motion (mō′shən) A change in an object's position compared to fixed objects around it. (p. 201)

motor neuron (mō′tər nûr′on) A nerve cell that carries commands from your brain and spinal cord to your muscles and glands. (p. 581)

mountain (moun′tən) A feature on the Moon like part of a mountain range on Earth, formed by impacts of debris from space. (p. 326)

mutation (mū tā′shən) A change in a gene. (p. 568)

N

natural selection (nach′ər əl si lek′shən) A theory that says organisms best adapted to their environment live longest and pass their traits to their offspring. (p. 566)

neap tide (nēp tīd) The slightest changes from high to low tide that occur when the Sun, the Moon, and Earth form a right angle or are perpendicular to each other. (p. 325)

nebula (neb′yə lə), pl. **nebulae** (-yə lē′) An enormous cloud of gas and dust in space that is the first stage of star formation. (p. 362)

net force (net fôrs) The combined effect of all the forces acting on an object. (p. 216)

neuron (nûr′on) An individual nerve cell. (p. 580)

neutron (nü′tron) A particle with no charge inside an atom's nucleus. (p. 22)

neutron star (nü′tron stär) The remnant of a supernova that has become an extremely dense star made up entirely of tightly packed neutrons. (p. 363)

New Moon (nü mün) A phase of the Moon in which none of its sunlit half is visible from Earth. (p. 320)

nuclear fission (nü′klē ər fish′ən) The splitting of a nucleus with a large mass into two nuclei with smaller masses. (p. 84)

nuclear fusion (nü′klē ər fü′zhən) The merging of nuclei with smaller masses into a nucleus with a larger mass. (p. 85)

nucleic acid (nü klē′ik as′id) One of the carbon compounds that contain codes that allow cells to build proteins. (p. 122)

nucleus (nü′klē əs), pl. **nuclei** (-klē ī′) 1. An atom's dense center, where most of its mass is. (p. 22) 2. The densest part of a cell, which controls a cell's activities. (p. 114)

nutrient (nü′trē ənt) Any of the substances in food that the body needs to grow, develop, work at its best, and stay healthy. (p. 618)

O

one-celled organism (wun seld ôr′gə niz′əm) A living thing that is made up of only one cell. (p. 118)

order (ôr′dər) One of the groupings of similar members within a class. (p. 157)

organ (ôr′gən) A group of different tissues working together to do certain jobs. (p. 105)

organ system (ôr′gən sis′təm) Different organs working together to do certain jobs. (p. 105)

organism (ôr′gə niz′əm) Any living thing that can carry out its life activities on its own. (p. 105)

original horizontality (ə rij′ə nəl hôr′ə zän′tə′lə tē) The idea that many kinds of rocks form flat, horizontal layers. (p. 388)

osmosis (oz mō′sis) The diffusion of water through a cell membrane. (p. 130)

outer planet (out′ər plan′it) One of the five planets farther from the Sun—Jupiter, Saturn, Uranus, Neptune, or Pluto. (p. 346)

output force (out′put′ fôrs) The force the machine applies to an object in response to our effort force. (p. 258)

ovary (ō′və rē) The female reproductive organ, which produces eggs. (p. 597)

oviduct (ō′vi dukt′) One of two narrow tubes through which egg cells pass from the ovaries to the uterus. (p. 606)

P

parallax (par′ə laks′) The apparent shift in an object's location when viewed from two positions. (p. 358)

passive transport (pas′iv trans′pôrt′) The movement of molecules through a cell membrane without the use of energy. (p. 129)

pedigree (ped′i grē) A chart used to trace the history of traits in a family. (p. 504)

penis (pē′nis) The male organ through which sperm is transferred out of the body. (p. 606)

perennial (pə ren′ē əl) A tree or shrub that lives from one year to the next and continues to grow and reproduce regularly. (p. 183)

phase of the Moon (fāz uv thə mün) One of the shapes of the lighted part of the Moon seen from Earth at any time. (p. 320)

photosphere (fō′tə sfîr′) The visible yellow surface of the Sun beneath the chromosphere. (p. 366)

photosynthesis (fō′tə sin′thə sis) A process in producers that makes food by using sunlight. (p. 132)

phylum (fī′ləm), *pl.* **phyla** (fī′lə) A main group within a kingdom, whose members share a main characteristic. (p. 156)

physical change (fiz′i kəl chānj) A change in size, shape, or state, without forming a new substance. See **chemical change**. (p. 8)

physical property (fiz′i kəl prop′ər tē) A property that can be observed without changing the identity of a substance. (p. 6)

placenta (plə sen′tə) A tissue through which the baby receives food and oxygen from its mother. (p. 608)

planet (plan′it) A large body orbiting the Sun or other star. (p. 334)

plateau (pla tō′) A large area of flat land of high elevation that was created by crustal movement. (p. 429)

plate tectonics (plāt tek ton′iks) The idea that Earth's surface is broken into plates that slide slowly across the mantle. (p. 393)

pollination (pol′ə nā′shən) The transfer of pollen from the male part to the female part of the plant. (p. 486)

population (pop′yə lā′shən) All the organisms of the same kind living in the same place. (p. 106)

position (pə zish′ən) The location of an object compared with things around it. (p. 200)

potential energy (pə ten′shəl en′ər jē) The energy stored in an object or material. See **kinetic energy**. (pp. 53, 244)

PRONUNCIATION KEY

a at; ā ape; ä far; âr care; e end; ē me; i it; ī ice; îr pierce; o hot; ō old; ô fork; oi oil; ou out; u up; ū use; ü rule; u̇ pull; ûr turn; hw white; ng song; th thin; th this; zh measure; ə about, taken, pencil, lemon, circus

pressure • secondary wave

pressure (presh'ər) 1. The force on each unit of area of a surface. (p. 68) 2. The weight that presses down on a layer of sediment. (p. 456)

primary wave (prī'mer ē wāv) One of the back-and-forth vibrations of rocks in an earthquake, called *P waves* for short. They travel faster than secondary waves. (p. 405)

probability (prob'ə bil'i tē) How likely it is for something to happen. (p. 498)

producer (prə dü'sər) Any green plant or one-celled organism that can make its own food. (p. 132)

protein (prō'tēn) One of the carbon compounds that are needed for cell growth and repair. (p. 122)

proton (prō'ton) A positively charged particle inside an atom's nucleus. (p. 22)

protostar (prō'tə stär') A young star that glows as gravity makes it collapse. (p. 362)

puberty (pū'bər tē) The time in life when a person begins to look like an adult and becomes physically able to reproduce. (p. 608)

pulley (pùl'ē) A grooved wheel that turns by the action of a rope in the groove. (p. 264)

pulsar (pul'sär) A neutron star that blinks on and off like the light from a lighthouse. (p. 363)

Punnett square (pun'ət skwâr) A table for predicting the outcome of crossing different forms of a trait. (p. 500)

purebred (pyùr'bred') When a self-pollinated organism shows the same form of a trait in all of its offspring for several generations of self-pollination. (p. 488)

Q–R

quasar (kwā'zär) An extremely bright, extremely distant high-energy source, shining with the light of a trillion suns. (p. 378)

radiation (rā dē ā'shən) The transfer of energy by electromagnetic waves. (p. 56)

ratio (rā'shē ō') A mathematical term that describes the relationship between two quantities. (p. 489)

recessive factor (ri ses'iv fak'tər) The trait masked in offspring when the factors in a pair are different. (p. 491)

recessive trait (ri ses'iv trāt) A form of a trait that is hidden, or masked, in the hybrid generation. (p. 489)

reflection (ri flek'shən) The bouncing of waves off a surface. (p. 294)

refraction (ri frak'shən) The bending of waves as they go from one substance to another. (p. 294)

relative age (rel'ə tiv āj) The age of a rock as compared with another rock. (p. 466)

relative dating (rel'ə tiv dāt'ing) Telling how old a fossil is based on the location of the sediment layer in which it is found. (p. 548)

reproduction (rē'prə duk'shən) The process in which organisms produce more of their own kind. (p. 143)

resistance force (ri zis'təns fôrs) The force that a machine acts against. (p. 258)

respiration (res'pə rā'shən) The release of energy from sugar molecules. (p. 133)

revolution (rev'ə lü'shən) One complete trip around the Sun. Earth completes one revolution in 365 days. (p. 312)

rift volcano (rift vol kā'nō) Volcanoes that form along the gaps at the edges of tectonic plates that are moving apart. (p. 414)

rock cycle (rok sī'kəl) Rocks continually changing from one kind into another in a never-ending process. (p. 460)

rotation (rō tā'shən) A complete spin on an axis. Earth makes a rotation every 24 hours. (p. 308)

S

scientific name (sī'ən tif'ik nām) A two-word term for a living thing, based on its classification. (p. 158)

screw (skrü) An inclined plane wrapped around a central bar. (p. 278)

sea-floor spreading (sē flôr spred'ing) The idea that new crust is forming at ridges in the sea floor, spreading apart the crust on either side of the ridges. (p. 390)

secondary wave (sek'ən der'ē wāv) One of the up-and-down vibrations of rocks in an earthquake, called *S waves* for short. They travel more slowly than primary waves. (p. 405)

Second Law of Motion, Newton's • star

Second Law of Motion, Newton's (sek′ənd lô uv mō′shən, nü′tənz) Force = mass × acceleration. (p. 227)

sedimentary rock (sed′ə men′tə rē rok) A rock that forms from pieces of other rocks that are squeezed or cemented together. (p. 456)

seedling (sēd′ling) A young plant that pushes up through the ground. (p. 182)

seismic-safe (sīz′mik sāf) The design of buildings and highways to keep them from collapsing in an earthquake. (p. 408)

seismic wave (sīz′mik wāv) A vibration that spreads out away from a focus when an earthquake happens. (p. 404)

seismograph (sīz′mə graf′) A sensitive device that detects the shaking of Earth's crust during an earthquake. (p. 406)

selective breeding (si lek′tiv brēd′ing) The process of crossing plants or animals to produce offspring with certain desirable traits. (p. 532)

self-pollination (self′pol′ə nā′shən) When the pollen produced by a flower pollinates the female parts of the same flower. (p. 486)

sensory neuron (sen′sə rē nûr′on) A nerve cell that picks up stimuli and sends impulses produced by the stimuli to the brain and spinal cord. (p. 581)

sex-linked gene (seks′lingkt′ jēn) A gene carried on an X chromosome but not a Y chromosome. (p. 528)

sexual reproduction (sek′shü əl rē′prə duk′shən) The production of a new organism from two parents. (p. 144)

shield volcano (shēld vol kā′nō) A wide, gently sloped cone that forms from flows of lava. (p. 416)

sill (sil) An underground structure that forms when magma hardens between horizontal layers of rock. (p. 419)

simple machine (sim′pəl mə shēn′) A machine with few moving parts, making it easier to do work. (p. 258)

soil (soil) A mixture of weathered rock, decayed plant and animal matter, living things, air, and water. (p. 432)

soil horizon (soil hə rī′zən) Any of the layers of soil from the surface to the bedrock below. (p. 433)

solar cell (sō′lər sel) A device that generates an electric current from sunlight. (p. 81)

solar eclipse (sō′lər i klips′) A blocking out of a view of the Sun when Earth passes through the Moon's shadow. (p. 323)

solar system (sō′lər sis′təm) A star, such as the Sun, and all the objects orbiting it. (p. 334)

solution (sə lü′shən) A mixture of one substance dissolved in another so that the properties are the same throughout. (p. 11)

space probe (spās prōb) A vehicle sent beyond Earth to study planets and other objects within our solar system. (p. 296)

species (spē′shēz) A group of similar organisms in a genus that can reproduce more of their own kind. (p. 157)

spectrum (spek′trəm) A band of colors made when white light is broken up. (p. 374)

speed (spēd) How fast an object's position changes with time at any given moment. (p. 202)

sperm (spûrm) A male sex cell. (p. 144)

spiral galaxy (spī′rəl gal′ək sē) A galaxy that is like a whirlpool in shape. (p. 372)

spore (spôr) A cell that can develop into an adult organism without fertilization. (p. 181)

spring tide (spring tīd) The greatest changes from high to low tide that occur when the Sun, the Moon, and Earth are lined up. (p. 324)

standard time zone (stan′dərd tīm zōn) A belt 15° wide in longitude in which all places have the same time. (p. 310)

star (stär) A large, hot ball of gases, which is held together by gravity and gives off its own light. (p. 358)

PRONUNCIATION KEY

a **a**t; ā **a**pe; ä f**a**r; âr c**a**re; e **e**nd; ē m**e**; i **i**t; ī **i**ce; îr p**ie**rce; o h**o**t; ō **o**ld; ô f**o**rk; oi **oi**l; ou **ou**t; u **u**p; ū **u**se; ü r**u**le; u̇ p**u**ll; ûr t**u**rn; hw **wh**ite; ng so**ng**; th **th**in; th **th**is; zh mea**s**ure; ə **a**bout, tak**e**n, penc**i**l, lem**o**n, circ**u**s

stimulus • vent

stimulus (stim′yə ləs), *pl.* **stimuli** (-yə lī′) Anything that causes a response. (p. 586)

structure (struk′chər) The way the pieces of materials in a mineral fit together. (p. 453)

subduction (səb duk′shən) The sliding of a denser ocean plate under another plate when they collide. (p. 396)

sunspot (sun′spot′) One of a group of darker patches on the Sun caused by the Sun's rotation and its powerful magnetic field. (p. 367)

supernova (sü′pər nō′və) A star that explodes, often a supergiant that has become unstable. (p. 363)

superposition (sü′pər pə zish′ən) The idea that in a series of rock layers, the bottom layer is the oldest and the top layer is the youngest. (p. 466)

surface wave (sûr′fis wāv) One of the wavelike vibrations of an earthquake that cause much of the damage to structures on Earth's surface. (p. 405)

synapse (sin′aps) The gap between neurons. (p. 580)

T

target organ (tär′git ôr′gən) The place in the body where a hormone acts. (p. 594)

telescope (tel′ə skōp′) A device that collects light and makes distant objects appear closer and larger. (p. 293)

temperature (tem′pər ə chər) The average kinetic energy of the molecules in a material. (p. 54)

testis (tes′tis), *pl.* **testes** (tes′tēz) The male reproductive organ, which produces sperm. (p. 597)

texture (teks′chər) How the surface of a mineral feels to the touch. (p. 453)

thermal expansion (thûr′məl ek span′shən) The expansion of matter when its temperature is raised. (p. 66)

thermal pollution (thûr′məl pə lü′shən) The excess heating of the environment. (p. 91)

Third Law of Motion, Newton's (thûrd lô uv mō′shən, nü′tənz) For every action force, there is a reaction force that is equal in strength and opposite in direction. (p. 230)

Third Quarter (thûrd kwôr′tər) or **Last Quarter** (last kwôr′tər) The phase of the waning Moon in which the left half is visible but growing smaller. (p. 321)

tide (tīd) The regular rise and fall of the water level along a shoreline. This twice-daily rise and fall of ocean-water levels is caused by the gravity of the Moon and the Sun. (p. 324)

till (til) A jumble of many sizes of sediment deposited by a glacier. (p. 446)

tissue (tish′ü) A group of similar cells working together at the same job. (p. 104)

transform fault (trans′fôrm′ fôlt) Boundaries where tectonic plates slide past each other. (p. 395)

trench (trench) A deep valley in the sea floor. (p. 390)

U

umbilical cord (um bil′i kəl kôrd) A ropelike structure that connects the placenta and the fetus during pregnancy. (p. 608)

unbalanced forces (un bal′ənst fôrs′əz) Forces that do not cancel each other out when acting together on a single object. (p. 217)

universe (ū′nə vûrs′) Everything that exists. (p. 292)

uterus (ū′tər əs) The organ where a baby develops. (p. 607)

V

vacuole (vak′ū ōl) A sac-like storage space in a cell's cytoplasm. Vacuoles can store such things as food or waste awaiting elimination. (p. 115)

valley (val′ē) Cigar-shaped depressions on the Moon's surface. (p. 326)

vaporization (vā′pə rī zā′shən) The change of a liquid to a gas as molecules break free from each other. (p. 70)

variation (vâr′ē ā′shən) The difference in appearance of an inherited trait in the members of a species. (p. 562)

velocity (və los′i tē) The speed and direction of a moving object. (p. 204)

vent (vent) The central opening in a volcanic area through which magma may escape. (p. 415)

virus (vī′rəs) A microscopic particle made of hereditary material and a protein coat; it can reproduce inside a living cell. (p. 175)

volume (vol′ūm) The amount of space an object takes up. (p. 4)

W

Waning Crescent (wān′ing kres′ənt) A phase of the Moon between the Third Quarter and the New Moon in which the visible part is growing smaller. (p. 321)

Waning Gibbous (wān′ing gib′əs) A phase of the Moon between the Full Moon and the Third Quarter in which the visible part is growing smaller. (p. 321)

wavelength (wāv′lengkth′) The distance from one peak to the next on a wave. (p. 295)

Waxing Crescent (waks′ing kres′ənt) A phase between the New Moon and the First Quarter in which the visible part is growing larger. (p. 320)

Waxing Gibbous (waks′ing gib′əs) A phase of the Moon between the First Quarter and the Full Moon in which the visible part is growing larger. (p. 320)

weathering (weth′ər ing) The breaking down of rocks into smaller pieces by natural processes. (p. 429)

wedge (wej) One or a combination of two inclined planes that is moved when used. (p. 280)

wheel and axle (hwēl and ak′səl) A simple machine made of a handle or axis attached to the center of a wheel. (p. 268)

work (wûrk) Force applied to an object times the distance the object moves in the direction of the force. (p. 248)

X-Z

X *and* Y chromosomes (eks and wī krō′mə sōmz) Chromosomes that determine a person's sex. (p. 528)

zygote (zī′gōt) A fertilized egg. (p. 607)

PRONUNCIATION KEY

a **a**t; ā **a**pe; ä f**a**r; âr c**a**re; e **e**nd; ē m**e**; i **i**t; ī **i**ce; îr p**ie**rce; o h**o**t; ō **o**ld; ô f**o**rk; oi **oi**l; ou **ou**t; u **u**p; ū **u**se; ü r**u**le; u̇ p**u**ll; ûr t**u**rn; hw **w**hite; ng so**ng**; th **th**in; th **th**is; zh mea**s**ure; ə **a**bout, tak**e**n, penc**i**l, lem**o**n, circ**u**s

INDEX

A

Absolute age, 470–471*, 548
  half-life, 470–471*
Acceleration, 202–205, 225*–226
Active transport, 131
Activity pyramid, 619
Adaptation, 562, 563*, 564–565
Adrenal glands, 597
AIDS, 611
Alloys, 11
Animals
  classification, 166–167
  evolution, 543–553*
  life cycles, 183
  metamorphosis, 184–185
  reproduction, 183
  species survival, 588
Aquifers, 434
Archaebacteria, 173
Asexual reproduction, 143
Asteroids, 340
Astronomy
  astronomical instruments, 291*, 293
  constellations, 359
  galaxies, 370–380
  light year, 358
  Milky Way, 370, 373
  natural satellites, 352–353
  origin of universe theories, 374, 375*, 378
  solar system, 301*–309, 312–315, 319–353, 366–373
  space flight, 300–301*
  space probes, 298, 302–303
  space shuttle, 299
  stars, 356–367
  stellar motions, 357*, 358*
  telescopes, 293, 296–297
  universe, 292
  U.S. space program, 302–303
  weightlessness, 235*–237
Atomic number, 23

B

Atoms
  differences among, 20
  history, 21, 23
  representations of, 20, 23
  structure of, 20, 22
  subatomic particles, 22

Background radiation, 376
Bacteria, 118, 173, 186*–187
Balanced diet, 123
Be a Scientist, S4–S20
Behavior, 586
Big bang, 375*
Biodiversity, 161
Biological feedback, 594–595*
Black holes, 363, 365
Body systems
  endocrine, 593*–599
  nervous, 579*–587
  reproductive, 605*–611
Boiling, 71
Boyle's Law, 69
Brain, 583, 589
Buoyancy, 3*, 14–15
Buttes, 429

C

Calderas, 415
Carbohydrates, 122
Careers
  astronomer, 292
  geologist, 476
  paleontologist, 572
Cell membrane, 114, 127*
Cell nucleus, 114

Cells
  animal, 117
  of animals, 103
  cancer, 147
  chemical composition of, 120
  chromosomes, 114, 142, 144–146
  discovery of, 102
  division, 140–142, 147
  energy for, 122–123, 132–133
  growth and development, 140–141
  Hooke, Robert, 102
  organization, 104, 105*, 113*
  organs, 105
  parts, 114–115, 127*
  plant, 116
  of plants, 102–103
  processing wastes, 134–135
  reproduction, 143–145
  sex, 144
  size, 139*–140
  structure and function, 113*–117, 119*
  systems, 105
  transport in, 127*–131
Cell wall, 116
Chain reaction, 84, 86*
Change of state, 7, 70–71
  boiling point, 7
  melting point, 7
Charles' Law, 69
Chemical bonds, 35–38
  covalent, 36
  ionic, 37
Chemical change, 12–13*, 33*
Chemical compounds, 34
  acids and bases, 42–43
  carbon compounds, 122
  organic, 132
Chemical equations, 40
Chemical formulas, 35, 39*
Chemical properties, 41

*Indicates an activity related to this topic.

Chemical reactions – Engines

Chemical reactions, 12–13*, 33*, 40
  energy relationships, 44
  types of, 13*, 40
  uses of, 40
Chlorophyll, 132
Chloroplasts, 132
Chromosomes, 114, 142, 144–146
Classes, 157
Colloids, 10
Comets, 350
Communities, 106–107
Competition, 567
Condensation, 71
Conduction, 57, 72–73*
Continental drift, 389
Convection, 57, 72–73*
Craters, 415
Cystals, 454
Cytoplasm, 115

D

Density, 3*, 5
  buoyancy, 3*, 14
  water displacement, 4
Deposition, 440*–447
Diabetes, 598
Diffusion, 128, 134–135
Dinosaurs
  extinction theories, 545, 558–559
  Mesozoic era, 552
Distance, 197, 201*
DNA, 160–161, 511*–517, 518*, 519

E

Ear, 585
Earth
  absolute age, 470–471*, 548
  atmosphere, 339, 346*
  continental drift, 389
  crust, 388
  earthquakes, 400–409
  eclipses, 322–323
  erosion, 429, 439*–447
  formation of, 377
  fossil record, 468, 543*–547, 552
  geologic columns, 466
  geologic eras, 472–474
  ice ages, 447, 473–474
  landforms, 427*–429, 439
  latitude effects, 314
  layers of, 388, 393
  magnetic field, 391
  mantle, 393
  minerals, 452
  original horizontality, 388
  Pangaea, 389, 397
  as a planet, 308
  plate tectonics, 387*–397
  relative age, 466–467, 548
  revolution, 312
  rock cycle, 460
  rotation, 308
  seasons, 312–313
  soil, 432–435
  superposition, 466
  time zones, 310*–311
  volcanoes, 390, 394–396, 412, 413*–421
  water cycle, 314
  weathering, 429–435, 439*–447
Earthquakes
  aftershocks, 404
  causes, 403
  epicenter, 404
  faults, 403
  focus, 404
  location of, 401*–402, 406
  magnitude, 407
  measuring instruments, 406*, 409
  Mercalli scale, 407
  prediction, 409
  preparedness, 408
  Richter scale, 407
  Ring of Fire, 402, 414
  seismic waves, 404–406
  tsunamis, 404
Eclipses
  lunar, 322
  solar, 323
Ecosystems
  biodiversity, 161
  communities, 106–107
  food chain, 108
  habitats, 109
  interactions, 106–109
  populations, 106
  producers, 132
Electric battery, 247
Electromagnetic spectrum, 295
Electrons, 22
Element, 20, 24, 25*–29
Emulsions, 10
Endocrine system
  biological feedback, 594–595*
  chemical reactions, 593*, 594
  diabetes, 598
  hormones, 594, 599–601
  insulin, 598
  metabolism, 596
  parts of, 596–598
Energy
  biomass, 83
  chemical, 246
  conservation, 252–253
  electric, 79*–81, 86, 89, 90, 246–247
  fossil fuels, 82, 90
  geothermal, 420–421
  hydroelectric, 89
  kinetic, 53, 245
  law of conservation of, 252–253
  light, 246
  mechanical, 246
  nuclear fission, 84, 86*, 87, 246
  nuclear fusion, 85, 87, 246
  potential, 53, 243*–244
  solar, 79*–81
  sound, 246
  thermal, 91, 246
  transformation, 246–247, 249*
  units, 53
  using, 80–81, 86
  wind, 88
Engines, gasoline, 74

INDEX

R41

Erosion – Heat

Erosion
  deposition, 440*–447
  glaciers, 444–447
  mass movement, 429, 439*–440*
  streams, 442–443
  wind, 441
Eubacteria, 173
Evaporation, 71
Evolution
  adaptation, 562–565
  competition, 567
  Darwin, 564–565
  evidence from embryonic development, 551
  evidence from fossils, 543*–545, 552
  evidence from molecular biology, 551, 568
  evidence from structures, 159, 550
  gradualism, 570
  of horses, 543*, 553
  human role in extinction, 571
  Lamarck, 564
  mass extinctions, 545, 558–559, 570–571
  mutations, 568
  natural selection, 566–567
  pace of evolution, 570
  speciation, 561*, 569
  variation, 562
Evolution of solar system, 377
Extinction of dinosaurs, 545, 558–559
Eye, 584

F

Families, 157
Fats, 122
Fermentation, 133
Fertilization, 145
Food chain, 108
Food Guide Pyramid, 618

Forces
  energy, 243*–247, 252–253
  friction, 209*, 211–213, 282–283
  gravity and weight, 214–215, 234–237
  inertia, 218–219*, 220*–221
  laws of motion, 218, 225*–231, 237
  and machines, 256–283
  momentum, 232–233
  net force, 216
  pushes and pulls, 210, 211
  unbalanced and balanced, 216–217, 220
  weightlessness, 235*–237
  work, 248–251, 275
Fossil fuels, 45, 82, 475
Fossils
  dinosaurs, 552
  formation of, 544
  fossil dating, 466–467, 548
  index, 469
  kinds of, 546–547
Freezing, 71
Frequency, 295
Fungi
  characteristics, 171
  classification, 170
  interaction with other organisms, 171
  life cycle, 171
  reproduction, 179*, 181
  usefulness to humans, 171

G

Galaxies
  classification of, 372
  expansion, 374, 378
  Milky Way, 370, 373
  motions, 380
  quasars, 378
  redshift, 374
Gas
  change of state, 7
  properties of, 9

Genera, 157
Genetics
  clones, 535
  gene splicing, 534–536
  genetic code, 511*, 516–519, 521
  genetic counseling, 537
  genetic disorders, 530–531
  genetic engineering, 533, 536
  selective breeding, 485–492, 532
Geologic eras, 472–474
Geologic time scale, 549
Geysers, 420
Glaciers
  composition, 445
  effects on land, 445
  formation of, 444
  glacial deposits, 446–447
  ice ages, 447, 473–474
Gradualism, 570
Gravity
  and weight, 214–215, 234–237
  weightlessness, 235*–237

H

Habitats, 109
Half-life, 470–471
Hearing, 585
Heat
  Boyle's Law, 69
  change of state, 70–71
  Charles' Law, 69
  conduction, 57, 72–73*
  convection, 57, 72–73*
  effects of, 56
  energy flow, 55–56
  expansion and contraction, 54, 65*–69
  heat transfer, 51*, 55–57, 59*, 72–73, 75
  insulation, 60–61
  kinetic theory, 51*–52, 67–71
  and pressure, 68
  radiation, 56, 72–73
  sources, 79*–90

R42

*Indicates an activity related to this topic.

specific heat, 58*–59
Sun as source of heat, 56
temperature, 52, 54
thermal energy, 51*–52
using heat, 61, 66, 67, 72–75, 80–81
Heat pumps, 75
Heredity
 blood type, 527
 Burbank, Luther, 492–493
 Carver, George Washington, 492
 cellular basis of, 511*–519
 changes in genetic material, 514–520, 534–537
 chromosomes, 512–519, 528–529*, 531
 DNA, 511*–517, 518*, 519
 dominant traits, 489–490, 506–507, 525*–527
 environmental factors, 520
 fertilization, 515
 human, 502–503*
 hybrids, 488
 inherited traits, 483*–486, 489*, 500–507
 meiosis, 514, 518
 Mendel's experiments, 485–491
 messenger molecules, 519
 patterns of, 483*, 506–507
 pedigree, 504–505
 predicting traits, 497*–501
 probability of inherited traits, 498–499
 Punnett squares, 497*, 500–501, 529*
 recessive traits, 489–490, 506–507, 525*–527
 sex–linked traits, 528–529*
History of science, 110–111, 124–125, 176–177, 206–207, 354–355, 398–399, 508–509
Hormones, 594, 599–601
Hot springs, 420
H-R diagram, 361
Human body
 body systems, 134, 579*–587, 593*–599, 605*–611
 cells, 103
 elements in, 121–122
 growth and development, 614–619

Human reproduction
 birth, 610
 development of embryo, 607
 female reproductive system, 606
 fertilization, 605*, 606
 male reproductive system, 606
 menstruation, 607
 pregnancy, 607
 puberty, 606
 STDs, 611
 twins, 609*
Humans
 life cycle, 615*–617
 reproduction, 605*–611
Humus, 435
Hypothalamus, 597

I

Ice ages, 447, 473–474
Igneous rocks, 454–455
Inertia, 218–221
Inner planets, 301, 333*–341

K

Kepler's laws, 341
Kinetic energy, 53, 245
Kinetic theory, 9
Kingdoms, 156, 174*

L

Landforms
 buttes, 429
 mass movement, 439
 mountains, 427*–428
 plateaus, 429

Lava, 415
Law of conservation of energy, 252–253
Laws of motion, 218, 225*–231, 237
Light
 electromagnetic spectrum, 295
 frequency, 295
 properties of, 294–295
 wavelength, 294–295
 waves, 294
Lipids, 122
Liquids
 change of state, 7
 properties of, 9
Living things
 activities of, 100
 biodiversity, 161
 cells, 101, 113*–122, 127–133
 characteristics of, 101, 153*–158, 561
 classification, 99*, 118, 153*–158, 160*, 165*, 174*
 DNA classification, 160–161
 heredity, 483–537
 homologous structures, 159
 interactions among, 106–109
 kingdoms, 156, 166–173, 174*, 175
 needs, 109
 nutrition, 123
 organisms, 105
 organs, 105
 reproduction, 179*–183
 systems, 105
 tissues, 104

M

Machines
 compound, 281
 efficiency, 282–283
 mechanical advantage, 262, 266–267, 277
 simple, 257*–261, 264–269, 278–280
 using machines, 267, 279

Magma – Planet

Magma, 390
Magnitude, 359
Main sequence stars, 362
Malnutrition, 620
Matter
  atoms, 18–23
  chemical bonds, 35–38
  chemical reactions, 12–13*, 40
  compounds, 34
  density, 3*, 5
  elements, 20, 24–29
  kinetic theory, 9
  mass, 4
  measuring instruments, 4
  mixtures, 10–11
  molecules, 38
  origin of, 376
  periodic table, 24–29
  properties of, 6, 9, 24
  states of, 7, 9
  volume, 4
  weight, 4
Mechanical advantage, 262, 266–267, 277
Meiosis, 144, 146*, 515
Melting, 70
Menstruation, 607
Mercalli scale, 407
Metabolism, 596
Metals, nonmetals, and metalloids, 27–29
Metamorphic rock, 458–459
Metamorphosis, 184–185
Meteors, 351
Microbes, 179*–180
Microscope, 110–111
Milky Way, 370, 373
Minerals
  crystal systems, 454
  Earth's crust, 452
Mitochondria, 115
Mitosis, 141–142, 146*, 514, 518
Mixtures, 10–11
  alloys, 11
  colloids, 10
  emulsions, 10
  solutions, 11
  suspensions, 10
Molecules, 38
Momentum, 232–233

Moon
  data from lunar landings, 327
  lunar eclipse, 322
  phases, 319*–321
  solar eclipse, 323
  surface features, 326
  tides, 324–325*
Motion
  acceleration, 202–203*, 204–205, 225*–226
  average speed, 199
  circular, 220
  direction, 200
  distance, 197, 201*
  gravitational acceleration, 205
  kinetic energy, 53, 245
  laws of motion, 218, 225*–231, 237
  paths, 196
  position, 196
  potential energy, 53
  speed, 195*, 198, 201*
  velocity, 200
Mountains, 427*–428
Mutation, 568

N

Natural selection, 566–567
Nebulae, 362
Nervous system
  brain, 583, 589
  central nervous system, 582
  learned behaviors, 586
  nerve cells, 579*–583
  neurons, 580–581
  reaction time, 587
  reflexes, 582
  senses, 584–585
  spinal cord, 582
  stimulus and response, 586, 588
  synapses, 580
Neutrons, 22
Neutron stars, 363
Nonrenewable resources, 82
Nucleic acids, 122

Nucleus
  electrons, 22
  neutrons, 22
  protons, 22
Nutrition
  activity pyramid, 619
  balanced diet, 123
  calories, 618
  carbohydrates, 122
  fats, 122
  Food Guide Pyramid, 618
  malnutrition, 620
  proteins, 122

O

Olfactory sense, 585
Orders, 157
Original horizontality, 388
Osmosis, 130, 131*, 134–135
Outer planets, 344–353

P

Pancreas, 598
Pangaea, 389, 397
Parallax, 358*
Parathyroid gland, 596–597
Passive transport, 129–130
Periodic table, 24–29
Phyla, 156
Physical change, 8
Physical properties, 6
Pituitary gland, 596
Planet
  identification of, 333*–334
  inner planets, 301, 333*–341
  Kepler's laws, 341
  natural satellites, 352–353
  outer planets, 344–353
  planetary atmospheres, 339, 346*
  planetary distances, 345*

R44

*Indicates an activity related to this topic.

Plants
    classification, 168
    fertilization, 182
    life cycles, 182
    photosynthesis, 132
    pollination, 486–487
    producers, 132
    reproduction, 182
Plateaus, 429
Plate tectonics
    continental drift, 389
    convection currents, 393, 396
    evidence, 389–397
    interactions, 393–396
    plate boundaries, 393–396, 414
    sea-floor spreading, 390–392*
    subduction, 396
Potential energy, 53, 243*–244
Pregnancy, 608
Producers, 132
Proteins, 122
Protists
    characteristics, 172
    classification, 172
    protozoans, 172
Protons, 22
Pulsars, 363

Q

Quasars, 378

R

Reaction time, 587
Red giants, 362
Redshift, 374
Reflection, 294
Reflexes, 582
Refraction, 294
Relative age, 466–467, 548
Renewable resources
    biomass, 83
    solar, 79*–81

Reproduction
    asexual, 143
    sexual, 144, 605*–611
Reproductive glands, 597
Reproductive system, 605*–611
Respiration, 133
Revolution, 312
Richter scale, 407
Ring of Fire, 402, 414
Rocks
    absolute age, 470–471*
    classifying, 453
    crystals, 454*
    cycle, 460
    histories, 461
    igneous, 454–455
    metamorphic, 458–459
    minerals, 452
    properties, 451*–453, 454*
    relative age, 466–467, 548
    sedimentary, 456*–457
    uses of, 461
Rotation, 308

S

Science skills
    classifying, 174*
    communicating, 39*
    defining terms, 263*
    interpreting data, 471*
    making measurements, 561*, R11–R17
    making models, 73*, 86*, 105*, 119*, 201*, 278*, 325*, 346*, 465*, 497*, 511*, 518*
    making predictions, 201*, 489*
    observing and inferring, 19*, 263*, 291*, 563*
    presenting data, R24–R26
    using numbers, 39*, 503*
Science, technology, and society, 16–17, 30–31, 46–47, 76–77, 87, 92, 136–137, 188, 222–223, 238–239, 254–255, 284, 342–343, 422–423, 436–437, 522–523, 538–539, 558–559, 600–601

Scientific instruments, 110–111, 291*, 293, 406*, 409, R6–R10, R20–R23
Scientific method
    experimenting, 19*, 99*, 335*, 465*, 497*, 587*
    hypothesizing, 392*, 555*
    separating and controlling variables, 59*
    thinking like a scientist, S4–S20
Seasons, 312–313
Sedimentary rock, 456*–457
Seismic waves, 404–406
Selective breeding, 485–492, 532
Senses, 584–585
Sight, 584
Simple machines
    inclined plane, 278–280
    lever, 257*–261
    pulley, 264–267
    wheel and axle, 268–269
Soil
    characteristics, 433
    conservation, 435
    erosion, 439*
    formation, 432
    and groundwater, 434
    horizons, 433
    types, 433
Solar cells, 81
Solar energy, 79*–81
Solar system
    asteroids, 340
    comets, 350
    eclipses, 322–323
    evolution of, 377
    inner planets, 301, 333*–341
    meteors, 351
    Moon, 319–327
    natural satellites, 352–353
    orbits, 335*, 341
    outer planets, 344–353
    revolution, 312
    rotation, 308
    scale of, 345*
    solar neighborhood, 371*, 373
    space probes, 302–303
    Sun, 307*, 309, 314–315, 366–367
    U.S. space program, 302–303

R45

Solid – White dwarfs

Solid
- change of state, 7
- properties of, 9

Solutions, 11
Space probes, 302–303
Species, 157, 561*, 569
Speed
- average speed, 199
- constant speed, 195*, 198, 201
- velocity, 200

Spinal cord, 582
Stars
- brightness, 361
- composition, 368–369
- constellations, 359
- distance, 357*, 358*
- H–R diagram, 361
- magnitude, 359
- parallax, 358*
- temperature, 360

STDs, 611
Stellar evolution
- black hole, 363, 365
- main sequence star, 362
- nebulae, 362
- neutron stars, 363
- pulsars, 363
- red giants, 362
- supergiants, 362
- supernovae, 364
- white dwarfs, 363

Stimulus and response, 586, 588
Sun
- atmosphere, 366
- location in sky, 307*, 309
- physical properties, 366–367
- as source of energy, 314–315

Supergiants, 362
Supernovae, 364
Suspensions, 10
Synapses, 580

T

Telescope, 296
Thermal pollution, 91
Thyroid gland, 596
Tides, 324–325*
Time zones, 310*–311
Tsunami, 404

U

Universe
- background radiation, 376
- big bang, 375*
- distances in, 375
- Doppler shift, 374
- expansion, 374, 378
- life in, 379
- quasars, 378

V

Vacuoles, 115
Vaporization, 70
Variation, 562
Vents, 415
Viruses, 175
Volcanoes
- activity, 418
- causes, 414
- geothermal energy, 420–421
- geysers, 420
- hot springs, 420
- kinds of, 416–417
- location of, 413*–414
- magma, 390, 415
- parts of, 415
- Ring of Fire, 414
- underground formations, 419

Volume
- of matter, 4
- units of measure, 4

W

Water
- properties of, 430*
- water cycle, 314
- water table, 434

Water cycle, 314
Watershed, 434
Wavelength, 294–295
Weathering
- agents of, 430*–431, 441–447
- chemical, 431
- mass wasting, 439*–440*
- mechanical, 430
- soil, 432–435

Weight, 4
Weightlessness, 235*–237
White dwarfs, 363

*Indicates an activity related to this topic.

CREDITS

Cover: printed from digital image ©1996 CORBIS

Maps: Geosystems

Transvisions: Richard Hutchings Photography (photography, TP1); Guy Porfirio (illustration)

Illustrations: Denny Bond: pp. 230, 281; Ka Botzis: pp. 483, 549, 565; Dan Clifford: pp. 196, 214, 233; Barbara Cousins: pp. 534, 551, 618–619; Paul Dempsey: pp. 41, 62, 93, 96, 188, 342, 354, 410–411, 432–434, 503, 513–518, R26; Brian Dugan: pp. 212, 216–218, 226, 260–261, 277; Simon Galkin: pp. 250–251, 259, 274–276, 309, 313; Pedro Julio Gonzalez: pp. 542, 544, 550, 553, 567, 570; Greg Harris: pp. 301, 340, 356, 370, 373, 374, 376–377; John Hovell: pp. 120, 122; Joel Ito: pp. 607, 610; John Karapelou: pp. 512, 580–581, 584–585, 598; Virge Kask: pp. 486–488, 490–491, 500, 506, 547–548, 552; George Kelvin: pp. 57, 84, 105, 114, 116, 129, 131–133, 140–144, 312, 314, 321, 324, 337, 350; Kristin Kest: pp. 156–157, 164, 166; Katie Lee: pp. 107–108, 145, 185; Joe LeMonnier: pp. 310–311, 391, 393, 418, 428, 431, 442–443; Steve Oh: pp. 582–583, 594, 606; Saul Rosenbaum: pp. 135, 158, 175, 294, 309, 313, 315; Nick Rotondo: pp. 203, 231, 237, 263, 278, 280; Wendy Smith: pp. 165, 181–182; Steve Stankiewicz: pp. 7, 15, 18–20, 35, 55, 72–74, 80, 90, 192, 219, 220, 225, 246–247, 262, 268, 295–296, 322–323, 342, 388, 401, 403–406, 408, 420–421, 424, 429, 434, 456–457, 465–468, 475, 477, 480, 564, R13; Art Thompson: pp. 4, 11, 61, 68–69, 87, 239, 284, 308, 320, 341, 360, 365–366, 390, 394, 396, 415–416, 419, 446, 454, 458, 460; Sally Vitsky: p. 121; Nina Wallace: pp. 200, 264, 265–267.

Photography Credits: All photographs are by Richard Hutchings Photography for McGraw-Hill School Division (MHSD) except as noted below:

iii: E.R. Degginger/Photo Researchers, Inc. iv: ©Mike Abbey/VU. v: Index Stock Imagery. vi: Digital Stock. vii: Lee F. Snyder/Photo Researchers, Inc. viii, ix: images copyright ©1999 PhotoDisc, Inc. S2–3: ©David M. Sanders. S4: *l.* Lambert/Archive photos; *m.* ©Jack Zehrt/FPG; *b.l.* ©Reuters/Scott Olson/Archive Photos. S5: Dave Mager/MHSD. S6: *m.l.* ©Wernher Krutein/LIAISON. *b.r.* Dave Mager/MHSD. S7: *t.r.* ©NASA. S8: Scala/Art Resource, NY. S9: *b.r.* ©Bruce Caines. S10: *t.* John Bova/Photo Researchers, Inc.; *b.* James L. Amos/CORBIS. S11: *t.r.* Frank Rossotto/TSM; *b.* Dave Mager/MHSD. S12: *m.l.* Robert Essel/TSM; *b.m.* Telegraph Colour Library/FPG. S13: *t.l.* ©Bruce Caines; *b.r.* ©Frank A. Cezus/FPG. S14: *b.l.* The Granger Collection, New York. *t.r.* Scott Goldsmith/TSI. S15: TSM; S16: *t.m.* ©NASA; *b.* Dave Mager/MHSD ©Telegraph Colour Library. S17: *t.r.* Frank Rossotto/TSM.; *m.l.* Bruce Forster/TSI. **Unit 1** 1: *bkgnd.* ©TSM/Rick Gayle; *r.* ©TSM/Myron J. Dorf. 2: Edward Parker/Still Pictures. 4: Martin Bough/Fundamental Photographs. 6: *l.* Arnold Fisher/Science Photo Library/Photo Researchers, Inc.; *m.r.* E.R. Degginger/Photo Researchers, Inc.; *r.* AURA/STScI; *b.r.* E.R. Degginger/Color-Pic, Inc. 8: *t.l.* Charles D. Winters/Photo Researchers, Inc.; *b.l.* A. Ramey/PhotoEdit. 9: *l.* ©Cabisco/VU; *t.r.* Tony Freeman/PhotoEdit; *b.r.* images copyright ©1999 PhotoDisc, Inc. 10, 12: *l.* Phil Degginger/Color-Pic, Inc. 12: *m.* Richard Megna/Fundamental Photographs; *r.* Charles D. Winters/Photo Researchers, Inc. 13: *l.* ©James W. Richardson/VU; *r.* Cesar Llacuna. 15: *m.* ©Science VU. 16: *l.* ©Ernest Braun/TSI; *r.* James L. Stanfield. 17: ©Frank Wing/TSI. 18: ©Doug Armand/TSI. 20: images copyright ©1999 PhotoDisc, Inc. 21: ©Science VU. 24: *t.r.* Aaron Haupt/Photo Researchers, Inc.; *m.l.* Cesar Llacuna; *b.l.* Charles D. Winters/Photo Researchers, Inc.; *b.r.* images copyright ©1999 PhotoDisc, Inc. 25: *t.l.* PhotoEdit; *t.r.* images copyright ©1999 PhotoDisc, Inc.; *b.l.* D. Young-Wolff/PhotoEdit. 28: *t.r.* Martyn F. Chillmaid/Photo Researchers, Inc.; *m.r.* Paul Silverman/Fundamental Photographs; *b.l., b.r.* Charles D. Winters/Photo Researchers, Inc. 29: John Walsh/Photo Researchers, Inc. 30–31: *bkgnd.* Scott Camazine/Photo Researchers, Inc. 30: *t.r.* ©Ken Lucas/VU; *b.l.* Musée des Beaux-Arts, Rouen, France/Lauros-Giraudon, Paris/SuperStock; *b.r.* Science Photo Library/Photo Researchers, Inc. 31: *t.l.* North Wind Picture Archive; *t.r.* Ken Edwards/Biografx/Science Source/Photo Researchers, Inc.; *b.* CORBIS/Bettmann. 32: ©Mark Newman/VU. 34: *t.* Charles D. Winters/Photo Researchers, Inc.; *b.l.* Tony Freeman/PhotoEdit; *b.r.* ©Inga Spence/VU. 35: Charles D. Winters/Photo Researchers, Inc. 36: Jim Steinberg/Photo Researchers, Inc. 37: ©Timothy Kerr/VU. 38: *l.* Sylvain Grandadam/Photo Researchers, Inc.; *m.* Cesar Llacuna; *r.* J.H. Robinson/Photo Researchers, Inc. 40: *t.l.* Phil Degginger/Color-Pic, Inc.; *t.r.* Charles D. Winters/Photo Researchers, Inc.; *b.l.* ©Tom Pantages; *b.r.* Phil Jude/Photo Researchers, Inc. 41: *l.* images copyright ©1999 PhotoDisc, Inc.; *r.* Blair Seitz/Photo Researchers, Inc. 42: *l.* images copyright ©1999 PhotoDisc, Inc. 43: *b.l.* ©Ron Chapple/FPG. 44: *t.* D. Young-Wolff/PhotoEdit; *b.* Charles D. Winters/Photo Researchers, Inc. 45: *m.* Mark Burnett/Photo Researchers, Inc. 49: *bkgnd.* Russell Illig Photography; *r.* ©TSM/Thomas Braise. 50: *m.* Tony Freeman/PhotoEdit. 52: Cesar Llacuna. 53: *l.* Jeff Greenberg/PhotoEdit. 54: *l.* Tony Freeman/PhotoEdit; *r.* Spencer Grane/PhotoEdit. 56: *t.* Tony Freeman/PhotoEdit; *b.* Dr. E.R. Degginger/Color-Pic, Inc. 59: Myrleen Ferguson/PhotoEdit. 60: *t.l.* ©Patrick J. Endres/VU; *t.r.* Dr. E.R. Degginger/Color-Pic, Inc.; *b.* Cesar Llacuna. 64: ©M. Long/VU. 66: *l.* Mark Burnett/Photo Researchers, Inc.; *t.r.* Cesar Llacuna. 68: Michael Newman/PhotoEdit. 73: Cesar Llacuna. 75: Tony Freeman/PhotoEdit. 76: *bkgnd.* ©Gerald & Buff Corsi/VU; *b.* Jeff Lepore/Photo Researchers, Inc. 77: *t.* David Parker/Science Photo Library/Photo Researchers, Inc.; *b.* Digital Stock. 78: *m.* ©A.J. Copley/VU. 81: *t.l.* Rosenfeld Images LTD./Photo Researchers, Inc.; *t.r.* Dana White/PhotoEdit; *m.r.* Tony Freeman/PhotoEdit; *b.r.* ©Ken Lucas/VU. 82: *t.r.* ©Derrick Ditchburn/VU; *m.* ©John D. Cunningham/VU; *b.* ©Arthur Hill/VU. 83: *t.* ©Hal Beral/VU; *m.* Tony Freeman/PhotoEdit; *b.* ©Larry Lefever/Grant Heilman Photography, Inc. 85: NASA. 86: *t.* images copyright ©1999 PhotoDisc, Inc.; *b.* ©Science VU. 88: *t., m.* ©Inga Spence/VU; *b.* ©Ken Lucas/VU. 89: *t.* Jerry Irwin/Photo Researchers, Inc.; *m.* Bachmann/PhotoEdit; *b.* ©R. Calentine/VU. 91: ©John Solden/VU. 92: *bkgnd.* John Mead/Science Photo Library/Photo Researchers, Inc.; *t.* Alan Pitcairn/Grant Heilman Photography, Inc.; *m.* Tony Freeman/PhotoEdit; *b.* ©John D. Cunningham/VU. **Unit 2** 97: *bkgnd.* Patti Murray/Earth Scenes; *r.* images copyright ©1999 PhotoDisc, Inc. 98: *l.* images copyright ©1999 PhotoDisc, Inc. 101: *t.* ©David M. Phillips/VU; *m.* ©Martha J. Powell/VU; *b* ©John D. Cunningham/VU. 102: *l.* ©Kevin Collins/VU; *r.* ©Science VU. 103: *f.t.r* Ray Simmons/Photo Researchers, Inc.; *t.l., t.r.; m.r., b.l.* ©John D. Cunningham/VU; *b.r.* ©Science VU. 104: *t.* Cabisco/Photo Researchers, Inc.; *t.m., b.m; b.* ©John D. Cunningham/VU; *f.b.* SIU/VU. 106: *t.* Walt Anderson; *b.* ENP Photography. 107: ©Jen and Des Bartlett/Bruce Coleman, Inc. 108: *t.* Patti Murray/Animals Animals; *b.* ©Joe McDonald/VU. 109: *l.* Ed Reschke/Peter Arnold, Inc.; *r.* S.J. Krasemann/Peter Arnold, Inc. 110: Leigh/Stock Imagery. 111: CNRI/Science Photo Library/Photo Researchers, Inc. 112: *t.* Michael Durham/ENP Photography; *b.* ©Dick Keen/VU. 113: *t.* ©Robert Calentine/VU; *m.* ©Kevin & Betty Collins/VU; *b.* ©Bernd Wittich/VU. 115: ©Don Fawcett/VU. 118: *t.* ©Mike Abbey/VU; *m.* ©David M. Phillips/VU; *b.* Joel Bennett/Peter Arnold, Inc. 123: Christine Coscioni/CO2, Inc. 124–125: *bkgnd.* images copyright ©1999 PhotoDisc, Inc. 124: *t.* ©Kevin Collins/VU; *b.l.* ©VU/Science VU; *b.r.* Cecil Fox/Science Source/Photo Researchers, Inc. 125: *t.* Gerard Mare/Petit Format/Photo Researchers, Inc.; *m.* W.&D. McIntyre/Photo Researchers, Inc.; *b.* Jacques Grison/Rapho/Liaison International. 126: *b.* Jeremy Stafford-Deitsch; *inset* Dave B. Fleetham/VU. 131: Ken Karp Photography. 135: ©SIU/VU. 136–137: *bkgnd.* ©Peter Cade/TSI. 137: *l.* Judy Gelles/Stock, Boston; *r.* ©Nick Vedros, Vedros & Associates/TSI. 138: ©Lindholm/VU. 140: ©A.M. Siegelman/VU. 141: Gerard Lacz/Peter Arnold, Inc. 142: *f.t., t., t.m., m.m., b.m., b.* ©Michael Abbey/Science Source/Photo Researchers, Inc.; *f.b.* ©Biology Media 1978/Photo Researchers, Inc. 143: *l.* ©Cabisco/VU; *r.* ©A.M. Siegelman/VU. 146: ©Cabisco/VU. 147: Manfred Kage/Peter Arnold, Inc. 148–149: *bkgnd.* GJLP/CNRI/PhotoTake. 148: *t.* ©Spike Walker/TSI. 149: Arthur G. James Cancer Hospital and Research Institute. 151: *bkgnd.* Fred Bavendam/Minden Pictures; *r.* images copyright ©1999 PhotoDisc, Inc. 152: *l.* ©Daniel W. Gotshall/VU; *m.l., r.* ©T.E. Adams/VU. 154: *t.l.* ©M. Abbey/VU; *t.r.* ©Fred Hossler/VU; *t.r.m.* ©Dick Poe/VU; *b.r.m.* ©James Richardson/VU; *m.l.* ©M. Abbey/Photo Researchers, Inc.; *m.r.* ©A.M. Siegelman/VU; *b.l.* ©Bill Keogh/VU; *b.r.* ©Doug Sokell/VU. 155: *t.l.* ©Bill Beatty/VU; *t.m.* ©Cabisco/VU; *t.r.* ©Gerard Lacz/VU; *m.l.* ©Gary Carter/VU; *b.l.* Jeremy Stafford-Deitsch/ENP Photography; *b.r.* Runk/Schoenberger/Grant Heilman Photography, Inc.; *f.b.r.* ©Joel Arrington/VU. 158: *f.t.* Blocker Collection/UT Medical Branch Library; *t.* ©Tom Edwards/VU; *m.* ©Art Morris/VU; *b.* ©Warren Stone/VU. 159: *t.* ©W. Ormerod/VU; *m.* ©Ken Lucas/VU; *b.* ©Glenn Oliver/VU. 160: *b.l.* Steve Gettle/ENP Photography; *b.r.* ©Kjell B. Sandved/VU. 161: ©WHOI-D. Foster/VU. 162–163: *bkgnd.* ©Manoj Shah/TSI. 163: images copyright ©1999 PhotoDisc, Inc. 168: *t.* Jim Strawser/Grant Heilman Photography, Inc.; *m.r.* ©Stephen P. Parker/Photo Researchers, Inc.; *r.* ©S.R. Maglione/Photo Researchers, Inc.; *b.l.* ©Ray Dove/VU; *b.m.* ©Jack M. Bostrack/VU.; *t.l.* Alan Pitcairn/Grant Heilman Photography, Inc. 169: *t.* ©George Hebren/VU; *t.m.* ©Kevin and Betty Collins/VU; *m.* ©Allen Benton/VU; *m.r.* Gerry Ellis/Ellis Nature Photography; *b.m.* ©Bill Beatty/VU; *b.* ©Dr. Gilbert S. Grant/Okapia/Photo Researchers, Inc. 170: *l.* ©John D. Cunningham/VU; *t.r.* ©Sherman Thomson/VU; *b.r.* Ed Reschke/Peter Arnold, Inc. 171: *t.* ©Larry Jensen/VU; *b.* ©David M Phillips/VU. 172: *f.t.l., t.r.* ©Arthur M. Siegelman/VU; *t.l.* ©M. Abbey/VU; *m.l.* ©David M. Phillips/VU; *m.r.* ©Cabisco/VU; *b.l.* ©Karl Aufderheide/VU; *b.r.* ©T.E. Adams/VU. 173: *t.l.* ©Charles W. Stratton/VU; *t.r., b.l.* ©David M. Phillips/VU. 175: ©Science VU. 176: *l.* LOC/Science Source/Photo Researchers, Inc.; *b.r.* images copyright ©1988 PhotoDisc, Inc.; *b.m.* Eastcott/Momatiuk/TSI; *b.l.* Alan D. Carey/Photo Researchers, Inc. 177: *t.* ©S. Lowry/Univ. Ulster/TSI; *b.* ©Laurie Campbell/TSI. 178: *l.* ©R. Cantentene/VU; *r.* ©Ken Wagner/VU. 179: *b.l.* David M. Phillips/VU. 180: *t.l.* ©Sylvia E. Coleman/VU; *m.l.* ©John D. Cunningham/VU; *b.l.* ©Stanley Flegler/VU; *b.r.* ©Cabisco/VU. 181: *t.l.* ©Sherman Thomson/VU; *t.r.* ©David M. Phillips/VU; *b.* Michael Viard/Peter Arnold, Inc. 183: Larry Lefever/Grant Heilman Photography, Inc. 184: *t.l.* ©J. Alcock/VU; *t.r.* ©Peter K. Ziminski/VU; *m.r.* Hans Pfletschinger/Peter Arnold, Inc.; *b.r.* ©Kevin & Betty Collins/VU. 187: Blocker Collections/UT Medical Branch Library. **Unit 3** 193: *bkgnd.* ©Doug Armand/TSI; *r.* images copyright ©1999 PhotoDisc, Inc. 194: *b.r.* ©Art Wolfe/TSI. 199: Dwight Kuhn/Folio, Inc. 200: *b.l.* ©Donald Johnston/TSI. 202: *t.l.* ©Paul Hurd/TSI. 203: *b.l.* ©E.B. Graphics/Liaison Agency. 204: *b.* ©TSM/David Lawrence; *b.r.* ©Thomas Zimmermann/TSI. 205: Chris Sorenson. 206: ©Alan R. Moller/TSI. 207: ©Peter Menzel/Stock, Boston/PNI. 208: *b.m.* Henry Horenstein/Stock, Boston. 210: *t.l.* ©NASA/Peter Arnold, Inc., *t.m.* ©TSM/Lewis Portnoy. 212: *b.m.* ©TSM/Michael Kevin Daly. 216: *b.m.* ©Max & Bea Hunn/VU. 221: *m.* ©Donald Johnston/TSI. 223: *bkgnd.* Diane Hirsch/Fundamental Photographs. 224: *b.* ©Jonathan Elderfield/Liaison Agency. 227: *r.* ©Science VU. 228: *t.* ©Erik Simonsen/TIB; *m.* ©ALLSPORT/Matthew Stockman; *m.l.* Bruce Wellman/Stock, Boston; *b.* ©Index Stock Photography. 229: *m.r.* ©ALLSPORT/Veronique Roux; *b.l.* ©Dagmar Fabricius; *b.r.* Calvin Larsen/Photo Researchers, Inc. 231: NASA/Peter Arnold, Inc. 232: *t.l.* Andy Levin/Photo Researchers, Inc. 234: *t.l.* Dr. Seth Shostak/Photo Researchers, Inc.; *t.r.* ©NASA/PhotoTake. 235, 236: NASA. 238: *bkgnd.* ©ALLSPORT/Clive Mason; *t.l.–t.r.* ©1998 AccuWeather, Inc. 241: *r.* ©Lester Lefkowitz/TSI. 242: *b.* ©Louie

Bunde/VU. 245: *b.l.* ©Zigy Kaluzny/TSI. 252: *t.* ©Gary Brettnacher/TSI. 253: *m.l.* ©Ken Sherman/VU. 254: *bkgnd.* Gamma-Liaison. 255: Courtesy Ford Motor Company. 256: *b.* ©Ned Therrien/VU. 258: *t.l.* Richard Megna/Fundamental Photographs. 264: *t.r.* ©Elena Rooraid/PhotoEdit. 268: images copyright ©1999 PhotoDisc, Inc. 269: *m.* © TSM/Chris Collins; *m.r.* Richard Megna/Fundamental Photographs. 270: *t.* ©K&K Ammann/Bruce Coleman, Inc.; *b.l.* Cesar Llacuna. 271: *l.* ©Erwin C. Nielsen/VU; *r.* Sandra Baker/Liaison International. 272: *b.r.* ©Manfred Mehlig/TSI. 279: *b.l.* ©Yoav Levy/PhotoTake; *m.r.* Chris Sorenson/Stock, Boston; *b.r.* ©Raymond Gendreau/TSI. 280: *t.l.* ©Novastock/PhotoEdit. 282: *m.l.* ©Chris Jones/TSM; *m.r.* ©K. Rehm/Camerique/H. Armstrong Roberts, Inc.; *b.l.* Fundamental Photographs. 283: *m.l.* ©TSM/C. Sorenson. 284: *b.* Dennis MacDonald/PhotoEdit. **Unit 4** 289: *bkgnd.* John Foster/Science Source/Photo Researchers, Inc.; *r.* images copyright ©1999 PhotoDisc, Inc. 290: *m.* NASA/JPL/Caltech; *b.* Sojourner (tm), Mars Rover (tm) and spacecraft design and images copyright ©1996–97, California Institute of Technology. All rights reserved. Further reproduction prohibited. 293: CORBIS/Bettmann. 294: Ronald Royer/Science Photo Library/Photo Researchers, Inc. 297: *t.* ©Dennis DiCicco/Peter Arnold, Inc.; *m.* Max-Planck Institute fur Radioastronomie/Photo Researchers, Inc.; *b.* NASA/Science Photo Library/Photo Researchers, Inc. 298: *b.l.* David Hanon; *b.r.* NASA/JPL/Caltech. 299: *t., b.l.* NASA. 300, 302: NASA. 304: *t.* ©Ira Block; *b.* CORBIS/Digital image ©1996 Corbis. Original image courtesy of NASA. 305: CORBIS/Roger Ressmeyer. 306: CORBIS/Joseph Sohm/Chromosohm, Inc. 308: CORBIS/Bettmann. 310: images copyright ©1999 PhotoDisc, Inc. 316: *all images*: images copyright ©1999 PhotoDisc, Inc. except *f.b.m.* Manfred Kage/Peter Arnold, Inc. *f.b.l.* ©Peter Cade/TSI. 317: *all images*: images copyright ©1999 PhotoDisc, Inc. except *f.b.* Grant Heilman/Grant Heilman Photography, Inc.; *t.l.* S. Fried/Photo Researchers, Inc.; *m.r.* Jim Zipp/Photo Researchers, Inc.; *f.b.* Manfred Kage/Peter Arnold, Inc. 318: David Hanon. 321: ©UCO Lick Observatory photo. 322, 323: *t.* ©Guillermo Gonzalez/VU; *b.l.* CORBIS/UPI. 324: Diego Lezama. 326: David Hanon. 327: images copyright ©1999 PhotoDisc, Inc. 328–329: *bkgnd.* images copyright ©1999 PhotoDisc, Inc. 328: *t.* Stephen P. Parker/Photo Researchers, Inc.; *b.* Fred Winner/Jacana/Photo Researchers, Inc. 329: *t.* Nancy Sefton/Photo Researchers, Inc.; *b.* Andrew J. Martinez/Photo Researchers, Inc. 331: copyright Anglo-Australian Observatory/Royal Observatory Edinburgh, photograph made by David Malin from UK Schmidt plates. 332: *bkgnd.* NASA; *l., r.* ©W.L. Sileth. 336: NASA/JPL/Caltech. 337, 338: NASA. 340: *b.r.* ©Allan E. Morton/VU.; *t.r.* NASA. 342–343: *bkgnd.* Digital Stock. 342: *l.* Leonard Lessin/Peter Arnold, Inc.; *r.* Tony Freeman/PhotoEdit. 346: NASA. 347: Courtesy Hubble Space Telescope Comet Team. 348, 349: NASA/JPL/Caltech. 350: ©Justin W. Virgerber/VU. 351: *t.* ©P. Bierenau/VU; *b.* ©D. Milon/VU. 352: *t.r.* NASA/JPL/Caltech. 353: Copyright ©1998 Calvin J. Hamilton. 355: *t.l.* Science Photo Library/Photo Library, Inc./Photo Researchers, Inc.; *t.r.* Detlev Van Ravenswaay/Science Photo Library/Photo Researchers, Inc.; *b.l.* CORBIS/Bettmann; *b.r.* LOC/Science Source/Photo Researchers, Inc. 362: Kim Gordon/Science Photo Library. 363: *l.* Material created with support to AURA/ST ScI from NASA contract NAS5-26555 is reproduced here with permission. Courtesy of B. Whitmore (ST ScI), and NASA; *r.* ©VU. 364: NASA. 365: *b.r.* ©Max-Planck Institut fur Extraterrestrische Physik/Photo Researchers, Inc. 367: *t.r.* ©Science VU. 372: *t.* ©VU; *b.* NASA/Photo Researchers, Inc. 378, 379: NASA/JPL/Caltech. 380: *bkgnd.* Material created with support to AURA/ST ScI from NASA contract. NAS5-26555 is reproduced here with permission. Courtesy of B. Whitmore (ST ScI), and NASA; *r.* ©TSM/Frank Rossotto. **Unit 5** 385: *bkgnd.* Douglas Peebles Photography; *r.* ©G. Brad Lewis/TSI. 388: ©Walter H. Hodge/Peter Arnold, Inc. 397: ©John Manno/Still Life Stock, Inc. 398: *t.* Steve McCurry; *b.* ©Stephen Frink/TSI. 399: CORBIS/NASA. 400: *l., r.* Culver Pictures. 403: Georg Cester/Photo Researchers, Inc. 404: Lynette Cook/Science Photo Library/Photo Researchers, Inc. 407: Mark Richards/Peter Arnold, Inc. 408: *t.* ©James Stanfield/NGS; *b.* ©Stephen Saks/Photo Researchers, Inc. 412: Catherine Ursillo/Photo Researchers, Inc. 413: ©Josef Beck/FPG. 416: *l.* ©John D. Cunningham/VU; *r.* C. Falco/Photo Researchers, Inc. 417: *l.* Krafft /Explorer/Photo Researchers, Inc. 420: ©Richard Thom/VU. 422–423: *bkgnd.* Superstock; *b.* John V. Christiansen/Earth Images; *m.* Bill Ingalls/NASA. 425: *bkgnd.* Superstock; *r.* images copyright ©1999 PhotoDisc, Inc. 426: *t., b.* ©William J. Weber/VU. 428: *t.* ©Mark E. Gibson/VU; *b.* ©Joel Arrington/VU. 429: ©John D. Cunningham/VU. 430: *r.* ©Ken Wagner/VU. 432: ©Science VU. 434: *l.* ©Ross Frid/VU; *r.* ©Ross Frid/VU. 435: ©Science VU. 436: *b.* ©John D. Cunningham/VU. 436–437: *bkgnd.* Runk/Schoenberger/Grant Heilman Photography, Inc. 437: *l.* Jacques Jangoux/Photo Researchers, Inc.; *r.* ©Science VU. 438: *b.r.* M. Richards/PhotoEdit. 440: *l.* Cesar Llacuna; *r.* ©John D. Cunningham/VU. 441: *t.* ©Martin G. Miller/VU. *inset* ©Martin G. Miller/VU. 442: G.R. Roberts/OPC. 443: *t.* Altitude/Peter Arnold, Inc.; *b.* Valmik Thalpar/Peter Arnold, Inc. 444: *bkgnd.* ©L. Linkhart/VU; *t.r.* ©Jeanette Thomas/VU; *b.* ©John Gerlach/VU. 445: *b.* ©Bill Kamin/VU. *inset* ©Martin G. Miller/VU. 446: ©Steve McCutcheon/VU. 447: ©Science VU. 448–449: *bkgnd.* ©Albert J. Copley/VU. 450: *t.* ©D. Cavagnaro/VU; *m.* ©Beth Davidow/VU; *b.* ©Gerald Corsi/VU. 451: *t.* ©A. Wambler/Photo Researchers, Inc.; *t.m.* Andrew J. Martinez/Photo Researchers, Inc. 452: *t.l.* ©Ken Lucas/VU; *t.m.* ©McKutcheon/VU; *t.r.* ©John D. Cunningham/VU; *b.l.* ©Elliot Kornberg/VU; *m.l.* ©Arthur R. Hill/VU; *m.r.* ©A.J. Copley/VU; *b., b.m.* ©Breck P. Kent/Earth Scenes; *b.r.* ©Thomas Hunn/VU. 453: *t.l., m.l., b.l., b.m.* ©A.J. Copley/VU; *t.m.* ©Doug Sokell/VU; *t.r.* ©McKutcheon; *b.r.* ©Arthur R. Hill/VU. 454: *b., m.* ©A.J. Copley/VU. 455: *r.* ©L.S. Stepanowicz/VU; *b.r.* ©Mark E. Gibson/VU. 456: *t.* ©Mark Newman/VU; *t.l.* ©Chris Bartlett/FPG; *m.* ©S. Callahan/VU; *b.* ©John Solden/VU. 457: *t.* ©John D. Cunningham/VU; *m.* ©S.J. Krasemann/Peter Arnold, Inc.; *b.* ©A.J. Copley/VU. 459: *f.t.l.* ©John D. Cunningham/VU; *f.t.r.* ©Martin G. Miller/VU; *t.m.l.* ©A.J. Copley/VU; *t.m., t.r.* ©John Solden/VU; *b.m.l.* ©Henry W. Robinson/VU; *b.m.r.* ©D. Cavagnaro/VU; *b.r.* ©Joyce Photographics/Photo Researchers, Inc.; *f.b.l.* ©Joyce Photographics/Photo Researchers, Inc.; *f.b.r.* ©Joyce Photographics/Photo Researchers, Inc. 461: *b.* ©Jonathan Nourok/PhotoEdit. 462–463: *bkgnd.* Omikron/Photo Researchers, Inc. 463: *t.* Superstock. 464: ©Jim Wark/Peter Arnold, Inc. 468: *b.* ©Don Fawcett/VU; *r.* ©A.J. Copley/VU. 469: *l.* ©Chip Clark/Smithsonian Institution; *b.r.* ©A. Kerstitch/VU; *t.r.* ©John D. Cunningham/VU. 471: Cesar Llacuna. 472: *l.* ©Jonathan Blair/NGS; *r.* ©Joseph Fontenot/VU. 473: *t.* ©Jonathan Blair/NGS; *b.* ©David Matherly/VU. 474: *l.* ©Lloyd Townsend/NGS; *r.* ©Jim Hughes/VU. 476: *bkgnd.* ©David Matherly/VU; *r.* Superstock. **Unit 6** 481: *bkgnd.* Tony Stone Imaging/TSI; *r.* CORBIS/Digital Art. 482: ©Superstock. 484: ©Bruce Berg/TSI. 485: *t.l.* ©James Richardson/VU; *b.* ©Tim Hauf/VU; *b.l.* ©Walt Anderson/VU. 486: ©Wally Eberhart/VU. 487: ©William J. Weber/VU. 489: *t.r.* ©M & D Long/VU; *b.l.* ©D. Cavagnaro/VU; *b.r.* ©D. Cavagnaro/VU. 492, 493: Culver Pictures. 493: *r.* David Cavagnaro/Peter Arnold, Inc. 494: *l.* ©Index Stock Photography, Inc./PNI; *r.* Fred Lyon/Photo Researchers, Inc. 495: ©Bob Daemmrich/Stock, Boston/PNI. 496: *l.* ©Seth Resnick/Stock, Boston; *r.* ©Cesar Llacuna. 498: *l.* ©VU; *r.* CORBIS/©Pablo Corral. 502: *b.l.* ©A.J. Copley/VU; *b.m.* ©Superstock; *b.r.* ©Terry Gleason/VU; *t.l.* ©SIU/VU; *t.m.* ©Bruce Berg/VU; *t.r.* ©Rosenthal/Superstock. 507: ©Dick Keen/VU. 508: *l.* Science Photo Library/Photo Researchers, Inc.; *r.* Science Photo Library/Photo Researchers, Inc. 509: *bkgnd.* ©D. Cavagnaro/VU. 510: *l.* ©William Palmer; *r.* CORBIS/Jim Sugar. 512: ©Dr. Gopal/PhotoTake. 513: *l.* ©Olney Vasan/TSI; *r.* ©Reed Williams/Animals Animals. 520: *b.m.* CORBIS/Niall Benvie; *m.l.* ©Cabisco/VU.; *t.l.* ©Renee Andrews/VU; *t.l. inset* ©Robert Cunningham/VU; *t.m.* ©Superstock; *t.r.* ©Doug Sokell/VU. 521: ©Mark E. Gibson/VU. 522–523: *bkgnd.* images copyright ©1999 PhotoDisc, Inc.; *b.* A. Barrington Brown/Science Source/Photo Researchers, Inc. 523: *t.l.* Science Source/Photo Researchers, Inc.; *t.r.* Science Photo Library/Photo Researchers, Inc. 524: ©Ellen B. Senisi/Photo Researchers, Inc. 526: *t.r.* ©Dr. Gopal/Photo Researchers, Inc.; *m.l.* ©Mark Burnett/Photo Researchers, Inc.; *b.l.* ©Jeff Kaufmann/FPG. 528: *l.* ©CNRI/Science Photo Library/Photo Researchers, Inc.; *r.* ©Biophoto Associates/Photo Researchers, Inc. 529: ©VU. 530: Culver Pictures. 531: *l.* Simon Fraser/RVI/Photo Researchers, Inc.; *r.* CNRI Science/Photo Researchers, Inc. 532: *l.* ©LINK/VU; *r.* ©Les Christman/VU. 533: *l.* ©Keith V. Wood/VU; *r.* ©D. Cavagnaro/VU. 535: ©Roslin Institute/PhotoTake. 536: *b.l.* Jim Strawser/Grant Heilman Photography, Inc.; *b.l. inset* ©Tom Myers/Photo Researchers, Inc.; *b.r.* Holt Studios/Photo Researchers, Inc.; *b.r. inset* ©Nigel Cattlin/Holt Studios International/Photo Researchers, Inc. 537: *m.r.* ©Ken Lax/Photo Researchers, Inc. 538: James King-Holmes/ICRF/Science Photo Library/Photo Researchers, Inc. 539: *bkgnd.* Philippe Hurlin/GLMR/The Gamma Liaison Network; l., *r.* Christian Vioujard/Gamma-Liaison. 541: *bkgnd.; r.* ©1977 Ron Kimball. 545: *t.r.* Tom McHugh/Photo Researchers, Inc. 546: *m.l.* ©John D. Cunningham; *b.l.* ©W. Ormerod/VU; *b.l.* CORBIS/Richard T. Nowitz. 547: *b.l.* ©Ken Lucas/VU; *b.r.* ©Kjell B. Sandved/VU. 552: *t.r.* ©John D. Cunningham/VU; *b.r.* ©Scott Berner/VU. 554: ©Kjell B. Sandved/VU. 555: *t.r.* ©Bruce Byers/FPG; *b.m.* John Reader/Photo Researchers, Inc.; *b.r.* ©Cabisco/VU. 556: *m.l.* ©Don W. Fawcett/VU; *b.l.* John Reader/Photo Researchers, Inc.; *b.r.* ©Science VU. 557: *t.r.* ©Science VU. 558–559: *bkgnd.* ©John D. Cunningham/VU; *l.* Francois Goheir/Photo Researchers, Inc. 559: *b.* ©John D. Cunningham/VU. 560: ©Jeri Gleiter/FPG. 562: *t.r.* ©Thomas Gula/VU; *l.* Richard Carlton; *b.r.* ©Richard Walters/VU. 564: *t.* ©Joe McDonald/VU; *b.* ©Science VU. 565: *t.r.* ©John Gerlach/VU; *l.* ©P. de Wilde/PhotoTake. 566: *t.* ©Michael Tweedie/Photo Researchers, Inc.; *b.* ©Michael Tweedie/Photo Researchers, Inc. 567: ©Roy David Farris/VU. 569: *l.* ©Erwin C. "Bud" Nielsen/VU; *r.* ©Bob Clay/TSI. 570: *t.* ©K. Pugh/VU; *b.* ©A.J. Copley/TSI. 571: *r.* ©Milton H. Tierney/VU. 572: *l., r.* all rights reserved, Photo Archives, Denver Museum of Natural History, photo by Rick Wicker, 1995. **Unit 7** 577: *bkgnd.* Emanuele Taroni; *r.* images copyright ©1999 PhotoDisc, Inc. 578: *b.* ©David Young Wolff/TSI. 586: *l.* David S. Waitz; *r.* ©Myrleen Ferguson. 588: *t.r.* ©TSM/Tom Tracy; *b.r.* ©TSM/Michele Burgess; *l.* Dwight Kuhn. 589: ©Bob Torrez/TSI. 590: *t.* ©Linda K. Moore/Rainbow/PNI; *b.* Jonathan Nourok/PhotoEdit. 591: ©Hank Morgan/Photo Researchers, Inc. 592: ©David K. Crow/PhotoEdit. 595: ©TSM/J. Sapinsky. 596: *l.* ©Jonathan Nourok/PhotoEdit; *r.* ©Lori Adamski/TSI. 599: ©David Hanover/TSI. 600–601: *bkgnd.* ©SIU/VU. 600: *b.l.* F.G. Banting Papers, Thomas Fisher Rare Book Library, University of Toronto. 601: *t.* Will and Deni McIntyre/Photo Researchers, Inc. 603: *bkgnd.; r.* Bob Schuchman/Phototake/PNI. 604: ©Suzanne Szasz/Photo Researchers, Inc. 607: C. Edelmann/Photo Researchers, Inc. 608: Photos Lennart Nilsson/Albert Bonniers Förlag, A CHILD IS BORN, Dell Publishing Company. 609: ©Paul Avis/TSI. 611: ©David M. Grossman/Photo Researchers, Inc. 612: *b.* M. Denis-Huot/Liaison International. 613: *t.l.* Gary Retherford/Photo Researchers, Inc.; *b.r.* Dale E. Boyer/Photo Researchers, Inc. 614: Bill Bachmann/PhotoEdit. 616: *l.* Ken Cavanagh/Photo Researchers, Inc.; *m.l.* ©George Shelley/Photo Researchers, Inc.; *m.r.* ©D. Young-Wolff/PhotoEdit; *r.* ©Index Stock Photography. 617: *t.* ©Dick Keen/VU; *l.* ©TSM/John Lei; *m., b.r.* SuperStock. 620: ©David Leeson/The Image Works. R9: *r.* NASA/Digital Stock. R10: *t. bkgnd., b.l., b.r.* images copyright ©1999 PhotoDisc, Inc. R16: *r.* Jim Harrison/Stock, Boston/PNI. R20: *b.l. bkgnd.* images copyright ©1988 PhotoDisc, Inc.; *b.l. inset* G.R. Roberts/Photo Researchers, Inc. R21: *t. inset* images copyright ©1999 PhotoDisc, Inc.; *b. inset* ©1998 AccuWeather.